THE APOCRYPHAL ACTS OF THOMAS

STUDIES ON EARLY CHRISTIAN APOCRYPHA

Edited by T. Adamik, J. Bolyki, J.N. Bremmer (*editor-in-chief*), A. Hilhorst and G. P. Luttikhuizen.

In recent years the so-called apocryphal literature has increasingly drawn the attention of scholars interested in early Christianity, ancient history and the ancient novel. New editions of the most important texts have already appeared or are being prepared. We are therefore pleased to announce a new series, *Studies on Early Christian Apocrypha* (formerly called *Studies on the Apocryphal Acts of the Apostles*). The editors welcome contributions on individual aspects of the main texts, be it proceedings of conferences or monographs.

1. *The Apocryphal Acts of John*, J.N. Bremmer (ed.), Kampen 1996
2. *The Apocryphal Acts of Paul and Thecla*, J.N. Bremmer (ed.), Kampen 1996
3. *The Apocryphal Acts of Peter: Magic, Miracles and Gnosticism*, J.N. Bremmer (ed.), Leuven 1998
4. *The Acts of John: a Two-stage Initiation into Johannine Gnosticism*, P.J. Lalleman, Leuven 1998
5. *The Apocryphal Acts of Andrew*, J.N. Bremmer (ed.), Leuven 2000
6. *The Apocryphal Acts of Thomas*, J.N. Bremmer (ed.), Leuven 2001

The

Apocryphal

Acts

of JAN N. BREMMER (Ed.)

Thomas

PEETERS

Contents

CONTENTS

Preface

After the fall of the Berlin Wall the Rijksuniversiteit Groningen decided to intensify contacts with universities in Eastern Europe. In 1991 the then Head of the Department of Church History, Professor Hans Roldanus, took this opportunity to forge links not only with the theologians of the Károli Gáspár University of Budapest but also with the classicists of the Loránt-Eötvös University of Budapest. The initiative seemed highly promising, as the world of early Christianity was receiving ever increasing attention from New Testament and patristic scholars as well as from ancient historians. Initially, it was decided to focus on the Apocryphal Acts of the Apotles, a genre of which various representatives had recently been re-edited or were (are!) in the process of being re-edited. As our series of yearly conferences now has completed the study of the major Acts and our initiative has been well received, we proceed with the major Apocalypses: the next volume in our series will focus on the *Apocalypse of Peter*. With the widening of the scope of our series we have also changed the title to *Studies in Early Christian Apocrypha*. The series will continue to publish the results of our conferences, but the editors also welcome other studies in this field, be it proceedings or monographs.

Following the volumes on the *Acts of John* (1995), the *Acts of Paul and Thecla* (1996), the *Acts of Peter* (1998) and the *Acts of Andrew* (2000), this volume is dedicated to the *Acts of Thomas*. The volume starts with the memoirs of the *Altmeister* Fré Klijn regarding his own role in the study of the Acts. He is followed by an analysis of the elusive phenomenon of Thomas Christianity. The major part of the book studies various aspects and passages of the *Acts*: narrative strategies, the heavenly palace, factors of plot, the Hymn of the Pearl, the serpent, women, and the connection of Thomas with India. As a kind of summary of the results of some of our investigations, the penultimate chapter takes a fresh looks at the authors, place, time and readership of the major Apocryphal Acts of the Apostles. As has become customary, the volume is rounded off by a bibliography and an index.

The conference which formed the basis of this book took place at the Rijksuniversiteit Groningen in the autumn of 1998. I would like to thank the Faculty of Theology and Science of Religion of the Rijksuniversiteit Groningen and the Onderzoekschool Rudolf Agricola, the Groningen Research School for the Humanities, for its financial support towards the conference. Ken Dowden, Stephen Harrison and Maryna Mews helped to correct the English; Ton Hilhorst and Gerard Luttikhuizen assisted in correcting the proofs, and Brenda Bartelink was a great help in making the index. I am grateful to them all.

Jan N. Bremmer   Groningen, Summer 2001

List of abbreviations

AAA	*Apocryphal Acts of the Apostles*
ANRW	*Aufstieg und Niedergang der römischen Welt*
Bremmer,	Jan N. Bremmer (ed), *The Apocryphal*
Acts of John	*Acts of John* (Kampen, 1995)
Bremmer,	Jan N. Bremmer (ed), *The Apocryphal*
Acts of Paul	*Acts of Paul and Thecla* (Kampen, 1996)
Bremmer,	Jan N. Bremmer (ed), *The Apocryphal*
Acts of Peter	*Acts of Peter* (Leuven, 1998)
Bremmer,	Jan N. Bremmer (ed), The Apocryphal
Acts of Andrew	*Acts of Andrew* (Leuven, 2000)
CIL	*Corpus Inscriptionum Latinarum*
JAC	*Jahrbuch für Antike und Christentum*
JTS	*Journal of Theological Studies*
NTA	W. Schneemelcher, *New Testament Apocrypha*, tr. and ed. R. McL. Wilson, 2 vols (Cambridge, 1992^2)
PG	*Patrologia Graeca*
PL	*Patrologia Latina*
RAC	*Reallexikon für Antike und Christentum*
RE	*Realencyclopädie der classischen Altertumswissenschaft*
SBL	*Society of Biblical Literature*
SEG	*Supplementum Epigraphicum Graecum*
TWNT	*Theologisches Wörterbuch zum Neuen Testament*
VigChris	*Vigiliae Christianae*
ZNW	*Zeitschrift für die neutestamentliche Wissenschaft*
ZPE	*Zeitschrift für Papyrologie und Epigraphik*

All translations, if not otherwise indicated, are from *NTA II* (by H.J.W. Drijvers

Notes on Contributors

Tamás Adamik b. 1937, is Professor of Latin at the Loránt-Eötvös University of Budapest. He is the author of the following studies in Hungarian: *A Commentary on Catullus* (1971), *Martial and His Poetry* (1979), *Aristotle's Rhetoric* (1982), *Jerome's Selected Works* (1991), *A History of Roman Literature* I-IV (1993-96), and *Ancient Theories of Style from Gorgias to Augustine* (1998). He is also the editor of new Hungarian translations of the *Apocryphal Acts of the Apostles* (1996), the *Apocryphal Gospels* (1996), the *Apocryphal Apocalypses* (1997), and the *Apocryphal Epistles* (1999).

János Bolyki b. 1931, is Professor Emeritus of New Testament Studies at the Károli Gáspár University of Budapest. He is the author of *Jesu Tischgemeinschaften* (1998), and of the following studies in Hungarian: *The Questions of the Sciences in the History of Theology in the 20th Century* (1970), *Faith and Science* (1989) and *The Table Fellowships of Jesus* (1992), *Principles and Methods of New Testament Interpretation* (1998²), and *The Ecological Crisis in Theological Perspective* (1999). He co-authored, in Hungarian, *Codex D in the Book of Acts* (1995) and *Revelation: Two Approaches* (1997).

Lourens P. van den Bosch b. 1944, is Associate Professor of History of Religion at the Rijksuniversiteit Groningen. He is the author of *Atharvaveda-parisista. Chapters 21-29: Introduction, translation and notes* (1978), *Inleiding in het hindoeïsme* (1990), and a forthcoming study on Max Müller.

Jan N. Bremmer b. 1944, is Professor of History and Science of Religion at the Rijksuniversiteit Groningen. He is the author of *The Early Greek Concept of the Soul* (1983), *Greek Religion* (1999²) and

The Rise and Fall of the Afterlife (2002); co-author of *Roman Myth and Mythography* (1987), editor of *Interpretations of Greek Mythology* (1987), *From Sappho to de Sade: Moments in the History of Sexuality* (1989), *The Apocryphal Acts of John* (1995), *The Apocryphal Acts of Paul and Thecla* (1996), *The Apocryphal Acts of Peter* (1998) and *The Apocryphal Acts of Andrew* (2000), and co-editor of *A Cultural History of Gesture* (1991), *Between Poverty and the Pyre. Moments in the history of widowhood* (1995) and *A Cultural History of Humour* (1997).

István Czachesz b. 1968, prepares a dissertation on apostolic commission at the Rijksuniversiteit Groningen. He is, in Hungarian, the author of *Gaia's Two Faces* (1996), co-author of *Codex D in the Book of Acts* (1995), editor of *Disciples, Wonderworkers, Martyrs* (1997: a volume of essays on the Apocryphal Acts of the Apostles), and translator of *Tyconius' Book of Rules* (1997).

A. Hilhorst b. 1938, is Associate Professor of Early Christian Literature and New Testament Studies at the Rijksuniversiteit Groningen. He is the author of *Sémitismes et latinismes dans le Pasteur d'Hermas* (1976) and co-author of *Apocalypse of Paul: a new critical edition of three long Latin versions* (1997), editor of *De heiligenverering in de eerste eeuwen van het Christendom* (1988), and co-editor of *Fructus Centesimus. Mélanges G.J.M. Bartelink* (1989), *The Scriptures and the Scrolls. Studies A.S. van der Woude* (1992), *Early Christian Poetry* (1993) and *Evangelie en beschaving. Studies Hans Roldanus* (1995).

A.F.J. Klijn b. 1923, is Professor Emeritus of Early Christian Literature and New Testament Studies at the Rijksuniversiteit Groningen. From his many books we mention *A survey of the researches into the Western text of the Gospels and Acts*, 2 vols (1949-69), *The Acts of Thomas* (1962), *Edessa, die Stadt des Apostels Thomas* (1965), (with G.J. Reinink) *Patristic evidence for Jewish-Christian sects* (1973), *Seth in Jewish, Christian and gnostic literature* (1977), *An Introduction to the New Testament* (1980²), *Der lateinische Text der Apokalypse des Esra* (1983), *Jewish-Christian gospel tradition* (1992), *Die Esra-Apokalypse (IV Esra)* (1992), *Jezus in de apocriefe evangelieën* (1999), *Apocriefe Handelingen van de Apostelen* (2001). He is the editor of *Apokriefen van het Nieuwe Testament*, 2 vols (1984-85).

Gerard Luttikhuizen b. 1940, is Professor of Early Christian Literature and New Testament Studies at the Rijksuniversiteit Groningen. He is the author of *The Revelation of Elchasai* (1985) and *Gnostische Geschriften* I (1986), editor of *Paradise Interpreted* (1999) and *The Creation of Man and Woman* (2000) and co-editor of *Stories of the Flood* (1998).

Monika Pesthy b. 1954, teaches Theology at the Vilmos Apor Catholic College. She is, in Hungarian, the author of *Origen: Commentary on the Songs of Songs* (1993), *Origen, Interpreter of the Bible* (1996), and translator of *Origen: De Principiis IV* (1998).

Philip Sellew b. 1953, is Associate Professor of Classical and Near Eastern Studies at the University of Minnesota. He is the author of *Early Collections of Jesus' Words: The Development of Dominical Discourses* (1986) and a contributor *to The Complete Gospels: Annotated Scholars Version* (1992; revised edition 1994). Since 1993 he has been co-editor of the journal *Currents in Research: Biblical Studies*. He is currently preparing a commentary on the *Gospel of Thomas* for the series *The Scholars Bible*.

I. The *Acts of Thomas* Revisited

A.F.J. KLIJN

The title of this contribution supposes a previous visit to the *Acts of Thomas*. First of all I would like to tell how this first visit came about. In the mid-fifties I was appointed as a lecturer in New Testament studies at the University of Utrecht. It was at the time that Van Unnik was flourishing[1]. Although he started as a scholar in the field of Syriac studies[2], he was intimately acquainted with the international New Testament scene and was widely invited to lecture abroad. In this same period Quispel was appointed to the chair of early Christian literature. Before long he became famous for his work on the Nag Hammadi writings and in particular the *Gospel of Thomas*[3].

It was also the time that German New Testament studies were dominated by the ideas of Bultmann, whose pupils held the most important New Testament chairs in Germany. All of them indulged in gnostic studies, especially Manichaeism and Mandaeism, at the basis of which they supposed to have discovered the system of the 'erlöste Erlöser'[4], an approach, which was strongly rejected by Van Unnik in spite of his excellent personal relationship with Bultmann and his followers.

[1] See *Woorden gaan leven. Opstellen van en over Willem Cornelis van Unnik (1910-1978)* (Kampen, 1979). This book was published on behalf of the Theological Faculty in Utrecht by A.J. Bronkhorst, O.J de Jong and J. Reiling and contains Van Unnik's bibliography. See also W.C. van Unnik, *Sparsa Collecta*, 3 vols (Leiden, 1973-83).
[2] See W.C. van Unnik, *Nestorian Questions on the Administration of the Eucharist, by Isho'yabh IV. A Contribution to the History of the Eucharist in the Eastern Church* (Diss. Leiden = Haarlem, 1937).
[3] See his bibliography in R. van den Broek and M.J. Vermaseren (eds), *Studies in Gnosticism and Hellenistic Religions presented to Gillis Quispel on the Occasion of his 65th Birthday* (Leiden, 1981) 1-12.
[4] See C. Colpe, *Die religionsgeschichtliche Schule. Darstellung und Kritik ihres Bildes vom gnostischen Erlösermythos* (Göttingen, 1961).

Quispel was tending more and more to the idea for a Jewish background of gnosticism; but initially, as a classical scholar, he lacked both the necessary knowledge of Semitic languages and – this especially applies to the study of the *Gospel of Thomas* – basic insights into New Testament textual criticism in general and into the harmonies of the Gospels in particular. Under these circumstances it was my privilege to work in the shadow of these two great scholars, although I originated from a quite different angle. The contents of my dissertation, which I defended in 1949[5], were in the tradition of another great Dutch scholar, Daniel Plooij, who devoted the greater part of his scientific work to the study of the text of the Liège *Diatessaron* which was, according to him, ultimately of Tatianic and Syriac origin[6].

My interest in textual criticism happened to be of some importance for the study of the contents of the *Gospel of Thomas*. However, it did not take long before Quispel was able to find his own way in the field of Diatessaric studies. I, therefore, decided to continue my work into a different direction. And it was in that period that Van Unnik drew my attention to the *ATh* and I decided to write a commentary on this work. It was his idea that these *Acts* had to be studied in the light of early Syriac literature. This meant that I had to keep some distance from *Mythos und Legende in den apokryphen Thomas-Akten* written by G. Bornkamm[7] who approached this work from a gnostic point of view in the tradition of Bultmann.

This was my first visit to the *ATh*. The results of my work were published in 1962[8]. I am thoroughly aware of its shortcomings and the occasional sloppiness of its contents. Nevertheless, after some forty years I am convinced that I happened to investigate some subjects that are still at the centre of scholarly interest.

---

[5] See Klijn, *A Survey of the Researches into the Western Text of the Gospels and Acts* (Diss. Utrecht, 1949).
[6] See D. Plooij with the assistance of C.A. Phillips, 'The Liège Diatessaron', *Verh. Kon. Nederl. Akademie van Wetenschappen*, Afd. Lett., NR XXXI, Part I-IV 1929-35; D. Plooij, C.A. Phillips and A.H.A. Bakker, Part V-VI 1938 and 1963, and D. Plooij and C.A. Phillips, A.H.A. Bakker, Part VII and VIII 1965 and 1970.
[7] See G. Bornkamm, *Mythos und Legende in den apokryphen Thomas-Akten* (Göttingen, 1933).
[8] Klijn, *The Acts of Thomas* (Leiden, 1962).

According to the Contents the following subjects are dealt with in this book: the text of the *ATh*; a comparison with other *AAA*; the question whether Thomas visited India; the beginnings of Christianity in Edessa; the doctrine of the *ATh*; the *Acts* and Syriac Christianity, and, finally, baptism and eucharist in the *Acts*. In any new commentary on the *ATh* these subjects would still have to be studied. At the moment it is almost universally accepted that the *ATh* have to be approached as a genuine product of Eastern Christianity[9].

In 1967 I was appointed to the chair of New Testament studies in Groningen and I had to dirct my attention to different subjects. But at that time I also became a colleague of such outstanding scholars as H.J.W. Drijvers and G.J. Reinink of the Groningen Semitic Institute who also happened to be interested in early Syriac Christianity and who were able to take over[10], where I decided to go a different way[11]. I am, nevertheless, grateful that I have been invited to revisit the *ATh* during a conference dealing with the *AAA* in general and at present especially with the *ATh*. It might seem to be reckless, but it is also appropriate to wonder what alterations would have to be made if a second and revised edition of my Commentary on the *ATh* of 1962 had to be prepared[12].

---

[9] Especially the so-called 'Hymn of the Pearl' (*ATh* 108-13) was supposed to be 'eines der schönsten Originalzeugnisse der Gnosis', according to Bornkamm, *Mythos und Legende*, 111 and cf. 117: 'Das Lied bringt also die Sendung und die prototypische Erlösung des selbst unter die Erlösergottheiten aufgenommenen Mani, indem auf ihn der alte, iranische Mythos vom erlösten Erlöser übertragen ist.' But see Klijn, 'The so-called Hymn of the Pearl (Acts of Thomas ch. 108-113)', *VigChris* 14 (1960) 154-64, and especially P.-H. Poirier, *L'Hymne de la Perle des Actes de Thomas. Introduction, Texte – Traduction, Commentaire* (Louvain-la Neuve, 1981); Luttikhuizen, this volume, Ch. VIII.

[10] Here I may refer only to H.J.W. Drijvers, 'The Acts of Thomas', in *NTA* II, 322-411, and H.J.W. Drijvers und G.J. Reinink, 'Taufe und Licht. Tatian, Ebionäerevangelium und Thomasakten', in T. Baarda *et al.* (eds), *Text and Testimony. Essays on New Testament and Apocryphal Literature in Honour of A.F.J. Klijn* (Kampen, 1988) 91-110, repr. in Drijvers, *History and Religion in Late Antique Syria* (Aldershot, 1994) Ch. IV.

[11] During my time in Groningen I went into the study of early Jewish Christianity.

[12] In the following I shall refer to publications which appeared after 1962. Because the invitation to revisit the *ATh* came as a surprise, I regret to say

1. *The Commentary*

In the edition of 1962 I decided to comment upon a Syriac text[13]. This decision was taken because I wanted to emphasize the Syriac origin of the *ATh*. However, in order to comment on the original text I had to refer to the Greek text very often, especially because the texts of the Greek manuscripts U (11th cent.) and P (11/12th cent.) are much better than the various Syriac texts. Thus I can understand why modern translations of this work are based upon the Greek text of R.A. Lipsius and M. Bonnet, which still is the only and best edition[14].

However, a commentary on the text of the *ATh* cannot be based on the Greek text only[15], since the Greek text shows that this work was written in an environment in which at least the Syriac language was well known. It appears that sometimes the Greek cannot be understood without the help of the Syriac version. We have to conclude that the work was written in a bilingual environment[16].

that I am not able to give an exhaustive summary of everything that has been published during the last forty years, but see Drijvers, *'Acts of Thomas'*, 322-39.

[13]   I used W. Wright, *Apocryphal Acts of the Apostles*, 2 vols (London, 1871; repr. Amsterdam, 1968) II.146-298.

[14]   *Acta Apostolorum Apocrypha* II (Leipzig, 1903) 99-288, cf. the translations of M. Erbetta, *Gli Apocrifi del Nuovo Testamento II: Atti e Legende* (Torino, 1966) 313-74; L. Moraldi, *Apocrifi del Nuovo Testamento II* (Torino, 1971) 1125-1350; Drijvers, *o.c.*; J.K. Elliott, *The Apocryphal New Testament* (Oxford, 1993) 439-511; F. Bovon and P. Geoltrain (eds), *Écrits apocryphes chrétiens* I (Paris, 1997) 1321-1470.

[15]   See A.J. Festugière, *Les Actes Apocryphes de Jean et de Thomas* (Geneva, 1983) 43: 'J'ai donc eu constamment sous les yeux la traduction (*scil.* of the Syriac text) de A.F.J. Klijn...'.

[16]   This is the opinion of B. Layton, *The Gnostic Scriptures* (London, 1987) 364; see also H.W. Attridge, 'The Original Language of the Acts of Thomas', in idem *et al.* (eds), *Of Scribes and Scrolls. Studies... presented to John Strugnell* (New York, 1990) 241-50 at 250: 'It is, however, clear that the range of witnesses now available to us ultimately depends on a Syriac original'. Drijvers, *o.c.*, 323, supposed that the *ATh* had originally been written in Syriac. However, in his 'Syriac Culture in Late Antiquity. Hellenism and Local Tradition', in *Mediterraneo Antico* 1 (1998) 95-113, he gives convincing evidence for the influence of Hellenistic culture in this area.

I remember that the form of the *Commentary* was inspired by that of J.H. Waszink's *De Anima*[17]. In the list of Abbreviations at the beginning of my work it is possible to discover what kind of references have been used. It is obvious that this list has to be corrected with the help of recent revisions of earlier editions and later discoveries like the Nag Hammadi writings[18]. Generally speaking. however, it remains necessary to limit oneself to that kind of sources which have been used in the Commentary.

2. Tradition of the Text

The first chapter of the Introduction deals with the tradition of the text. At that time I apparently tried to give a complete survey of all the available texts both in Greek and other languages. I assume that such an effort is now impossible. But it also seems to be unnecessary in order to write a commentary on the text, since most of the Greek manuscripts and those of the translations offer a secondary text which has to be studied in its own right. This appears from some recently published works on the *AAA*[19]. Nevertheless a number of interesting contributions to the translated versions of the *ATh* have been published recently[20]. But even if we use the Greek version as the *texte de base* we shall have to have continuous recourse to the Syriac version.

[17] J.H. Waszink, *De Anima* (Amsterdam, 1947).
[18] It seems to me, however, that the contribution to the commentary of recently discovered writings is limited.
[19] E. Junod et J.-D.Kaestli, *Acta Iohannis*, 2 vols (Turnhout, 1983); J.-M. Prieur, *Acta Andreae*, 2 vols (Turnhout, 1989).
[20] For the Greek text see M. Lipinski, *Konkordanz zu den Thomasakten* (Frankfurt am Main, 1988). See also K. Zelzer, *Die alten Lateinischen Thomasakten* (Berlin, 1977); M. van Esbroeck, 'Les actes apocryphes de Thomas en version arabe', *Parole de l'Orient* 14 (1981) 11-77; P.-II. Poirier, *La version copte de la Prédication et du Martyre de Thomas*; avec une contribution codicologique au corpus copte des Acta Apostolorum apocrypha, par Enzo Lucchesi (Brussels, 1984); L. Leloir, *Écrits apocryphes sur les Apôtres. Traduction de l'Édition Arménienne de Venise* (Turnhout, 1992) 531-646.

6   A.F.J. KLIJN

3. Comparison with other AAA

The second chapter of the Introduction deals with a 'Comparison with other Apocryphal Acts'. At that time my main interest was to discover the chronological relationship between the various AAA^{21}. Starting from the oldest dated AAA I tried to discover the origin and possible dependence of the other ones. But here we can speak of a considerable development. And this does not only apply to the ATh but also to the other ones. With regard to the ATh, scholars are aware that its author produced a work of art. He was able to give a 'symbolic presentation of salvation'[22]. The five ancient AAA are presenting a literary *genre* of a narrative character which has to be studied with modern methods[23].

4. Thomas and India

The third chapter of the Introduction deals with Thomas and India. I had to decide about a possible visit of Thomas to India. At the moment I very much doubt whether Thomas has ever been in that country, especially because I am impressed by the critical view expressed by Dr. L.P van den Bosch[24]. However, a few questions remain. The most important is why the author neglected the ancient traditional view according to which Thomas visited Parthia. Nevertheless the Parthian influence on the contents of the ATh, especially the Hymn of the Pearl, is considerable. I may suggest that the author deliberately chose a far-away country with imaginary royal courts[25],

[21] See now Bremmer, this volume, Ch. XI.
[22] See Drijvers, *o.c.*, 327.
[23] See L. van Kampen, *Apostelverhalen* (Diss. Utrecht, 1990); W. Rordorf, 'Terra Incognita. Recent Research on Christan Apocryphal Literature, especially on some Acts of Apostles', in his *Lex Orandi – Lex Credendi* (Freiburg, 1993) 432-438.
[24] See van den Bosch, this volume, Ch. X.
[25] See H.J.W. Drijvers, 'Apocryphal Literature in the Cultural Milieu of Osrhoëne', *Apocrypha* 1 (1990) 231-47 at 233 = Drijvers, *History and Religion*, Ch. III: 'The royal Court had a central function in local urban culture', and Klijn, 'Der Einfluss der politischen Lage auf die Literatur in Edessa in den ersten Jahrhunderten der christlichen Ära', in J. Irmscher (ed), *Die Literatur der Spätantike, polyethnisch und polyglottisch betrachtet: eine Aufsatzsammlung* (Amsterdam, 1997) 135-44.

well known in the region in which the *Acts* originated. In addition to this I would like to draw attention to the composite character of the *ATh*. For this reason it is impossible to conclude that this work is supposed to be simply a coherent story about a visit to 'India'[26].

5. The Beginnings of Christianity in Edessa

In the year 1962 I was still convinced that the *ATh* was written in Edessa. As a title of one of my books I chose 'Edessa, die Stadt des Apostels Thomas'[27]. However, it seems that Edessa did not show interest in the Apostle Thomas before the fourth century[28]. Since we have to study the *ATh* against the background of newly discovered writings like the *Gospel of Thomas* and *Thomas the Contender*, we now realise that stories about Judas Thomas were spread over a considerable time and space with roots in Aramaic-speaking Christianity[29]. I suppose that the situation is much more complicated than is usually assumed. Drijvers writes that the *ATh* were written in 'East Syria'[30]. If we speak about Edessa we may say that it was located on the cross-roads of various cultures and a variety of religions. We know that here Tatian went to live but he called himself an Assyrian. Earlier we spoke about the Parthian influence in the *ATh*.

---

[26] It is evident that at *c*.62 the story starts again. See also Y. Tissot, 'Les Actes apocryphes de Thomas: exemple de recueil composite', in Bovon, *Les Actes Apocryphes des Apôtres*, 223-32.
[27] Neukirchen 1965, but see also the Introduction to the translation of the *ATh* in Bovon and Geoltrain, *Écrits apocryphes chrétiens* I, 1325: 'Rédigés sans doute à Edesse...'; Bremmer, this volume, Ch. VI.
[28] See J. Wilkinson, *Egeria's Travels: newly translated (from the Latin) with supporting documents and notes* (London, 1971) 224-5. In the Greek text of the *ATh* the name of the city of Edessa is absent even at the end at which it is said according to the Greek text that the body of Thomas has been brought to the 'West' or 'Mesopotamia'.
[29] See Layton, *Gnostic Scriptures*, 357-409 ('The School of St. Thomas'); P.-H. Poirier, 'Évangile de Thomas, Actes de Thomas, Livre de Thomas. Une Tradition et ses Transformations', *Apocrypha* 7 (1996) 9-26; Klijn, 'John XIV 22 and the Name Judas Thomas', in *Studies in John. Presented to J.N. Sevenster* (Leiden, 1970) 88-96; J.J. Gunther, 'The Meaning and Origin of the Name 'Judas Thomas',' *Le Muséon* 93 (1980) 113-48.
[30] See Drijvers, *o.c.*, 323, and 'Syriac Culture in Late Antiquity'.

If we look at the literary products of this area like the *Odes of Salomon*, the *Gospel of Thomas* and the *ATh*, we are always dealing with the same problems of original language, date and place of origin. Now we may conclude that 'The Beginnings of Christianity in Edessa' does not help us to solve the problems regarding the origin of the writings connected with the name of Thomas.

6. *The Doctrine of the ATh*

In a fifth chapter of the Introduction I went into the doctrine of the *ATh*. Here I tried to give a survey of the contents without going into the question of origin and parallel passages. It clearly showed that we are dealing with Christian doctrines that can certainly not be called gnostic. In my article on John 14.22 and the name of Judas Thomas, mentioned above, I was especially impressed by the influence of what I named the *morphê*-christology. This means that the heavenly Christ appeared in the 'form' of Jesus. But he can also appear in the form of Judas the apostle. It is clear that the *ATh* supposes a distinction between the incorrupt heavenly world and the corruptible earthly life. At that time I omitted to define the doctrine of the *ATh*. At the moment it seems that scholars are looking for a form of encratism[31].

7. *The ATh and Syriac Christianity*

In accordance with the idea of an Edessene origin, I dealt with the *ATh* and Syriac Christianity. I mentioned a number of authors and writings, like the *Liber Graduum*, Bardaisan and Tatian. It appears that now especially Drijvers is keen to demonstrate the relation between these writers, especially Tatian, and the *ATh*[32]. Recent works on Tatian and Bardaisan have made it possible to go into the religious background of these *Acts*.

---

[31] See already G. Blond, 'L'encratisme dans les actes apocryphes de Thomas', *Recherches et Travaux* 1.2 (1946) 5-25, and especially Y. Tissot, 'L'encratisme des Actes de Thomas', in *ANRW* II 25.6 (Berlin and New York, 1988) 4415-30.
[32] In addition to articles mentioned earlier I may refer to Drijvers and Reinink, 'Taufe und Licht'.

8. Baptism and Eucharist

Finally I had to discuss the Baptism and Eucharist in the *ATh*. I was able to show that the order of Baptism in the *Acts* agrees with what is found in ancient Syriac literature[33]. I am glad to say that the study of the sacraments in Syria and especially Armenia has now been pursued. However I suppose that the epicleses still require further study[34].

Conclusion

If we consider what has been said here we wonder what would have to be done if a second edition of my commentary on *ATh* had to be prepared. First of all we have to study this work within the wider framework of what we may call Eastern Christianity, with roots going back to the early Aramaic-speaking Church. Next, a number of corrections has to be made, and especially the commentary has to be revised and amplified with references taken from recently discovered writings. It is a matter of consideration whether this has to be based upon the Greek or the Syriac text. The evidence of the translations asks for a special treatment. The chapter about the relation with other *AAA* has to be rewritten in the light of modern approaches to narrative texts. Since the discovery of a number of writings bearing the

---

[33] See Klijn, 'An ancient Syriac Baptismal Liturgy in the Syriac Acts of John', *Novum Testamentum* 6 (1963) 216-28.
[34] See G. Winkler, 'The Original Meaning of the Prebaptismal Anointing and its Implications', *Worship* 52 (1978) 24-45 and 'Zur frühchristlichen Tauftradition in Syrien und Armenien unter Einbezug der Taufe Jesu', *Ostkirchliche Studien* 27 (1978) 287-306; S. Brock, *The Holy Spirit in the Syrian Baptismal Tradition* (Bronx NY, 1979); L. Leloir, 'Symbolisme dans la Liturgie Syriaque primitive. Le Symbolisme dans le Culte des Grandes Religions', in *Homo Religiosus* II (Louvain-la Neuve, 1985) 247-63; H. Kruse, 'Zwei Geistepiklesen der syrischen Thomas-Akten', *Oriens Christianus* 69 (1985) 33-53; G. Rouwhorst, 'La célébration de l'eucharistie selon les Actes de Thomas', in Ch. Caspers and M. Schneiders (eds), *Omnes Circumstantes. Contributions towards a History of the Role of the People in the Liturgy* (Kampen, 1990) 51-77; E. Boone, 'L'onction pré-baptismale: sens et origine. Un exemple dans les *Actes de Thomas*', *Studia Patristica* 30 (Leuven, 1997) 291-5.

name of Thomas, it is necessary to go into their common background and its development. Finally, the *ATh* represents one aspect of Eastern Christianity and we have to realise that an apostle who happened to bear the name of 'Twin' was, therefore, bound to attract the interest of various cultural and religious groups in that region.

II. Thomas Christianity: Scholars in Quest of a Community

PHILIP SELLEW

Some recent scholarship suggests that standing behind the literature composed by the ancient church in connection with Judas Thomas was a particular sort of Christianity or even an identifiable school of thought[1]. This supposed community is given the label 'Thomas Christianity,' a term that suggests an identifiable and distinct social group, presumably with some level of organizational structure as well as a corporate history and a characteristic ideology. According to one leading advocate of this view, Gregory J. Riley, there existed a 'Thomas community which looked to this apostle for inspiration and spiritual legitimacy and created the Thomas tradition.... It produced the Gospel of Thomas and the Book of Thomas (the Contender)....'. Riley goes on to say that 'The Acts of Thomas are in conscious continuity with this tradition'[2]. In what follows I want to examine this proposal of a 'Thomas tradition' that looks to an apostolic figure and forms a 'Thomas community' still visible in those three books: the *Gospel of Thomas*, the *Book of Thomas (the Contender)*, and the *ATh*. Riley's thesis is the most provocative and far-reaching version of this construct being offered to scholars today.

---

[1] See e.g. B. Layton, *The Gnostic Scriptures* (Garden City, 1983) 359-64 ('The School of St. Thomas'); S.J. Patterson, *The Gospel of Thomas and Jesus* (Sonoma, 1993) 121-57 ('Thomas Christianity: A Social-Historical Description'); and most recently G.J. Riley, 'Thomas Tradition and the *Acts of Thomas*', *SBL Seminar Papers* 30 (Atlanta, 1991) 533-42 and *Resurrection Reconsidered: Thomas and John in Controversy* (Minneapolis, 1995), as well as the 'Thomasine Christianity' research group within the North American Society of Biblical Literature.

[2] Riley, 'Thomas Tradition and the *Acts of Thomas*', 533.

1. *Thomas books and Thomas Christianity in recent scholarship*

Scholars have of course been drawing attention to the possible relationship of these three Thomas books for quite some time. Ever since the study of Codex II of the Nag Hammadi corpus first began in the 1950s, and even more since the Coptic text of the entire collection became available to the world late in the 1970s, researchers have noted some intriguing links. Henri-Charles Puech drew attention to the interesting double form of the apostle's name as given in both the *Gospel* and the *ATh*, as well as the apostle's 'privilege... of being the confidant of the most secret teachings of Jesus' at various points in the *ATh* (10, 39, 47, 78), as well as in the prologue and statement 13 of the *Gospel of Thomas*[3]. From this and other observations about themes shared between the two books Puech drew the widely accepted conclusion that the *ATh* show both a knowledge and a deliberate use of the *Gospel of Thomas* (though some other scholars, like Günther Bornkamm writing in the Hennecke-Schneemelcher collection, did not find all the proposed thematic links quite so convincing)[4]. Puech made only a tantalizingly brief mention of the *Book of Thomas* (still unpublished when he was writing) that was included in the same Nag Hammadi codex as the Coptic *Gospel of Thomas*.

In his dissertation written at Duke University and published in 1975, John D. Turner made a more explicit linkage of the *Gospel, Book,* and *ATh*. Turner's main concern was to argue that the *Book of Thomas* from Codex II was composed by combining two originally separate documents, the first (Section A) being a dialogue between the risen Savior and his twin brother Thomas. But in the conclusion of his book Turner pointed out that 'all three [Thomas books] contain the ascetic theme, possess a dualistic anthropology, and regard Judas

---

[3] H.-C. Puech, 'Une collection de paroles de Jésus récemment retrouvée: l'Évangile selon Thomas', reprinted in his *En quête de la Gnose*, vol. 2: *Sur l'Évangile selon Thomas* (Paris, 1978) 43-4; 'Doctrines ésotériques et thèmes gnostiques dans l'Évangile selon Thomas', *ibid.*, 210-6, 242, and 'Gnostic Gospels and Related Documents', 286f.

[4] G. Bornkamm, 'The Acts of Thomas,' in *NTA* II, 427; cf. also B. Ehlers (later Aland), 'Kann das Thomasevangelium aus Edessa Stammen?', *NovT* 12 (1970) 284-317; A.F.J. Klijn, 'Christianity in Edessa and the Gospel of Thomas', *Novum Testamentum* 14 (1972) 70-7.

Thomas as the twin (*didymos*) of the Savior and recipient of his most secret revelations.... In view of these common themes and particularly of the Thomas-tradition central to all three works, section A of *Thomas the Contender* occupies a median position in the stream of the ascetic Syrian Thomas-tradition as we move from the *Gospel of Thomas* to the *ATh*'. His analysis led Turner to 'postulate the existence of a tradition centered on the apostle Thomas, the twin of Jesus and recipient of his secret words, which increasingly regards Thomas as champion and contender in the cause of abstinence from all that is worldly, especially sex'[5].

Both Puech and Turner made connections between documents that they saw as dating from the second and third centuries, and traced the origins of these connections to Syrian Christianity. The location of the Thomas tradition in eastern Syria had also been emphasized as early as 1965, in agreement with Puech, by Helmut Koester in his article on the diversification of ancient Christian belief and practice, which was a deliberate effort to update and refine Walter Bauer's thesis about the 'non-orthodox' character of Syrian Christianity before the third century, especially in the east[6]. Though Koester was most interested in the *Gospel of Thomas*, he also considered the other factors pointed to by Puech as indicating not only that the *ATh* was 'the direct continuation of the eastern Syrian Thomas tradition as it is represented in the second century by the *Gospel of Thomas*,' but that 'the Thomas tradition was the oldest form of Christianity in Edessa, antedating the beginnings of both Marcionite and orthodox Christianity in that area'. 'Thomas was the authority for an indigenous Syrian Christianity....'[7]. In later publications Koester would push the possible composition date of the *Gospel of Thomas* back into the first century[8].

---

[5] J.D. Turner, *The Book of Thomas the Contender from Codex II of the Cairo Gnostic Library from Nag Hammadi* (Missoula, 1975) 232-7, 233, 235, respectively.

[6] H. Koester, 'GNOMAI DIAPHOROI: On the Origin and Nature of Diversification in the History of Early Christianity', *HTR* (1965), reprinted in *idem* & J.M. Robinson, *Trajectories through Ancient Christianity* (Philadelphia, 1971) 114-57 at 128-41.

[7] *Ibid.*, 129, 133.

[8] Koester, 'Apocryphal and Canonical Gospels,' *HTR* 73 (1980) 105-30; 'Introduction [to Tractate Two: The Gospel According to Thomas]', in

In his commentary published on the *ATh* in 1962, which quickly became the standard resource on the book, A.F.J. Klijn confirmed the location of the *Acts* within Syrian Christianity with a wealth of philological and thematic evidence[9]. Though he considered the question of the relations of the *ATh* with other apocryphal apostolic acts and with such authors of Syriac Christianity as Tatian, Bardaisan, and Ephrem, Klijn spent little time in his commentary on possible connections of the *Acts* with other Thomasine literature[10]. Layton has also accepted the general association of these three Thomas books with eastern Syria, and although he titled a section of his anthology of Gnostic scripture 'The School of St. Thomas, he acknowledged both that the Thomas literature is not especially Gnostic, and furthermore that it shares many of its central values and themes with other early Christian texts typically associated with other apostolic figures. In Layton's careful phrasing, he says that:

> 'the Thomas works were composed and transmitted in one or more Christian communities of the Mesopotamian region. Edessa was one of the main centers for the diffusion of Christian literature composed in this region; this fact, together with its claim to possess the bones of St. Thomas, makes it the most obvious home for a 'school' of writers who honored St. Thomas as their patron saint. Since there is nothing especially sectarian about the Thomas scripture, it must have been a part of the normal canon of scripture read by Mesopotamian Christians in the second and early third centuries. It would have been read along with works such as the *Odes of Solomon* and Tatian's *Harmony (Diatessaron)*...'[11].

B. Layton (ed), *Nag Hammadi Codex II, 2-7*, vol. 1 (Leiden, 1989) 39 ('possibly even in the first century AD'). Patterson, *Gospel of Thomas and Jesus*, 120, cautiously suggests a composition date for the *Gospel of Thomas* sometime around the decade of AD 70-80 based on such factors as genre, appeal to personal (not corporate) apostolic authority, and (less persuasively) the book's 'primitive' christology. I. Dunderberg suggests a slightly later period based on structural and ideological analogies between *Thomas* and the *Gospel of John* (see n. 26).

[9] A.F.J. Klijn, *The Acts of Thomas* (Leiden, 1962) 30-3, 38-53; see also Klijn, this volume, Ch. I.

[10] Klijn confirmed the connection of the name Judas Thomas with eastern Syria in his article 'John XIV 22 and the Name Judas Thomas,' in *Studies in John* (Leiden, 1977) 88-96.

[11] Layton, *The Gnostic Scriptures*, 361.

These judgments would accord in many respects with those expressed by H.J.W. Drijvers. In addition to his extensive treatment of the *ATh* for the fifth edition of Schneemelcher's *Neutestamentliche Apokryphen*, in which he has made important advances in explaining both the literary structure and the ideological basis of the *ATh*, Drijvers has published some trenchant remarks about the 'romantic and nostalgic picture' that he judges has overly influenced scholars like Koester and Gilles Quispel in their reconstructions of early Syrian Christianity, especially in their suppositions about the antiquity of the Thomas traditions there[12]. Drijvers explains the similarities of theme and content in the *Gospel* and *ATh* as arising from the characteristic elements of Syrian Christian theology (both east and west) as exemplified by Tatian and the *Odes of Solomon*, and not as the remnant of any real connection of the origins of the church in eastern Syria with either an historical apostle Thomas or any first-century movement attached to his name. Indeed Drijvers has identified the origin of the Judas 'the Twin' symbol itself in second-century Syria in the person of Tatian and his *Diatessaron*[13].

In his recent essay on Thomas writings and the Thomas tradition, presented at a symposium in Philadelphia marking the fiftieth anniversary of the discovery of the Nag Hammadi codices, Paul-Hubert Poirier, well known for his work on the *Hymn of the Pearl*, provides a succinct and helpful summary of recent Thomasine research. Poirier begins, however, by repeating the more conventional view, in contrast to Drijvers, that the entire Thomasine tradition can ultimately be derived from the ascription (which he considers original) in the *Gospel of John* of the phrase 'the one called Twin' (*John* 11.16, 20.24, 21.2)[14]. Poirier says, 'It is clear that the

---

[12] H.J.W. Drijvers, 'East of Antioch: Forces and Structures in the Development of Early Syriac Theology', reprinted as chapter I of his collected essays: *East of Antioch: Studies in Early Syriac Christianity* (London, 1984).

[13] Drijvers, 'East of Antioch,' 16; he is a bit more cautious in his contribution 'The Acts of Thomas,' in *NTA* II, 324, where he gives much of the evidence but withholds the inference that Tatian was the first to call Judas the twin (of Jesus?).

[14] P.-H. Poirier, 'The Writings Ascribed to Thomas and the Thomas Tradition', in J.D. Turner and A. McGuire (eds), *The Nag Hammadi Library after Fifty Years: Proceedings of the 1995 Society of Biblical Literature Commemoration* (Leiden, 1997) 295-307 at 295-6.

Johannine double name is one of the main sources of the Thomasian apocryphal traditions, all of which portray Thomas as Christ's double, or twin, and, consequently, as Christ's privileged spokesperson'[15]. After stating this assumption about the names of Thomas and their import, which he acknowledges requires 'fresh examination', Poirier in effect reverses Riley's argument that the *Gospel of John* is engaged in polemics against the claims of Thomas Christians who were already in existence and posed a threat to the Johannine style of Christianity (see further below).

Poirier's main point in his essay, however, is to draw into question the supposed homogeneity of the Thomasine tradition, a task which he accomplishes effectively, and also to make some suggestions about the relationships and relative chronology of the Thomas literature. In particular, Poirier argues that John Turner's thesis that the *Book of Thomas* stands in a mediating relationship between the incipient Thomasine Christianity of the *Gospel* and the fully realized portrait of the apostle in the *ATh* is faulty.

Hans-Martin Schenke had already pointed out in his own edition and commentary of *Das Thomas-Buch* that, though the wording of the opening lines of the *Book of Thomas* shows a clear literary borrowing from the prologue of the *Gospel of Thomas*, the rest of the book gives no clear indication of any significant influence from that text: 'Mit anderen Worten, der Verfasser würde hier Zitate benutzen, ohne sie literarisch einwandfrei in sein Werk zu integrieren. Das würde übrigens zugleich bedeuten, daß der Verfasser (vergleichbar dem Verfasser des neutestamentlichen Judasbriefes) die Judas Thomas-Tradition zwar kennt, sehr gut kennt, aber nicht selbst in ihr steht. Er scheint die Gestalt des Judas Thomas nur literarisch zu benutzen'[16]. Schenke's judgment that the *Book of Thomas* is not truly representative of Thomasine Christianity in the same way or as

---

[15] *Ibid.*, 296. A bit later in his essay Poirier (*ibid.*, 302) concedes the possibility that John received the double name from non-Johannine sources: 'In this creative process [viz., the production of the Thomas Didymus figure], the *Acts Thom.* are indebted to a tradition of which the *Gos. Thom.* is the earliest witness, but which ultimately goes back to John, or the tradition echoed by John'.

[16] H.-M. Schenke, *Das Thomas-Buch (Nag-Hammadi Codex II,7)* (Berlin, 1989) 65.

thoroughly as are the *Gospel* and *ATh*, though not shared completely by Poirier, does support the latter's position that the literary and historical relationship between the *Book of Thomas* and the *ATh* needs to be reconsidered. In Poirier's opinion, the *Book of Thomas* borrowed the motif of the twinship of Thomas with Jesus the Savior from the *ATh* rather than the other way around. Poirier points out that the use of the twin symbolism, so thoroughly integrated into both the story and ideology of the *ATh*, is employed in the *Book of Thomas* merely to emphasize and exploit the authority of Thomas as the recipient of the Savior's hidden words[17].

To sum up this review of scholarship, Riley's thesis about the existence of a specific brand of ancient Christianity that could be labeled 'Thomasine' is in effect a sharpening and extension of Turner's proposal, with the differences that Riley, largely in accord with Koester, sees the genesis of the Thomas traditions as beginning already in the first century, as not necessarily originating within or restricted to Syrian Christianity, and as displaying a special interest in the issue of the physical resurrection of Jesus and thus of the faithful. Far from seeing the literary figure of Thomas as created from a second- or third-century reading of the 'Doubting Thomas' pericope in the *Gospel of John*, as Poirier still presupposes, or as expressing a typically Syrian Christian view of soteriology, as Drijvers proposes, Riley suggests that the power of Thomas as an apostolic figure of major importance already predated John's narrative, and indeed that it was this first-century version of Thomasine Christianity that provoked John's unflattering and polemical image of Thomas in an attempt to undermine his authority and possibly his appeal to the Johannine Christians.

Whether Turner is correct that the *Book of Thomas* provided the intermediate step between the relatively sparse development of the character of the apostle in the *Gospel* and its full development in the *ATh*, or Poirier is right instead that the *ATh* suggested the twin brother motif as a vehicle for authority to the otherwise only lightly Thomasine *Book of Thomas*, in either case Riley would assert the existence and importance of a Thomasine brand of Christianity that produced and preserved this literature. So now my task is to query what more precisely would be meant by this 'Thomas Christianity.'

[17] Poirier, 'The Writings Ascribed to Thomas,' 303-5.

2. Point of Comparison: Gospels and Their 'Communities'

To make progress on this issue we must first try to determine what is meant by an early Christian 'community.' Students of the New Testament and Patristic literature are familiar with the notion of a 'school' model to explain the Pauline and Deutero-Pauline churches, to begin with, and Paul's letters and those of his imitators do reveal an actual set of historical people organized as a cult of Jesus Christ who looked to Paul as their founder and guide[18]. Some reasonable analogies might be drawn with the various schools of Hellenistic philosophy that Justin Martyr tells us, in the biographical introduction to his *Dialogue with Trypho the Jew*, that he has sampled before he came upon the perfect philosophy, Christianity[19]. And of course ancient heresy fighters like Irenaeus, Tertullian, or Epiphanius felt quite justified in claiming that the varieties of Christian, Jewish, Gnostic, Encratite, or Manichaean belief and practice that they were attacking could be traced, somewhat like the virus of modern day medical epidemiology, to schools gone bad, often inspired or led by ambitious or even demented individuals of shocking morality.

As is well known, Flavius Josephus makes a conscious effort to present the major parties of Palestinian Judaism, namely the Sadducees, Pharisees, and the Essenes, within the framework of philosophical schools or *haireseis*, especially in his account of the Jewish-Roman War[20]. Josephus also claims to have sampled the schools of thought in his youth[21]. And indeed the scrolls found near Qumran, whether they should be identified as Zadokite or as Essene in origin and theology, do reflect a highly developed group consciousness and ethos that few would dispute have the flavor of a school of thought or distinct community. The archaeological information found at Qumran provides the historian another sort of data entirely outside the texts that can help us to understand the group's way of life: the

---

[18]   See for example D.R. MacDonald, *The Legend and the Apostle: The Battle for Paul in Story and Canon* (Philadelphia, 1983), and W.S. Babcock (ed), *Paul and the Legacies of Paul* (Dallas, 1990).
[19]   Justin Martyr, *Dial.* 2.
[20]   Josephus, *Bellum* 2. 8 (119-66), with brief notices elsewhere, e.g., *Antiq.* 13. 5 (171-3).
[21]   Josephus, *Vita* 2.10-2.

settlement's size; its eating, bathing, and sleeping arrangements; burial practices; and much of the other 'stuff' of lives actually lived. Only some small portion of that material picture could be adequately inferred from a reading of the literary productions of the group, which are often symbolic and always self-conscious.

We often hear mention of specific 'communities' that are thought to lie behind the writing and the reading of the various gospels of the New Testament. But the contrast with the Dead Sea Scrolls should help make my point: we have far fewer texts, and little or no material remains to connect with any of the surviving literature. The corpora that we do have are nearly all the secondary products of collectors, editors, and forgers. The people who collected, edited, and published Paul's letters sometime in the second century, by point of comparison, created a specific character and theological outlook for that apostle that, as an entirety, offers only a poor or at best distorted portrait of the historical person[22]. Those who selected, combined, and harmonized the gospels of the emerging New Testament canon by that very process have also repositioned and thus redirected our readings of the *Gospel of Mark* vis-à-vis *Matthew* or *Luke* vis-à-vis *John*.

Nor do we have the words of contemporary observers, like those of Josephus on the Essenes or Philo on the Therapeutae, to explain who the authors of these gospels were and what they were like. There are hints of competing sorts of Christians or Jesus believers in Paul, the New Testament *Acts*, Ignatius, and even the *Apocalypse of John*, to be sure, but little to go on beyond those tantalizing bits, which are often cloaked in the strained rhetoric of invective or condemnation. Therefore the work of 'constructing a community' behind any particular early Christian narrative like the biblical or apocryphal gospels and acts will primarily involve the task of reading and drawing sensible inferences with a disciplined imagination.

Of those gospels within the canon of scripture it is easiest to imagine an actual, living sect involved with the generation and redaction of the *Gospel of John*, especially when it is read alongside at least two of the Johannine letters. But before I discuss *John* it may be instructive to consider the less promising circumstances of the Synoptic Gospels, whose origins and literary relationships make the issue of a generative 'community' rather more complicated.

---

[22] See e.g. the essays in Babcock, *Paul and the Legacies of Paul*.

The oldest surviving gospel, that ascribed to Mark, certainly has many aspects of sectarian consciousness: questions of who really belongs inside and outside the group are frequently discussed, for example, and there is also a sense of a community history, largely marked by disappointment and even failure[23]. Furthermore there is a very clear sense of hope for divine intervention and vindication in a time of stress. Thus it makes sense for us to imagine a group of Christians in a time of trouble who represent both the bearers of the Marcan traditions of Jesus and those for whom the *Gospel of Mark* was first composed and recited. Presumably these were Gentile believers, given the explanations of Jewish customs and cavalier attitudes toward the Law of Moses displayed in chapter 7. But more than this is difficult to say with any clarity or hope of achieving consensus: guesses about the place of writing (Rome, Antioch, even Galilee) or the social location of the audience (urban or rural?) range far and wide.

Estimates also vary widely about the size and social-status profile of most early Christian congregations in the first three centuries. Keith Hopkins, who writes Roman historical studies using sociological and statistical models, and who has recently turned to examining early Christianity, prefers to use the term 'house-church' rather than 'community,' on the grounds that the term 'community' misleadingly suggests a larger, more highly developed organization[24]. Thus the group that produced or first heard the *Gospel of Mark* might have consisted merely of a few families and their close associates, meeting in the domestic quarters of whichever member of the group (like the Chloe or Philemon visible in the Pauline correspondence) might have space.

It is difficult enough to reach even a low level of confidence in what is admittedly a very sketchy and abstract portrait of a 'community' of believers for Mark's gospel; the task is just as difficult for either *Matthew* or *Luke*. In the case of *Luke*, in fact, specialists are still divided on the question of whether the author is fundamentally

---

[23] See e.g. H.C. Kee, *Community of the New Age* (Philadelphia, 1977) and J. Marcus, *The Mystery of the Kingdom of God* (Chico, 1986); further P. Sellew, 'Oral and Written Tradition in Mark 4. 1-34', *NTS* 36 (1990) 234-67, and the literature cited there.
[24] K. Hopkins, 'Christian Number and Its Implications', *JECS* 6 (1998) 185-226.

opposed to Judaism, as some see the case, or else, on the other side, so thoroughly a Jew as to be identified as a member of the Pharisaic party[25]. But no doubt in both *Matthew* and *Luke* we still find considerable evidence of group formation: the church order rules of *Matthew* chapters 16 and 18, for example, or the community ethics preached through Jesus' parables of the last judgment in *Matthew* 24 and 25.

Luke's gospel displays various themes that might relate to a community behind the text. His famous interest in the disadvantaged members of society is prominent, though probably too generalized to construct the specifics of his group. Though no doubt an idealized narrative, the Lucan *Acts of the Apostles* is chock-full of vivid sketches of community origins—programmatic aims, leaders chosen by divine lot, instructions offered them through visions and dreams, and leadership councils that pass legislation that is then communicated by letter. This *hairesis* (*Acts* 24.14) even has two new names for itself: their own or 'insider' name, the 'Way' (ἡ ὁδός), used especially in the context of conflict or persecution (*Acts* 9.2; 19.9, 23; 22.4; 24.14, 22), and the name given them by outsiders, the 'Christians' (11.26). The big problem is that we have little or no proof that either the author of *Luke–Acts* or whomever we can imagine reading his text (including the enigmatic Theophilus, the addressee mentioned in the prefatory sentence) had any direct connection with the groups pictured in Jerusalem or Antioch, and even the more specifically Pauline churches are shown mostly in a set of anecdotes and sketches without much detail. The author displays a marvelous verisimilitude, of course, and clearly was a resident of the Aegean who quite likely had a personal acquaintance with some of the congregations founded by Paul: but that acquaintance does not make a community.

The *Gospel of John*, to now move more closely to the spirit and thought-world of the Thomas literature[26], betrays its in-group orientation with its use of 'we' language in both the prologue ('We have

---

[25] Contrast e.g. the views of J.T. Sanders, *The Jews in Luke-Acts* (Philadelphia, 1987) with those of J. Jervell, *Luke and the People of God* (Minneapolis, 1972) and D.L. Tiede, *Luke: Augsburg Commentary* (Minneapolis, 1988).
[26] S. Davies, G. Riley, A. DeConnick and others have discussed the possible relationship or connections between the 'communities' of John and Thomas in different ways; for a good review see I. Dunderberg, 'John and Thomas in Conflict?', in Turner and McGuire, *The Nag Hammadi Library*

beheld his glory,' 1.14) and the epilogue ('We know that his testimony is true,' 21.24). Many other specific features of the text have
suggested to scholars a sectarian group identity for the writers and
audience of this gospel. I need mention only a few items: there is the
insistence on an ethos of love for one's fellow group members, with
a corresponding suspicion or even demonization of opponents; there
is the sense of exclusion from the ordinary arenas of Jewish life,
especially the synagogue; or the use of a set of pictorial and symbolic vocabulary. The Johannine epistles provide further evidence of
this apparent community in their continued stress on group cohesion
and cooperation[27].

One further symbol of import in the narrative of the *Gospel of
John* might also signal its place in a closed, sectarian group, namely
the enigmatic figure of the 'Beloved Disciple'. Whoever or whatever
that cipher may be, the presentation of the character within the gospel
story constructs a special and idealized authority figure for the group
writing and reading this literature. The rather close analogies offered
by the Socrates of Plato or, better, the Teacher of Righteousness of
Qumran underline my point. In a way this unexplained, even teasing
use of the anonymous Beloved Disciple as the linchpin of the authoritative Johannine memory and meaning of Jesus provides us a key as
to the function of apostolic witnesses in other early Christian literary
circles. Most of those other authorities will be named, to be sure, such
as James, Peter, or our own Thomas, but their historical reality may be
no more or less tangible than that of John's Beloved Disciple[28].

after Fifty Years, 361-80; *idem*, '*Thomas*' I-sayings and the Gospel of
John', in R. Uro (ed), *Thomas at the Crossroads: Essays on the Gospel of
Thomas* (Edinburgh, 1998) 33-64. In the latter article Dunderberg (p. 64)
concludes that 'the coincidences between the Gospel of John and the I-sayings of the *Gospel of Thomas* do not betray any especially intimate relationship between these writings or the communities behind them' but rather
point 'to a common setting in early Christianity from 70 CE to the turn of the
first century'.
[27]   There are good discussions in R.A. Culpepper, *The Johannine School*
(Missoula, 1975); R.E. Brown, *The Community of the Beloved Disciple*
(New York, 1979) or Brown's Anchor Bible commentary on *The Epistles of
John* (Garden City, 1982).
[28]   J.H. Charlesworth, *The Beloved Disciple: Whose Witness Validates the
Gospel of John?* (Valley Forge, PA, 1995), has made the unlikely suggestion that the Beloved Disciple in John's Gospel is none other than Thomas.

Yet to make progress from the general recognition that a narrative reveals a sense of group identity among its tradents, composers, and audience, to a more specific understanding of the flesh and bones of some specific human group called conveniently a 'community' or 'congregation' or 'Gemeinde' is more problematic than is usually acknowledged. There are both epistemological and literary difficulties of major consequence in reading these texts as the historically legible scripts of specific Christian congregations. Hopkins has this 'word of caution,' as he calls it:

> 'Community', like the term 'Christian', is a persuasive and porous category. In modern histories of the early church, *community* is often used as a category of expansion and idealism. For example, when we have a text, it is understandably tempting to assume that the author and his immediate audience constituted a 'community'. Hence the commonly touted concept of Pauline communities, Johannine communities, Gnostic communities; each text is assumed to have had a matching set of the faithful, who formed solidary communities, and these communities putatively used particular texts as their foundation or charter myths[29].

A recent collection edited by Richard Bauckham also raises the issue of 'communities' in gospel scholarship at length and with some acuity[30]. Though I do not share much of the ideological agenda of some of the authors in Bauckham's collection who question the reality of specific 'communities' behind specific Biblical texts, especially their quite unabashed theological intent to rescue the gospels from any limited historical significance to help them regain their exalted status as Holy Scripture that may speak to all believers in all places, and grant us once again a direct or at least an uncomplicated 'unity' between the gospel literature and the historical Jesus[31], the essays in

---

Dunderberg, in Uro, *Thomas at the Crossroads*, 65-88, offers sensible criticism of Charlesworth's proposal and discusses the analogies between the figure of Thomas in the *Gospel of Thomas* and that of the Beloved Disciple in *John* in his article 'Thomas and the Beloved Disciple'.

[29] Hopkins, 'Christian Number', 198-9 (emphasis in original).

[30] R. Bauckham (ed), *The Gospels for All Christians* (Grand Rapids, 1998).

[31] F. Watson, 'Toward a Literal Reading of the Gospels', in Bauckham, *The Gospels for All Christians*, 195-217. Watson argues most strenuously against Bultmann and Marxsen, claiming that their form-critical and redaction-critical work is essentially a modern form of allegorical interpretation.

Bauckham's book do raise pertinent and telling criticisms of the standard model of supposing that 'behind every Gospel stands a particular community.'

We must first of all be attentive to issues of literary type and function. As Bauckham remarks[32], we sometimes jump from the rather well-attested communal concerns visible to us in Pauline letters like *1st Corinthians* to the assumption that similar issues must be in view in the gospels and acts. Though even the letters have narrative elements and can be read as stories with profit[33], we can presume that at least the authentic letters are addressing actual, living people who have real, pressing concerns like sexual ethics, the conduct and import of rituals such as baptism and the Lord's Supper, or the promised *parousia* of the Lord.

When narratives like the *ATh* display through the device of story-telling similar concerns with sexuality or sacraments, on the other hand, does this necessarily mean that the story's author and first readers needed immediate advice on these issues, or was another goal being addressed? When the disciples of Jesus ask him anxiously who will lead them after his departure, as we read in *Gos. Thom.* 12, and he tells them to 'go to James the Just, wherever you are, for heaven and earth came into being for him!' is this to be read as evidence for an actual connection and feeling of respect for some type of 'James Christianity,' as is most often suggested, or is it instead an ironic comment on the limitations of these all-too-human authority figures, stranded in this material world bounded by 'heaven and earth'?[34]

One of the key questions of method to ponder, therefore, is whether or how we can use a literary narrative as a transparent 'window' through which to gaze on some other world, or, less optimistically perhaps, as a reflective 'mirror' by which we at least

---

[32] Bauckham, 'For Whom Were the Gospels Written?', in *The Gospels for All Christians*, 26-30.

[33] An excellent example is N.R. Petersen, *Rediscovering Paul: Philemon and the Sociology of Paul's Narrative World* (Minneapolis, 1985).

[34] Patterson, *Gospel of Thomas and Jesus*, 116-117, 151 (as others), still takes the reference to James in *Gos. Thom.* 12 as indicating an interest in or even a possible connection with Christians who appealed to that apostle's authority. For my suggestion cf. *Gos. Thom.* 86, which situates humanity between above (the realm of the birds) and below (the dens of the foxes).

get glimpses, admittedly distorted, of that other world[35]. The assumption of much discussion of the 'communities' lying behind early Christian texts seems often to be that the narratives can indeed function as one of these types of glass. For example, scholars like Krister Stendahl or, more recently, J. Andrew Overman have moved beyond the géneral abstractions to read the *Gospel of Matthew* persuasively as telling the story of a Jewish-Christian congregation (*ekklêsia*) engaged in active competition with a prosperous group of Pharisees or proto-Rabbis[36]. This reading depends on understanding the furious invective hurled by Jesus in the text against the hypocritical Pharisees (esp. *Matthew* 23) as having more to do with the situation of Matthew's day and the circumstances of his original audience than that of the days of Jesus. Of course this historical judgment is in itself presumably correct: the issue is to determine more precisely just *how* the gospels function as primary evidence for their authors' situations. Another example is how Theodore J. Weeden and others have seen the strongly negative portraits of the disciples of Jesus drawn in the *Gospel of Mark* to have a historical basis in the distrust of Mark's community in the leadership offered by Jerusalem-centered individuals who claimed connection with Jesus' family or original followers[37]. Yet scholars of a rather more literary inclination have explained the treatment of the disciples as models (both positive and negative) for Mark's readers, or as part of the author's narrative strategy for implicating the audience in the value systems, actions, and thus also the challenges and failures of Jesus' first followers[38].

---

[35] S. Barton addresses this issue in his essay 'Can We Identify the Gospel Audiences?', in Bauckham, *The Gospels for All Christians*, 173-94 at 176-9. Patterson acknowledges the hermeneutical difficulties in determining '*why* one should expect that a particular text might be able to inform the historian about the social context in which it was written and used, and *how* such information is to be wrung from the text in question' (*Gospel of Thomas and Jesus*, 121-5, emphasis in original).

[36] K. Stendahl, *The School of St. Matthew*, rev. ed. (Philadelphia, 1968); J. A. Overman, *Matthew's Gospel and Formative Judaism* (Minneapolis, 1990); *idem, Church and Community in Crisis: The Gospel According to Matthew* (Valley Forge, 1996).

[37] T.J. Weeden, *Mark: Traditions in Conflict* (Philadelphia, 1971).

[38] See e.g. R.C. Tannehill, 'The Disciples in Mark: The Function of a Narrative Role,' *J. Rel.* 57 (1977) 386-405, followed in part by P. Sellew, 'Composition of Didactic Scenes in Mark's Gospel,' *J. Bibl. Lit.* 108 (1989) 613-34.

Halvor Moxnes has recently raised this very point of method in connection with interpreting the *Gospel of Luke* and the New Testament *Acts*:

> How can we move from the text of Luke's Gospel to the social situation of his first readers? This problem in Gospel research has not yet been solved....the Lukan text creates a narrative world, and it is this world we examine as we analyze the social relations, ethos, and symbolic universe of Luke. Still, this does not mean that we now have a 'window' that opens onto the social situation of Luke's historical community[39].

It is quite possible, then, that the function and significance of characters and events within a narrative, such as the stereotyped 'hypocritical Pharisees' in *Matthew*, or the blundering and half-blind disciples of Jesus in *Mark*, are as much symbol or token as they are meant to represent the socio-historical reality of a particular congregation or set of churches in second- or third-generation Mediterranean Christianity.

Bauckham's own suggestion is that the gospels were intended to be read more broadly, by a network of churches, and figure in a larger literary, historical and theological conversation than the focus on some single generative community might suggest. The comparisons that Bauckham makes with *1st Clement* and the Ignatian epistles (to which one might add the letters addressed to the seven churches of Asia in *Revelation* 2–3) are suggestive of the notion of a network of congregations that are in frequent communication. Nonetheless Bauckham's approach to this literature seems uninformed by the insights of Walter Bauer's work on the highly diversified and non-centralized nature of Christian groups in the first two centuries. Bauckham calls his book 'The Gospels for *All* Christians', but his vision of early Christianity is anything but all-inclusive: he seems to have forgotten the readers of 'Q' and the *Gospel of Thomas* and the *Acts of Paul*, and has adopted the perspective of Bishop Eusebius of Caesarea wholesale.

---

[39] H. Moxnes, 'The Social Context of Luke's Community', *Interpretation* 48 (1994) 379 (quotation taken from Barton, 'Can We Identify the Gospel Audiences?', 188).

The important point to carry from this methodological consideration that I have given to the canonical gospels and their possible origins in specific Christian communities is as follows. What we can be most sure about is the theological outlook (and possibly the sociological profile) of the group that generated a particular narrative; perhaps we may sketch out a bit of the character and expectations of their early audiences. But we must be very cautious about constructing a detailed history of such a postulated group from a symbolic reading of the story's people and events. General notions of such things as the group's stance toward possessions, or the acceptability of remarriage, or of circumcision, can be safely inferred; but constructing a more tangible and detailed portrait of this community may be risky. While we can glean quite a bit about the 'contours' of the groups portrayed within the text, and then move on to identify more precisely and vividly 'the social location of the beliefs and behaviors of the characters and groups presented in the [...] narratives', moving further away from that narrative world by using the text as a window into the life of a particular set of people is a hazardous step difficult to control[40].

3. *Evidence for a 'Thomas Community'?*

With these perspectives in mind, we can return to the question of the 'Thomas community' or 'Thomas Christianity' that Riley claims was not only responsible for creating the tradition still visible in Syrian Christian literature, but in fact was active from the first century as a major strand within the varieties of early Christian ideology. This 'community' produced the three texts the *Gospel of Thomas*, the *Book of Thomas*, and the *Acts of Thomas*, though in this last case with considerable influence from the emergent 'orthodox' Christianity.

Riley constructs his case for a 'Thomasine Christianity' using familiar blocks[41]. He apparently takes the notion of 'community' for granted (following the general tradition of gospel scholarship in this

---

[40]   On this point I am in general agreement with Barton.
[41]   Riley's essay 'Thomas Tradition and the *Acts of Thomas*' provides a convenient summary of his views.

regard) since he never explains or seeks to justify his presumption that such a group existed. Many of Riley's indicators are philological and literary: the use of the name 'Judas' alongside the name 'Thomas' in the *Gospel, Book,* and *Acts of Thomas*; the apostle's status as the recipient of Jesus' hidden words in all three works; the designation of the apostle as Jesus' twin brother in the *Book* and *Acts of Thomas.* All of these observations go back as far as Puech, Klijn, and Turner. Unfortunately this sort of evidence need not point to anything beyond the existence of a literary influence (and presumably also an ideological influence) of one or two of these books on the others. Readers and authors can recognize and encourage these similarities and allusions without such features necessarily requiring a distinct community of Thomas faithful to be understood.

Riley builds more of his case for 'Thomas Christianity' on the basis of the encratite attitude toward the body so visible in these three books, and especially on their denial of the physical resurrection. Riley's book on these traditions, entitled *Resurrection Reconsidered: Thomas and John in Controversy,* develops this theme in the Thomas literature with clarity and conviction. No doubt the *Gospel of Thomas,* the *Book of Thomas,* and the *ATh* do share a strongly negative attitude toward the physical world, and, in the latter two books, a special hatred of sexuality. Turner was right on target when he argued that over the course of the writing of these three books, the figure of the apostle becomes more and more active as the hero of encratism. In fact Thomas plays no such rôle at all in the *Gospel of Thomas,* though Jesus does make a few disparaging if indirect remarks about sex and especially its consequences (birth) that would be read by an encratite Christian with pleasure[42].

Nonetheless it is clear that distrust of the material world, denigration of the body of flesh, and even this horror of the doctrine of the physical resurrection are not at all distinct to the Thomas books. Similar attitudes are promoted by much of early Christian literature, including the other *AAA,* and are notably visible in Syrian Christianity. Paul already dealt at Corinth with new believers who shared precisely these values: they were unsure or suspicious of sexuality (1 Cor. 7); they denied the (physical) resurrection of the body (1 Cor. 15). Many Christian Gnostic texts adopt a similar ideology.

[42] See e.g. *Gos. Thom.* 29; 55; 79; possibly also 15; 87; 114.

Another thematic similarity that Riley and other scholars point to as shared across these three Thomas texts is their symbolic vocabulary of paired opposites: and we may agree that all three do insist on the fundamental ethical and existential contrasts between such categories as below and above, the visible and invisible, what is perishable and what is eternal, the illusory and the real, and the fundamental contrast among humans, the ignorant vis-à-vis the wise or intelligent or perfect. Klijn's discussion in his commentary of these systematic polarities in the *ATh* would apply with very few changes to their similar use in the *Gospel of Thomas* or, perhaps less obviously, in the *Book of Thomas*[43]. Yet once again this discourse of opposites does not define the Thomas literature over against other important streams within early Christianity: as we all know, both Paul and the *Gospel of John* also deployed these contrasts to great effect, as indeed did many Platonist, Hermetic, and Gnostic writings.

Though scholars have had difficulty identifying concrete evidence of specific community concerns in the *Gospel of Thomas*, its generic character as a sayings collection leads us to expect an active and involved readership[44]. Some limited signs of group consciousness are visible, as might be the case with questions posed in the text about the correct attitude to adopt toward fasting, prayer, and almsgiving in *Gos. Thom.* 6, 14, and 104[45]. But it may be easier to reconstruct plausible ancient readings of the text than its generative community[46]. Karen King has identified an ethos of community embedded in the language of the 'kingdom' in many of the

[43] Klijn, *The Acts of Thomas*, 34-7.
[44] To this point I agree with Patterson, *Gospel of Thomas and Jesus*, 122, though I find the work too enigmatic to sense the 'air of utility' that he ascribes to it.
[45] See P. Sellew, 'Pious Practice and Social Formation in the Gospel of Thomas', *Forum* 10 (1994) 47-56; and now also A. Marjanen, '*Thomas* and Jewish Religious Practices', in Uro, *Thomas at the Crossroads*, 163-82. I do not agree with Patterson, *Gospel of Thomas and Jesus*, 147-8 n. 111, that *Gos. Thom.* 104 contradicts the earlier statements to the extent that one must reckon on a 'late secondary influence from the synoptic text' in this instance.
[46] One example is B. Lincoln's reading of the *Gospel of Thomas* as a handbook for mystical initiates: 'Thomas-Book and Thomas-Community: A New Approach to a Familiar Text', *Novum Testamentum* 19 (1977) 65-76.

statements made by Jesus in the *Gospel of Thomas*[47]. She interprets the symbolic function of the frequent references to 'kingdom' as fostering the self-definition of a community of Thomas Christians in such key areas as social boundaries, community ethics, and conflict with outsiders; she understands the theme of searching and finding as conveying a strong sense of the 'salvific sense of belonging' to the group. King's close reading of the 'kingdom' theme is suggestive of how a group of ascetical readers of the *Gospel of Thomas* might well have understood its message. Nonetheless, the dominant theme of the text is not community rules but rather an intense focus on individual identity, on one's 'solitary' salvation[48]. Entrance into the group ('finding the kingdom') would thus involve salvation, but the mechanisms of how the group managed its affairs remain vague[49].

Such a conclusion is actually supported even by the observations of Stephen J. Patterson, who has made the most sustained attempt to date at defining a 'Thomas community' that might have produced the gospel or otherwise explain its origins[50]. The social description that Patterson offers in his thoughtful book is an extension of Gerd Theissen's thesis about the formative rôle played by itinerants or 'wandering charismatics' in the early generations of the Syro-Palestinian Jesus movement[51]. But while Theissen used primarily the

---

[47] K. King, 'Kingdom in the Gospel of Thomas', *Forum* 3 (1987) 48-97.

[48] It is intriguing however that the insistence on salvation offered to the ⲘⲘⲞⲚⲀⲬⲞⲤ or single ones running throughout the text (as in *Gos. Thom.* 16, 49, 75) typically uses the plural term. *Gos. Thom.* 49, e.g., reads: 'Blessed are those who are alone (ⲚⲘⲞⲚⲀⲬⲞⲤ) and chosen.' It is debated whether the Coptic terms ⲞⲨⲀ or ⲞⲨⲀ ⲞⲨⲰⲦ ('one,' 'single one': *Gos. Thom.* 4, 11, 22, 23, 106) are synonymous with the transliterated ⲘⲞⲚ-ⲀⲬⲞⲤ. Patterson has a good discussion along with earlier literature in *Gospel of Thomas and Jesus*, 152-153. ⲞⲨⲀ *simplex* seems used specifically when paired with ⲤⲚⲀⲨ ('two').

[49] King agrees with S. Davies and J.Z. Smith that such sayings as *Gos. Thom.* 22 refer to a baptismal rite which functioned to create 'children of the living Father,' i.e., members of the Thomas group.

[50] Patterson, *Gospel of Thomas and Jesus*, esp. chap. 5, 'Thomas Christianity: A Social-Historical Description,' 121-57, and chap. 6, '"Thomas Christianity and Itinerant Radicalism: Be Passers-By,' 158-70.

[51] G. Theissen, 'Wanderradikalismus: Literatursoziologische Aspekte der Überlieferung von Worten Jesu im Urchristentum', *ZThK* 70 (1973) 245-71, and *Soziologie der Jesusbewegung* (München, 1977).

Synoptic Gospels and especially the 'Q' traditions to build his reconstruction of itinerants like Jesus and his first followers moving
among settled base communities of 'sympathizers,' Patterson shows
that Theissen's insights fit the *Gospel of Thomas* better than they do
the redacted forms of the Q materials as we now see them deployed
in the *Gospel of Matthew* or the *Gospel of Luke*[52].

Patterson takes the enigmatic statement of *Gos. Thom.* 42 'Be
passers-by' (ϣⲱⲡⲉ ⲉⲧⲉⲧⲛ̄ⲣ̄ⲡⲁⲣⲁⲅⲉ) in a programmatic fash-
ion[53]: Thomas Christians are itinerant radicals, indeed 'homeless
beggars' who are urged to despise ordinary life and the values of the
commercial world. Patterson sees further evidence of Thomas Christianity's itinerant identity in *Gos. Thom.* 14, with its behavioral
instructions to readers when they 'go into any district and walk from
place to place' (though he also admits the statement's composite
nature), and scattered calls to cut family ties and adopt an attitude of
disdain for material wealth[54]. Patterson argues that these and other
statements in the *Gospel of Thomas*, which do of course fit an attitude of denial of the world, reflect or even support a group (?!) of
alienated, homeless, wandering loners. Patterson in effect constructs
his 'Thomas Christians' by reifying the implied audience of Jesus'
commands within the text (adapting Bultmann's formal categories of
'legal sayings' and 'community rules'). But when it comes to
describing his 'Thomas Christianity' in any detail beyond this rather
straightforward historicization of admittedly enigmatic and at times
contradictory commands and exhortations, even Patterson has to
grant that there is 'precious little material with which to work', and
that 'there is little in Thomas that provides for community organization or structure: there is no Thomas community *per se*, but rather a
loosely structured movement of wanderers'[55]. Instead Patterson
demonstrates how smoothly the 'Thomasine' ethos of ascetic indi-
vidualism fits with emergent forms of Syrian Christianity[56].

---

[52] See in particular Patterson, *Gospel of Thomas and Jesus*, 163-70.
[53] The translation 'Become (*or* Come into Being) as you pass by' is also
possible. No parallel survives among the Greek fragments.
[54] E.g., *Gos. Thom.* 27, 54; the parables 63-65, 95; possibly 8, 55, 76, 86, 107.
[55] Patterson, *Gospel of Thomas and Jesus*, 151.
[56] Patterson, *Gospel of Thomas and Jesus*, 166-8, drawing on the work of
A. Baker, A. Vööbus, G. Kretschmar, and J. M. Robinson.

In view of all these difficulties in describing the socio-historical 'community' in which the *Gospel of Thomas* was (first) written, a more promising task would be to construct a probable *readership* for the *Gospel of Thomas*. As I have suggested in two recent articles[57], it is not difficult to understand the appeal of the late-second and early third-century Oxyrhynchos *Thomas* fragments in ascetical circles of Greek-reading Egyptian Christianity, or to imagine fourth-century monks puzzling over the esoteric and contradictory statements of the Coptic translation of the *Gospel of Thomas* (and *Book of Thomas*) in Nag Hammadi Codex II. This approach could then exploit King's suggestions about how reading the symbolics of 'kingdom' and other themes in the *Gospel of Thomas* could serve the process of (individual and) group formation[58].

Once we pose the question of readership rather than of the identity of some generative community, we can begin to open up the dynamics of this literature as a conversation among authors, iconic characters, scribes, translators, and readers. A fruitful manner of sketching out the relationship and special character of the literature associated with Thomas is to analyze the way the figure of the apostle himself develops in and across these books—from the mere attachment of his name as the putative narrator or author, which could well be incidental (as in the so-called *Infancy Gospel of Thomas*) toward the development of a special Thomasine persona and rôle. In the *Gospel of Thomas*, he is named the confidant of Jesus and is shown to be reluctant to serve as spokesperson for the One Who Lives; he is in no way a representative or replacement for Jesus (in contrast to the polymorphism on display in the *ATh*)[59]. Within the

[57] Sellew, 'Death, the Body and the World in the Coptic Gospel of Thomas', *Studia Patristica* 31 (1997) 530-4, and 'The Gospel of Thomas: Prospects for Future Research', in Turner and McGuire, *The Nag Hammadi Library after Fifty Years*, 327-46.
[58] King, 'Kingdom in the Gospel of Thomas.' King observes that nearly all the parables of the kingdom in *Thomas* mention an individual person, which she understands as referring to actual or idealized members of the Thomas community. The metaphoric language is likely rather more fluid than this approach allows.
[59] Riley has a fascinating and convincing discussion of the theme of polymorphism and docetism in the *ATh*: 'Thomas Tradition and the *Acts of Thomas*', 538-41; see now also P. J. Lalleman, 'Polymorphy of Christ,' in Bremmer, *Acts of John*, 97-118.

gospel text itself, Thomas figures only at statement 13; it may be that the prologue (and also the subscript) were derived secondarily from this scene of private and secret conversation, an idea which I unfortunately cannot develop here for reasons of space[60].

In the *Book of Thomas*, the apostle plays the rôle of Jesus' special interlocutor, the one who poses the questions that he (and presumably his readership) want the Savior to address. So in that book, though Thomas is still not Christ's spokesperson, he does an effective job of eliciting his teaching. The apostle is more prominent in the dialogue there than in the *Gospel of Thomas*: indeed he is the only conversation partner that Jesus addresses by name (though others seem present beyond the Mathaias of the prologue).

In the lengthy narrative of the missionary career of Judas Thomas (the *ATh*) we at last get a full and quite interesting characterization of the apostle. A much more powerful sense of an author's voice emerges on reading the *ATh*, produced by a talented creator of narrative. The author constructs the character in part through description, when he shows us Thomas's actions, in part by what other individuals in the story say to and about him. In other words, the author of the *ATh*, an otherwise unknown writer resident in early third-century Syria[61], has composed a work that exemplifies the Christian sector of popular literature in Late Antiquity, the 'early Christian fiction' compared so aptly in recent years to the Greek novels of the Roman Imperial period[62]. The more successfully the narrative art of fiction is

[60] Patterson, *Gospel of Thomas and Jesus*, 117, argues that *Gos. Thom.* 13 has 'a secondary status', and that 'the basic Thomas collection was already in existence when the Prologue, Thom 13, and Thom 114 were added...'. I treat this topic at length in my book on the *Gospel of Thomas*, currently in preparation for the Polebridge series *The Scholars Bible*.

[61] Beyond these two items (locating the *ATh* in third-century Syria, possibly Edessa) little is known about the historical circumstances behind the text, but see also Bremmer, this volume, Ch. VI. On the relative anonymity of the authors of the *AAA*, see Bremmer, this volume, Ch. XI.1.

[62] M.A. Tolbert and others use the term 'popular literature' to describe early Christian prose in close comparison with the Greco-Roman novels (in Tolbert's case, particularly Xenophon of Ephesus and the *Gospel of Mark*: *Sowing the Gospel: Mark's World in Literary-Historical Perspective* (Minneapolis, 1989) 48-79; see also R.F. Hock, J.B. Chance and J. Perkins (eds), *Ancient Fiction and Early Christian Narrative* (Atlanta, 1998). R. I. Pervo, *Profit with Delight: The Literary Genre of the Acts of the Apostles*

employed, of course, the ever more dangerous it becomes to read too
much between the lines to find something 'historical' behind or
beyond the story.

The character in the *ATh* that seems to know the most about the
apostle is the talking colt of an ass in *Praxis* 4 who invites him to ride
back into the city on its back after Thomas has revived a youth. The
colt addresses him as 'twin brother of Christ, apostle of the Most
High, initiate into the hidden word of Christ, who receives his secret
utterances, fellow worker of the Son of God' (39). Thomas gives
glory to God for the wonders of his creation and then ponders how
this animal came to know what he calls things 'hidden from many'
(40). These details of the Thomasine persona are of course available
to the Thomas aficionado in the *Gospel* and *Book* that carry his
name: maybe the colt can read as well as it can talk! It turns out that
the colt is descended from the prophetical race of asses that trace
their ancestry to the stable of Balaam himself, and it seeks the special
spiritual reward that will come if it can persuade Thomas to mount
and ride it. After some hesitation, the apostle does ride the colt, and
the animal does appear to receive its reward—when Thomas dis-
mounts at the city gate, the colt promptly dies on the spot (41)[63].

Should we read the prophetic beast as a symbol of scholars in
search of Thomas and his hard-to-find 'community' of Thomasine
Christians? There is no doubt that in Syria many early Christians
revered the person of this apostle. But the profile of Thomasine literature and theology that we have been offered is shared also by the
Gospel of Philip, the *Pistis Sophia*, and many other ancient Christian
and even some not-so-Christian writings. We cannot simply confine
the varieties of Syrian Christianity to a 'Thomasine' church. The *ATh*
may reveal nothing more than the deployment of this beloved
and available apostolic figure for the author's own literary and

(Philadelphia, 1987) 122-31, classified the *AAA* as novels, particularly 'historical novels'; the comparison with 'romantic fiction' is driven home more
fully by him in *idem*, 'The Ancient Novel Becomes Christian', in G.
Schmeling (ed), *The Novel in the Ancient World* (Leiden, 1996) 685-711,
overlooked by J. N. Bremmer, 'The Novel and the Apocryphal Acts: Place,
Time and Readership,' in H. Hofmann and M. Zimmermann (eds), *Groningen Colloquia on the Novel IX* (Groningen, 1998) 157-80 at 158.
[63] The fate of the colt who carried Jesus into Jerusalem in the canonical
gospels is unrecorded.

theological ends. The learned and witty writer of the *ATh* had read
the *Gospel* and probably also the dialogue book bearing his name and
had drunk deeply from that well (that 'bubbling spring,' *Gos. Thom.*
13) and taken those lessons to heart. The legendary follower of Jesus
who may have doubted his resurrection was able to become – via his
literary career – first his Savior's scribe, then his interlocutor and
spokesman, and finally, through the divine mysteries of twinship and
polymorphism, his earthly representative to the faithful. But this journey and transformation were not the result of impersonal forces at
work on an anonymous Thomasine community. Rather than reduce
the achievement of the artist behind this masterly romance of the
saint to the archival level of community records, we should be grateful for his inspiration and applaud his creative genius.

III. The Bride of the Demon. Narrative Strategies of Self-Definition in the *Acts of Thomas*

ISTVÁN CZACHESZ

In this study we will examine a conspicuous narrative pattern in the *Acts of Thomas* (*ATh*) and some literary parallels. The plot of these stories can be summarized in one sentence: A demon loves a woman and tortures her until the man of God drives him out[1]. We may also read about the demon's jealousy and his murders of the men who approach the woman; and the story often concludes with the celebration of baptism, eucharist, or marriage. The pattern described here resembles the plot of a romance, but it also differs from it in that within our narratives there is always a jealously loving demon, while romantic love and marriage are not necessarily parts of the story.

The three passages on which we will focus are found in the *cc.* 30-8, 42-50, and 62-81 (third, fifth, and seventh to eighth acts in the numbering of the Greek text). The third act relates that the apostle Thomas finds the corpse of a handsome young man beside the road, and begins to pray. Soon a serpent, or more correctly, a dragon (*drakôn*), comes forth from the bushes and recounts how he killed the man, because he made love to a beautiful woman whom the dragon loved. The apostle then converses at length with the dragon and commands him to suck out the poison from the corpse. The dragon obeys and bursts. The apostle in turn raises the young man from the dead, who then becomes a follower[2].

---

[1] Since the demons in our stories appear in the shapes of male figures and lovers of women, we will use the male pronoun 'he' in connection with them.
[2] See also Adamik, this volume, Ch. IX.

In the second episode, a woman tells the apostle of her encounter with a troubled young man, who came up to her after she left the baths, and asked her to sleep with him. She refused him, but he appeared to her in dream and had sexual intercourse with her. This goes on for a long time, until she meets the apostle. The mysterious lover turns out to be a demon, who negotiates for a while with the apostle, but then leaves his 'fair wife'. The woman is baptized and celebrates the eucharist with the other followers of Thomas.

The third episode is the lengthiest, and actually includes two 'acts'. A king's general (identified as 'Siphor' in c. 100) comes up to the apostle and asks him to cure his wife and daughter. Both had been attacked by a man and a boy on the street many years ago. Since then they are unexpectedly struck down to the ground from time to time. While the apostle and the general are on the way to the general's house, they catch sight of a herd of wild asses beside the road. Thomas tells the general to call the asses to him, and the asses obey. When they enter the city, Thomas sends one of the asses as a delegate into the courtyard to call out the demons[3]. The woman and her daughter come out, and Thomas begins to converse with the demon in the woman. The demon turns out to be the one expelled from the other woman in cc. 42-50. When the demons finally leave, the two women fall to the ground, but Thomas cures them and they become his followers. The wild asses witness the whole procedure, until the apostle sends them back to their pasture.

First we will pursue a short narrative critical survey of the selected passages, then seek for ancient literary parallels, and finally interpret the passages in the context of the *ATh* and the parallel texts with the help of a typological scenario.

1. *Narrative analysis: plot, rhetoric and characterization*

The *ATh* can be divided into two halves of approximately equal length. The second half consists of cc. 82-170, and tells the story of Mygdonia, who becomes a follower of Thomas and refuses to sleep with his husband Charisius, kinsman of the king. Other women of the royal court and family join the apostle, and this leads finally to the martyr-

---

[3]   Cf. the big dog as Peter's delegate in the *APt* 9.

dom of the apostle. This is basically the recurring pattern of the end-
ings of the *AAA*, where women of high social stance follow the teaching of the apostles and begin to practise chastity; their mighty and jealous husbands, in turn, give over the apostles to trial and death.
The first half of the *ATh* (1-81), on the other hand, contains a
chain of shorter episodes, most of which are based on the theme of
marriage. Both halves contain a hymn, the 'Hymn of the bride' (6-7),
and the famous 'Hymn of the pearl' (108-13), respectively. Though
women, marriage and demons play an important role in all of the
AAA[4], the *ATh* handles the subject in an especially concentrated manner. After a short introduction of how Jesus sent the apostle to India,
we find him already at a wedding celebration, where he sings his
'Hymn of the bride'. It is in this context that the three episodes of
women and demons are situated.
This is the basic plot of the three stories: The apostle meets one
of the characters on his journey. He listens to the story of the mis-
deeds of the demon. He then summons the demon, who talks about
his origin and deeds. The apostle, in turn, talks about his mission and
the mighty deeds of God, and expels the demon. The demon leaves,
and the apostle cures the victims. The victims talk about wondrous
experiences and visions, praise God and become followers. Baptism
and eucharist may close the story.
The largest part of the narratives contains direct speech of the
characters, mainly about mythological themes. The speeches are
made up of a dualistic vocabulary: God and his followers stand in
opposition with the devil and his followers; the demon's power with
the apostle's power, light with darkness. The speeches are also set up
in pairs so as to express this dualistic contrast. In *c*.32, the dragon
tells the history of humankind from his own perspective: his father
made himself like God; rules everything that is created under
heaven; spoke with Eve in Paradise; incited Cain to kill Abel;
caused the heavenly beings to marry the daughters of men, caused
the sons of Israel to rebel in the desert and make the golden calf;
stirred up Caiaphas, Herod, and Judas against Jesus.

---

[4]   See the articles by J.N. Bremmer in Bremmer, *Acts of John*, 37-56; *Acts
of Paul*, 36-59; *Acts of Peter*, 1-20, and this volume, Ch. VI; see also the
contributions by M. Misset-van de Weg, in Bremmer, *Acts of Paul*, 16-35
and *Acts of Peter*, 97-110.

Two chapters later the young man, restored to life, talks at length about his experience of seeing light and being delivered from the anxieties of the night. He destroyed the one that is of the same birth as the night and found the one who is similar to the light (*pheggodês*, or perhaps rather *pheggoeidês*[5]) to be his relative. He found him whose works are light, and was delivered from the one whose fraud is permanent, and even his veil radiates darkness etc. In the Syriac version he even retells the whole history of humankind from God's point of view.

A similar balance of the satanic and divine perspectives can be seen in the other story, where the speech of the demon (45) is contrasted to the apostle's hymn of Jesus (48). It is interesting that the demons also use a dualistic rhetoric, and compare the people of God to the people of the devil. A peculiar phrase that marks the difference between the two realms is 'what have we to do with you'[6]. Though the demons do not deny their destructive nature, they also claim to respect certain positive laws: the dragon affirms that he killed the young man, because he did unlawful things with the woman, and especially because he did that on the day of the Lord (31). This means that the narrative provides the demons with a dynamic character: they are evil and destructive, but also just and jealously loving. Their role in the story is more than simply being the means by which Thomas demonstrates his wondrous powers, as was the case with Simon in the *APt*.

Other mythological themes are also abundant throughout the narrative. There is an account of the origin of evil in *c.* 32. The curious reference in the Greek text to 'the one who injured and hit the four brothers who were standing' gave much headache to the interpreters. The motif is also present in rabbinical literature: 'Four died because of the injury of the serpent'[7]. The dragon also relates that the devil

[5] Cf. M. Lipinski, *Konkordanz zu den Thomasakten* (Frankfurt/M, 1985) 457.
[6] *ti humin kai soi*. Demons use this phrase in Mk 1.24, 5.7, Lk 4.34, Jesus in Jn 2.4. In the NT it is probably a translation of the Hebrew *mah-li walak* (2Kings 16.10 etc). It also occurs in the *AA*, cf. Bremmer, *Acts of Andrew*, 28f.
[7] See A.F.J. Klijn, *The Acts of Thomas* (Leiden, 1962) 224f. Lipsius suggested that it would be a reference to the four elements of the universe. Klijn himself suggests that the word 'standing' should be taken in the sense of 'righteous'.

'braces the sphere (that is, of the world)', and is out of the ocean, with his tail in his mouth. Jewish sources, as well, describe the outside darkness as a dragon surrounding the world. The sexual interest of demons toward women, the basic motivation of these stories, also gains mythological depth. It was the dragon, who 'threw the angels down from above', and 'bound them with the desires of women'. The prototype for all demonic possessions of women would thus be the episode of the birth of giants in *Genesis* 6.4.

Alongside the lengthy theological discourses there is an interesting handling of the narrative voices. From time to time the narration of the text is given over to different characters. Thus the narrative offers multiple perspectives of the affair of the demon and the woman. It is always to the apostle that one of the characters tells the story, and Thomas behaves like a judge listening to the parties presenting their cases.

The dragon's story (31): In the first episode it is the dragon who reports the events to the apostle. Already the first sentence betrays that he will deliver a forensic speech, an apology: 'I will tell before you for what reason I killed him'. He depicts the beauty of the woman and his love toward her. Then he vehemently attacks the inferior and fleshly nature of the young man, her lover. He even intimates confidence and cooperation when he talks about their deeds: 'It would be easy for me to describe everything to you, but I know that you are the twin brother of Christ.' Finally he defends his own act: he did not want to disturb the lovers, and waited until the young man was going home in the evening, and only killed him then. He justifies the murder with the fact that they sinned on the day of the Lord. The apostle appears as a judge also in the later parts of the story.

The woman's story (42-3): The second episode is told from the opposite angle, mainly from the point of view of the woman possessed by the demon. The woman's report also reveals some rhetorical traits. She greets Thomas as 'the apostle of the new God', and praises him as the healer of all who were tortured by the enemy. Then she begins her story: Earlier she had a peaceful life 'as a woman'[8]. On her way home from the bath she met the demon:

---

[8]   This might emphasize her female role in a marriage, although her claim she refused to sleep with her fiancé because she did not want to get married (43) may suggest just the opposite.

public baths frequently were places of demonic presence[9]. While the woman saw the demon in the shape of a young woman, her maidservant saw an old man. This is a remarkable case of polymorphy, a recurring motif in the *AAA*. Thomas also calls the demon 'polymorphous' (44), and the *AJ* talks about the 'polymorphous Satan', too (*AJ* 70). But Thomas is also said to 'have two forms' in the previous story (34), and he calls Christ 'polymorphous' in *c*.48. Polymorphy always seems to go together with superhuman nature and abilities in the *ATh*[10].

The woman then tells that the demon used to torture her over and over again by night, and confesses her belief that the apostle has power over him. She asks him to pray and drive out the demon, so that she may be free, gain back her 'original nature' (*tên archaiogonon phusin*), and receive the gift which is given to those who are of the same birth (*suggeneis mou*). While the story of the dragon presents the eternal triangle[11], the woman's story contains little reference to her human relations, possible marriage or family background. Demonic possession does not appear as a disturbance of social life, as it will appear in the next story, but as a religious and psychological complex. It does not distract the victim from her husband, groom, or family, but poses the theological problem of belonging to the family of the Satan, or to the family of God. Therefore, unlike the other two cases, the healing is explicitly completed by baptism and eucharist.

The story of the husband and father (62-4): The third story is told from the perspective of the husband and father of the victims, but further interesting changes of perspective are also applied in the narrative. An officer of high standing, described as the right hand of the king, lived a peaceful family life with his wife and daughter, until he had to send them to a great wedding banquet given by a close friend. He was reluctant to do so, but the close friends, and possibly also influential ones, came and had invited them personally[12]. Late in

---

[9] Bremmer, *Acts of Andrew*, 26.
[10] For a thorough investigation of polymorphy see P.J. Lallemann, 'Polymorphy of Christ', in Bremmer, *Acts of John*, 97-118.
[11] See J. Bolyki, 'Triangles and what is beyond them', in Bremmer, *Acts of Andrew*, 70-80.
[12] The translation of the text should be then: 'They came and honored me by calling her and her daughter'.

the evening the general sent servants to the banquet to escort his wife and daughter home. While he was standing out in the street waiting, the servants turned up weeping. At this point, there is a shift of voice in the narrative, and we hear the words of the servants as reported by the general. They saw a man and a boy, who laid their hands on the woman and her daughter, and then ran away. In the same moment the wife and the daughter fell, gnashing their teeth and dashing their heads on the ground. The servants wanted to defend them, but their swords fell on the ground. This act scarcely makes the father any happier, and serves only as a self-defense of the servants before their master.

Here the general speaks again in his own words, and describes his reaction: he tore his clothes, beat his face with his hands, and ran down the street like a madman. After he had brought his family home and they had recovered, he asked his wife about what had happened. This time the general reports his wife's words: on the way to the banquet they passed a fountain, where they saw a black man and a boy like him. The man was looking at them with a strange face (*upogrulizôn*)[13]. The teeth of the man and boy were white like milk and their lips black like coal[14]. The demons appear close to the water, again. On the way

[13] The word *hupogrulizô* seems to be a hapax legomenon. Lampe's, *Patristic Greek Lexicon*, 1446B gives 'reprove gently' which is hard to interpret in this context. Liddel, Scott, Jones, *Greek-English Lexicon*, 361B has an entry only for *grulizô*, meaning the 'grunting' of swines. We might imagine the black men sounding like pigs, although they were at some distance from the women. The word is best understood as a description of some strange and ugly facial expression (cf. the problem of the black figures below, esp. note 14).

[14] The serpent killing the lover was also black. Klijn, *Acts of Thomas*, 223 refers to the general idea of the devil being black (although we have to note that this is not the case in many cultures). For black as the colour of demons see Bremmer, *Acts of Peter*, 8. We have to remember that the heroine in c. 55 was also lead to the hell by an ugly black figure (*apechthês te idea, melas holos*). We suspect here the influence of a stereotyped description of African people, perhaps Ethiopians. The name 'Ethiopian', was originally a mythological name of sun-burnt people of the East in Homer. It was later given to different people, especially to the people of Nubia, but also of India. See 'Aithiopia', in K. Ziegler and W. Sontheimer (eds), *Der kleine Pauly* I (München 1975) 201-4 at 201. The image of Ethiopians relied primarily on mythological notions. Cf. K. Kerényi, *Die griechisch-orientalische Romanliteratur* (Darmstadt, 1962²) 50-1. Egypt was called black after

home from the banquet, the daughter catches sight of the two men, and
runs to her mother. Here the Greek text is unclear: a possible reading
is that the servants ran away and the demons struck the two women on
the ground. If this reading, supported also by the translations, is the
correct one, the wife's version of the story destroys the self-defense of
the servants. The general concludes the story by reporting it happened
three years earlier. Since then his wife and daughter have had to be
kept locked up in a room, and have not even eaten a meal together.
Here the narrative of the father ends.

2. Ancient literary parallels

The most direct literary parallel to our stories can be found in the *Book
of Tobit* (esp. 3, 6, 8). Sarah, the daughter of Raguel in Ecbatana, suffers from a demon that has already killed seven of her grooms on the
honeymoon night. In the former part of the book we also read about
the pious old Jew Tobit, who lost his sight. God sends the archangel
Raphael to heal both of them. Raphael, disguised as Tobit's kinsman,
escorts the young Tobias to Sarah's house, and advises him how to
drive away the demon by burning the heart and liver of a fish.

This story is told by one omniscient narrator[15], and combines the
narrative perspectives. We can see Sarah praying in her upper room,
Raphael driving the demon to the upper part of Egypt and binding
him there, and Raguel worrying for the young couple all night and
digging a grave for Tobit. The story of Sarah thus unites the motives
of the three episodes of the *ATh*.

First we can read the story from the demon's perspective. It is
similar to the first passage in the *ATh*. The jealous demon Asmodeus
kills the husbands of Sarah. That the demon is in love with Sarah, is
told by Tobit in the shorter text (6.15)[16]. The demon does no harm to

its soil (Plutarch, *De Iside* 33); both Egypt and Ethiopia were important
spots of Hellenistic novels and legendary narratives (e.g. Philostratus, *Vita
Apollonii* 6).
[15] For the narrators in the *Book of Tobit* see I. Nowell, 'The Narrator in the
Book of Tobit', *SBL 1989 Seminar Papers* (Atlanta, 1989) 27-38
[16] The main witness of the longer text of Tobit is the *Codex Sinaiticus*, of
the shorter text the *Codex Vaticanus*, cf. J.D. Thomas, 'The Greek text of
Tobit', *JBL* 91 (1972) 463-71.

the girl, but he kills the men who enter her chamber. This is similar to the situation of the beautiful girl in *ATh* 30-8, and the jealous demon that kills her lover. We have no information about the grooms, except that there were seven of them. Unlike the young man in *ATh*, none of them were raised from the dead.

Secondly, we take the women's perspective, like in the second passage of the *ATh*. Sarah's intelligence, braveness, beauty, and ancestry are praised by the archangel Raphael (6.12). Unlike the beautiful girl of the *ATh*, however, she keeps her virginity, because her demon acts before she can sleep with her husbands. And unlike the other woman in *ATh*, she is not actually attacked by the demon, though she also suffers much from him. Her conflict is about her social role and status: this is explicitly spoken of in her concern about her father's reputation (3.10). She is concerned about her 'embedded honor'[17].

The father's perspective is similar to the third text in the *ATh*, and is represented by Raguel, father of Sarah. Though he belongs to the rural middle class, rather than to high social milieu, he is also afraid lest they 'become stock of ridicule and blame' (8.10). He is concerned about the reputation of his family, much like the general in the *ATh*. Like the general, he also appears as a caring family man with a wife, only girl, and servants.

The healing man of God is actually an angel in this story. Raphael disguises himself as a humble travelling companion of Tobias, and does not 'show off' like Thomas. He remains an allegorical figure, the tool of divine providence, who submits his knowledge of magic to the young Tobias. At first sight a character like Tobias seems to be missing from the *ATh*, where none of the three exorcisms ends with a wedding ceremony. We have to seek this motif in the first chapters of the *ATh*, where the king's only daughter and her husband spend their honeymoon night in the company of the Lord, who appears them in the shape of Thomas (11-3). The story of the newly married couple and the worried parents is based on a similar setting as in the *Book of Tobit*.

---

[17]   For embedded honor, see B.J. Malina, *The New Testament World* (Louisville, 1993) 28-62. For the application of social-science models in the *APt*, see I. Czachesz, 'Who is Deviant?', in Bremmer, *Acts of Peter*, 84-96.

There may be a cultural reason that this wedding celebration is not present in the case of the three exorcisms. While the heroes of the *Book of Tobit* embody the Jewish piety of the post-exilic priestly restoration of Israel, with family values in the center, the protagonists of the *ATh* illustrate a (gnostic?) contempt for all earthly ties. The man raised from the dead, and the exorcised women, will find new bonds only in the community of the apostle Thomas. We will have to come back to this problem in the third part of our paper.

Though no other piece of ancient literature deals with our subject as thoroughly as the *Book of Tobit*, we still have a few more parallels. Philostratus in his *Vita Apollonii* (4.45) tells the following story: It happened in Rome that a girl died in the hour of her wedding. Apollonius touched the girl, told her something, and raised her from 'seeming death' (*tou dokountos thanatou*). The girl returned to the house of her father. The text suggests that the wedding went ahead in the end. Even if there is no mention of demons in these texts, the situation is similar to the previous cases. Death intervening at the hour of the wedding fulfils here the same narrative function as jealous demons in the other stories. We have to remember that in a narrative plot different characters may fulfil the same function.

There are three other parallel passages in the New Testament. In *Acts* 16.16-19 we read about a young demonized girl, who brings much profit to her masters by telling the future. When she sees Paul and his companions, she identifies them as the agents of the Most High God. Paul drives the demon out of the girl, who loses her ability to tell the future, to the anger of her masters. At first sight, the only motif connecting this episode to our passages is that a demon abided in a girl for a long time. But the demon is also classified more closely in the text, namely as a 'spirit of foretelling' (*pneuma puthôn*). It is notable that the word *Python* as a proper name originally designated the dragon that lived at the oracle of Delphi (*Python*), until Apollo killed it[18]. In *Python* we have a typical dragon figure, as the black serpent in the first story in the *ATh*. In ancient literature, dragons and serpents often appear as sexual

---

[18] For a brief discussion of this figure see 'Python', *Der kleine Pauly* IV, 1280-1. For Python in *Acts* 16 and the *Sibylline Oracles* see J.W. van Henten, 'Python', in K. van der Toorn *et al.* (eds), *Dictionary of Deities and Demons in the Bible* (Leiden, 1999²) 669-71.

symbols: demons and deities in this form have intercourse with women[19].

Another parallel is found in the synoptic gospels. In Mk 5.21-43 the raising of the daughter of Jairus is combined with the healing of the woman with haemorrhage. The pericope is preceded by the driving out of the demon in Gerasa, whose words 'what have I to do with you' (Mk 5.7) are echoed in the healing of the woman in our second passage (45). We should assume that the insertion of the woman's story into the story of the raising of Jairus' daughter has a serious purpose. We are definitely not content with the explanation that it is a mere stylistic maneuvre, a means of heightening tension in the narrative. We suggest that the healing of the young girl and the woman represent two aspects of the same problem. They are women and they are sick, both of them lacking power over their lives. The girl has not yet had time to become a woman, and the adult woman has had illness in her female organs for twelve years. It is certainly not by chance that the girl is also twelve years old. Not only is this the span of time that the woman has been ill, but it is also the age of sexual maturity and readiness for marriage[20]. Both recover their health and the chance to live a full life as women, according to the standards of their society.

The illnesses of the girl and the woman thus both resemble each other and the instances of other demonic possessions in *ATh*. Moreover, as a pair they resemble the mother and the daughter in the story of the general. The exasperated father also appears on the scene, and his perspective is to be taken seriously. It is from Jairus' perspective that the whole story is told. As the head of the synagogue, he is an important person in the local hierarchy. The concerns of the general

---

[19]   A great number of illustrations is provided by O. Weinreich, *Antike Heilungswunder* (Giessen, 1909; repr. Berlin, 1969) 93-4 and A. Dieterich, *Eine Mithrasliturgie* (Leipzig and Berlin, 1923³, reprint Darmstadt, 1969) 123. The best known story is perhaps the birth of Augustus in Suetonius, *Octavianus* 94, itself based on the Alexander novel. There are also parallels from China: see Weinreich, *Antike Heilungswunder*, 94 (footnote).

[20]   There are no absolute rules in the Old Testament when girls are to get married in Israel. Talmudic tradition suggests twelve or thirteen years, the Roman law at the time of Augustus prescribed twelve years as a minimum. See 'Marriage' in D.N. Freedman *et al.* (eds), *The Anchor Bible Dictionary* IV (New York and London, 1992) 559-72; Bremmer, *Acts of Peter*, 2.

about his family could also have been related by him, since he equally appears in a numerous household as well as in a circle of friends and acquaintances. In his case, it is again the integrity of the family and social life that is endangered. But the girl is only 'seemingly dead', as in the story of Apollonius. She is finally raised from the dead, and the integrity of Jairus' family, or, as we can also say, the integrity of Jairus' life is restored. We must conclude, that the Markan story is not only about the restoration of hope of the three individuals, but also has a complex overall perspective, from which we must interpret these healings as one continuous story.

Before we proceed further, let us make a quick reference to another woman who was exorcised by Jesus, namely, Mary Magdalene, from whom he drove out, according to Luke, no less than seven demons (Lk 8.2). In all the three synoptic gospels she is one of the women who witness the empty tomb. We do not know much about the nature of her demonic possession. Her seven demons remind us of the seven husbands of Sarah. The tradition of the Church, by conflation with other stories, colored her life as a prostitute. But we think that she represents the religious aspect of exorcism in Luke's story, just as the woman in the bath in the *ATh*. She had demons, was healed by Jesus, and became one of the most faithful female followers.

3. *Typological interpretation*

In our selection of the texts we mostly have stories of women, loved by jealous demons that damage their lives. Most of the time the stories of these women are not told from the women's perspectives. The narrative point of view in the texts is either that of the demon, the lover, the father, the groom, the masters, or the healers. Most of these female figures are alienated and objects in the hands of other agents in the stories. To different degrees, they are mishandled by their environment. This misuse of their bodies and souls is represented by demonic possession.

The beautiful girl is the sexual object of the young lover. In fact the moral conflict does not present itself until the dragon gives his interpretation of the deeds of the young couple. The dragon symbolizes the knowledge of good and bad, the end of the state of moral innocence. The dragon, as the moral judge of the young couple, bears a mythological symbolism. As he explicitly states, it was he who talked to Eve in the garden, and told her what his father entrusted him to tell. He is, mythologically, the origin of moral dilemmas and *aporiae*.

Another young girl in *Acts* is also misused by a dragon-like demon, the one foretelling the future. Her exploitation is explicitly signified by the money her masters make from her demonic illness. The sexual complex, however hidden, is recognizable also here, and is implied by the allusion to the mythological dragon of Delphi, too. Also in the case of Sarah's demon in the *Book of Tobit* we find an allusion to his relationship with dragons: it is the killing of the huge fish, and the burning of its inner parts, that drives the demon away.

The demons further symbolize the ties of these women to their fathers or masters, which hinders them from living a full life as women. This is what we call the 'Electra complex', the female pair of the 'Oedipus complex'. Rather than only an incestuous lust, it means paralyzing bonds to the father and the family. It can be seen in the demonic possession of Sarah and the general's daughter; in Philostratus' story of the girl raised by Apollonius of Tyana; and perhaps, also in the case of Jairus' daughter, the woman with hemorrhage, and the prophesying girl from *Acts*. It is divine intervention in each case, which breaks this paralyzing bond, and makes normal and complete life possible for these women.

Now let us turn our attention to the male perspectives of the narratives. It is not only women that have to kill their demons of incest, family bonds, and usurpation, with the help of divine characters. At least two protagonists, the young lover and Tobias, also have to fight dragons. In fairy tales it is usually the male hero, typically the smallest son of the king, who has to find and then overcome the monster. That the demons are typologically complex figures, was already seen in the case of the black serpent. In one narrative character, he embodied original sin, the moral agony of the human soul, as well as sexual exploitation and alienation. In addition to that, he was not only a jealous demon in the girl's story, but also the dragon in the story of the young man, who overcame him only with the help of a divine agent, the apostle Thomas. In the case of Tobias, it is even easier to recognise the double roles of the demon. There is a separate agent, the huge fish, as an *alter ego* of the demon Asmodeus. The black dragon and the fish of Tobit are phallic symbols, the pictures of the destructive drives of the two young men[21]. This is also symbolized by the river Tigris; the inner parts of the fish; the bursting of the dragon; his poison sucked out from his victim, which is then poured out onto the ground, together with gall, where it eats out a big hole.

Just as the poison and gall of the dragon are poured into the ground, and the heart and liver of the fish are burnt, the primary drives of these young men are sublimated and transformed into creative powers. It is interesting to notice that while the demonization of women was of an interpersonal nature most of the time (dependence on fathers, masters and families), the possession of these two young males represents rather the destructive drives of their own personalities. Although the bond to family and mother presents itself in the *Book of Tobit* and in the 'Hymn of the pearl', an analysis of these two texts from this angle is beyond the scope of this paper.

We have already referred to the two hymns in the *ATh* sung by the apostle Thomas. Without a deeper analysis of the 'Hymn of the pearl', perhaps the best known and most discussed part of the *ATh*[22], we can make the observation that its young hero is the archetypal relative of Tobias and the other young man in the *ATh*. He is the son of a fabulously rich king from the East, and is sent to Egypt for a study trip. He returns after various adventures, puts on his decorated robe and participates in the kingdom of his father. The first episode of the *ATh*, including the 'Hymn of the bride', also leads us to a royal family, with the king and his only daughter in the center of the story. Worried father, wedding celebration, young couple praying on honeymoon night, all are present in this first scene. In addition, we have a fountain, where a lion (sexual symbol) and a black dog (demonic symbol) attack the cup-bearer[23], who abused Thomas at the wedding. Almost the whole inventory of the exorcism episodes is anticipated here.

---

[21] For the symbolism of dragons in general see note 18 above. For the interpretation of the fish in *Tobit* see Drewermann, 'Gott heilt – Erfahrungen des Buches Tobits', in H. Becker and R. Kaczinsky (eds), *Liturgie und Dichtung* II (St. Ottilien, 1983) 359-404 at 397.

[22] See Luttikhuizen, this volume, Ch. VIII.

[23] Cf. the black figures discussed above (note 14). For the lion as a sexual symbol see T. Adamik, 'The baptized lion' in Bremmer, *The Acts of Paul*, 60-74 at 67, who quotes Pliny, *Naturalis historia*, 8.42.

Already the first act lines up the basic themes of the *ATh*, and delineates the basic narrative plot, which is later decomposed into minor conflicts in the individual scenes. The three demonic stories that we selected from the narrative of the *ATh*, and interpreted with the help of other literary parallels, are in fact nothing else than variations of the main plot of the *ATh*.

The king is the key figure of this story: he is a corporate person, embodying collective identity. Families, kingdoms and households fulfil the same role throughout the *ATh*. The king symbolizes also the upper level of the hierarchy of personality, the realm of the conscious. Kings, royal officers and fathers have the same typological function in our stories. In the center of the plot we also find princesses, beautiful girls, and women. They represent the opposite sex, and are associated with cultural values, as well as the psychological resources of personality. In C.G. Jung's terminology, they stand for the *anima* aspect of the unconscious[24].

From this complex perspective, the characters in our stories play the roles of different factors of an organic psychological process. The circular repetition of plots and subplots, on the other hand, offer different approaches to the one ultimate problem of restoring integrity of the personality. This integrity is most beautifully expressed by the heavenly palace, which Thomas builds for the king in his second act (17-29). The *ATh* first describes the marriage of the royal couple and the construction of the heavenly palace, and only then does it come back to the difficult details.

How shall we understand the narrative pattern of the 'bride of the demon' in the context of this archetypal scenario? From this perspective we have to interpret demonic possessions as the dominance of the destructive powers of the unconscious over creative forces, which are, in turn, represented by the female figure of the *anima*. In the first story, the young man loses the fight against the paralyzing Oedipal aspects of personality, and is unable to keep his *anima* partner. As we have already mentioned, this story signifies the sexual and moral aspects of the basic psychological complexes the most directly.

---

[24]   See C.G. Jung, 'Über den Archetypus mit besonderer Berücksichtigung des Animabegriffes', in *idem*, *Die Archetypen und das kollektive Unbewusste* = Gesammelte Werke 9/1 (Olten and Freiburg in Breisgau, 1985[6]) 67-87.

The members of the personality remain disintegrated in a primeval mythological chaos.

The general's daughter and wife are not much luckier either. In this story, if possible, we have a more fundamental problem. While the young man at least possessed half his *anima* for a while, the two women in the general's story live locked up in a room of his house. Typologically this means that the general, symbol of the aged and powerless conscious, is completely separated from the *anima* aspects of the self, which could fill the 'house' of the personality with new life and energy. It is also evident from the story, that the wild asses stand for the 'shadow' forces of the unconscious[25]. They first have to be mastered by the apostle, before the two women are able to leave their bondage. It is the uncontrolled powers of the unconscious, which prevent the integration of the *anima* into the household of the psyche. Not only the wild asses, but also the black dragon, the two black men, the bath, and the fountain symbolize these forces.

The second woman, also an *anima* character, is loved by the same demon. During his visit of the inferno, she has the chance to see various representations of the dark side of the human psyche. Her successful return from this journey also means that the positive powers of the unconscious are liberated from the destructive ones. She has no male partner at all in the story. Her liberation concludes in baptism and eucharist.

It is remarkable, that in none of these stories have we the classical fairy-tale solution, the young hero killing the dragon and marrying the princess! The successful young hero, the symbol of the integrated and restored self, for example Tobias in the *Book of Tobit*, is completely missing from the plot. Could it be Thomas, who takes the role of the young prince in the *ATh*? At the wedding celebration in the first act he seems for a minute to play the role of the young hero in the eyes of the Hebrew flute player. But it is there Thomas himself, who refuses to continue this role.

In Thomas we have rather a typical helper figure. His polymorphy also corresponds to this role. Let us remember the benevolent helpers of the fairy tales, who appear sometimes as magicians,

---

[25] 'Shadow' is the name of the destructive aspect of the unconscious in Jung's terminology. For theriomorphic symbols of the 'shadow' and the unconscious, see especially his 'Phänomenologie des Geistes im Märchen', in *Archetypen*, 221-69 at 246-58.

sometimes as old men, and sometimes as animals[26]. The apostle
Thomas raises the dead, heals the sick and steers events toward a
positive conclusion: the integration of the fragmented personality.
But he is not the young hero, the real groom of the princess, the symbol of the restored self.

The answer to our question is found in the 'Hymn of the bride':
'And they look to their Bridegroom who shall come, / and they shall
shine with His glory, / and shall be with Him in the kingdom / which
never passeth away' (8.35-9)[27]. From these and the coming lines, it is
clear that the young hero, the one who leads back the bride to the
palace of the father, is the Bridegroom of the 'Hymn of the bride'.
We should look for no other 'self' symbol in the later episodes either.
Even where we have a 'real' bridegroom, as in the scene of the royal
wedding, he does not fulfil his function of leading home the *anima*,
taking the place of the aged king, and becoming the renewed center
of the integrated self. The marriage of the young couple is prevented
precisely by the savior figure, who is the only legitimate bridegroom
of the soul in the imagery of the *ATh*.

This is symbolized by the religious initiation of the exorcised
women. The 'marriage' of the conscious and unconscious aspects of
personality, the union of the young hero and the *anima*, which Jung
called the process of 'individuation', gives way in these stories to the
reformation of the personality in a mystical experience.

This is the narrative plot of self-identification into which the *ATh*
invites the reader. The moral, social, and religious 'demons' of these
stories are all overcome by one and the same person. In the various
attempts at reintegrating the self, we find one common character, the
collective figure of the saviour. The narrative ways of reconstructing
the self, the various exorcisms and healings, point toward a transcendent centre of personality. The solution offered here is the formation
of an 'excentric' type of personality, a mystical union described also
by Paul (*Galatians* 2.20): 'it is no longer I who live, but it is Christ
who lives in me'.

---

[26]   See again Jung, 'Phänomenologie des Geistes im Märchen'.
[27]   The translation is from Klijn, *Acts of Thomas*, 67-8.

IV. The Heavenly Palace in the *Acts of Thomas*

A. HILHORST

In its first and second Acts, the *ATh* contains a story about palace-building which can be summarized as follows[1]: Gundaphorus, an Indian king, sends his merchant, Abbanes, to Jerusalem to engage a skilled architect. There he meets Jesus. Jesus sells him his slave, Thomas, who is an accomplished craftsman. Abbanes and Thomas embark for India (2-3). After a stop at Andrapolis (4-16), an episode which we will not address here, they arrive at the royal court, where Thomas is presented to the king. The king invites him to build him a palace, which he agrees to do. They discuss plans and visit the place where the work is to be carried out. Thomas takes a reed, measures the place and designs a draft; all this convinces the king of Thomas' competence. Although he is somewhat surprised at Thomas' determination to build in winter rather than in summer, he departs, leaving a considerable amount of money with Thomas to meet the building costs. Thomas, however, distributes the money among the poor; at the same time, he reports to the king that he is building the palace. Finally, the king, who has received alarming messages from his friends, wants to inspect the progress of the work personally, whereupon Thomas gives the startling answer, 'Now you cannot see it, but you shall see it when you depart this life'. The king is furious. He casts Thomas into prison and considers by what death he will kill him. The king's brother, Gad, is so shocked at what he regards as Thomas' insult to the king that he grows ill and dies. Angels take his soul up into heaven (17-22). Then the text continues in this way:

---

[1] My starting-point is the Greek text edited by M. Bonnet.

Angels received the soul of Gad, the king's brother, and took it up into heaven, showing him the places and mansions there, asking him, 'In what place do you wish to dwell?' And when they came near the edifice of the apostle Thomas, which he had erected for the king, Gad, upon beholding it, said to the angels, 'I entreat you, my lords, let me dwell in one of these lower chambers.' But they said to him, 'In this building you cannot dwell.' And he said, 'Why not?' They answered, 'This palace is the one which that Christian has built for your brother.' But he said, 'I entreat you, my lords, allow me to go to my brother to buy this palace from him. For my brother does not know what it is like, and he will sell it to me.' (22; trans. J.K. Elliott)

Then the soul of Gad is permitted to return to his body. He asks his brother to sell his heavenly palace to him. At first, the king does not understand anything of what his brother says, but after Gad explains, the king decides to keep his palace and refers his brother to Thomas, who will build a still better palace for him (23-24). Needless to say, both Gad and Gundaphorus become Thomas' converts in the meantime.

This story must have made a lasting impression on its readers. It was retold by the Syrian poet Jacob of Sarug (*ca.* 451-521)[2] and much later by Vincent of Beauvais and Jacobus de Voragine[3]; it was also represented in medieval Latin and vernacular rewritings of the *ATh*[4] and mentioned in medieval Latin historiography and poetry[5]. We find Thomas represented in art as a carpenter, and the story has earned him the dignity of being the patron saint of architects, surveyors, bricklayers and stonemasons[6]. Scholarship, however, has been

---

[2]   Cf. R. Schröter, 'Gedicht des Jakob von Sarug über den Palast, den der Apostel Thomas in Indien baute', *Zeitschrift der Deutschen morgenländischen Gesellschaft* 25 (1871) 321-77.

[3]   *Speculum Historiale* 9.62-5 (edition of 1624 = 1965) and *Golden Legend* 5.12-87 ed. Maggioni, respectively.

[4]   See M. Geerard, *Clavis Apocryphorum Novi Testamenti* (Turnhout, 1992) 148-51; F. Wilhelm, *Deutsche Legenden und Legendare: Texte und Untersuchungen zu ihrer Geschichte im Mittelalter* (Leipzig, 1907) pass.

[5]   Ordericus Vitalis *Hist. Eccl.* 2.14; A. Poncelet. 'Hymni, sequentiæ aliaque carmina sacra hactenus inedita', *Analecta Bollandiana* 6 (1887) 353-404 at 403-4, where the eighth strophe of the poem on Thomas reads: *Es palacii fundator, / fratris regis suscitator, / ipsum regem sic repente / acquiris cum ipsa gente.*

[6]   Cf. M. Lechner, 'Thomas, Apostel', in E. Kirschbaum and W. Braunfels (eds), *Lexikon der christlichen Ikonographie* 8 (Rome etc., 1976) 468-75;

less generous and much remains to be done[7]. In this paper, I will look for some of the motifs and ideas that shape the story, namely the protagonist as a manual worker, pious fraud, and heavenly palaces for individual persons. Alms-giving, which plays a role in virtually all of the material, will not be dealt with separately; it will be taken for granted that charity, of little importance in the Graeco-Roman world, is a major obligation in Early Judaism and Christianity[8]. Once we know what is traditional in the story, we will be in a position to establish its measure of originality.

1. Manual work

Early Christianity has a positive appreciation of manual labour, which contrasts strongly with Graeco-Roman views. In Greece, the ideal is the free, well-to-do citizen who can spend his time working for the common good and his own interests, while the ordinary work is being done by immigrants (μέτοικοι) and slaves. In Rome, a similar mentality can be observed. The Christian attitude was destined to get the upper hand and to maintain itself in later centuries as well, especially in monasticism (ora et labora)[9]. Paul is important in this

L. Goosen, *Van Andreas tot Zacheüs: Thema's uit het Nieuwe Testament en de apocriefe literatuur in religie en kunsten* (Nijmegen, 1992) 280-3.
[7] There is little explanation in R.A. Lipsius, *Die apokryphen Apostelgeschichten und Apostellegenden* I (Braunschweig, 1883), 225-347; E. Preuschen – R. Raabe, 'Thomasakten', in E. Hennecke (ed.), *Handbuch zu den Neutestamentlichen Apokryphen* (Tübingen, 1904) 562-601; A.-J. Festugière, *Les Actes apocryphes de Jean et de Thomas* (Geneva 1983); P.-H. Poirier and Y. Tissot, 'Actes de Thomas', in F. Bovon and P. Geoltrain (eds), *Écrits apocryphes chrétiens I* ([Paris], 1997), 1323-470. Only G. Bornkamm, *Mythos und Legende in den apokryphen Thomas-Akten* (Göttingen, 1933) 18-23 and A.F.J. Klijn, *The Acts of Thomas* (Leiden, 1962) treat the passage in some depth.
[8] J. Hahn, 'Almosen', *Der Neue Pauly* 1 (1996) 529-31.
[9] Cf. F. Hauck, 'Arbeit', *RAC* 1 (1950) 585-90; C. Schneider, *Geistesgeschichte des antiken Christentums* (Munich, 1954) I 509-10, 621-2, 695-7; several authors, 'Handwerk', *Der Neue Pauly* 5 (1998) 134-50 at 145. Monasticism: *Regula Benedicti* 48; several authors, *Théologie de la vie monastique* (s.l., 1961) 226, 375, 377, 440, 443, 456. B. van den Hoven, *Work in Ancient and Medieval Thought* (Amsterdam, 1996), tones down the differences between ancient and medieval attitudes toward labour.

respect, stressing that he works for his living with his own hands[10]. In the Gospels, Peter and Andrew, and James and John, are portrayed as fishermen (Mt 4.18-22 par). We even see Jesus as a carpenter (τέκτων) in Mark 6.3 or the son of a carpenter in Matthew 13.55[11], a feature which Simon the Magician uses to make Peter lose face with the Romans in the *APt* 23. And the *Protevangelium of James* offers a picture of Joseph working with an adze (9.1) and building houses (9.3; 13.1).

In the *ATh* it is essential that Thomas is a τέκτων (2). Indeed, this quality is duly stressed. Thomas himself gives a survey of his skills twice (3, 17) and he is actively engaged in the preparation of the building plans (18). Interestingly, a connection is found between the carpentership of Joseph and Thomas, for when selling Thomas, Jesus draws up a bill of sale beginning with the words: 'I, Jesus, son of the carpenter Joseph, declare that I have sold my slave' etc. (2).

Our story bears a certain resemblance to the legend of saints Laurus and Florus, which may be summarized as follows:

> Florus and Laurus were twin-brothers, stonecutters, who had learnt their craft from the martyrs Proclus and Maximus. They settled in a city of Illyricum, where they worked for the governor of the province, Lycon. Licinius, the son of empress Elpidia, writes him a letter, asking to send him skilled workers to build a magnificent temple. And so it happens. Licinius engages them, draws a plan for the temple and furnishes them with funds to execute it. The saints take the money and spend it on the poor; by day they work at the building, by night they give themselves to prayer. When the work is nearly finished, the chief priest of the temple becomes a believer in Christ, his son having been cured of blindness by the twin-brethren. After the building has been finished, Licinius fills the temple with idols, but the twins come by night with the poor they had supported and destroy them. The poor and later the twin-brothers suffer martyrdom[12].

---

[10]   1 Cor. 4.12, cf. 1 Thess. 2.9; 2 Thess. 3.8; Acts of the Apostles 18.3; 20.34.

[11]   P. Nagel, 'Joseph II (Zimmermann)', *RAC* 18 (1998) 749-61; for the allegorical meaning cf. Bornkamm (n. 7) 19-21; Klijn (n. 7) 163-4.

[12]   Partly after J. Rendel Harris, *The Dioscuri in the Christian Legends* (London, 1903) 5. For an edition of the text, see F. Halkin, 'Une Passion inédite des saints Florus et Laurus. *BHG 662z*', *Jahrbuch der Österreichischen Byzantinistik* 33 (1983) 37-44.

This story shares with the Thomas narrative the element of saints as craftsmen and builders commissioned by a pagan ruler, the building plan drawn, the diversion of construction funds to relieve the needs of the poor, and the conversion of a prominent heathen. However, it is something of an overstatement to call both accounts, as Günther Bornkamm does, 'most closely related'[13], if only because with Florus and Laurus there is no matter of a palace in heaven.

2. Pious fraud

Although the preparations for the building of the palace seem to be in earnest, in the end we become aware that Thomas is misleading the king. When the moment of truth arrives, his promise turns out to be true in a very different way than his employer had imagined: The palace is a palace in heaven, and the money needed for its building serves to bestow alms to the poor and needy. This is an instance of pious fraud that we meet more often in hagiographical texts.

A well-known example of this motif is the story about St Laurence, who held the office of deacon in Rome in the middle of the third century. This story is sung in a famous Ambrosian hymn, *Apostolorum supparem*, and is related in several other sources[14]. The deacon had the task of collecting and distributing the alms; in Rome, this might create the impression of big business. During the persecution under Valerian, the deacon was asked by the prefect of Rome to deliver up the treasure of the Church, whereupon he assembled the poor among whom he had distributed the ecclesiastical possessions and presented them to the prefect, saying 'These are the treasure of the Church'.

Another instance occurs in Palladius' *Lausiac History*, ch. 6, where a monk, Macarius, in order to free a rich woman from her attachment to material things, promises to buy her precious stones. However, he uses her money to pay for the costs of a hospital. When

---

[13]   Bornkamm (n. 7) 22 n. 1.
[14]   Cf. J. Fontaine (ed), *Ambroise de Milan, Hymnes* (Paris, 1992) 549-59; T. Sternberg, '»Aurum utile«. Zu einem Topos vom Vorrang der Caritas über Kirchenschätze seit Ambrosius', *JAC* 39 (1996) 128-48; 'Laurence, St', *The Oxford Dictionary of the Christian Church* (Oxford, 1997³) 958 (bibliography).

the woman wants to see the stones, he shows her the patients nursed by her money[15].

In pagan tradition, there is a more or less comparable anecdote about Alexander the Great. Ammianus Marcellinus transmits a dictum by the Emperor Julian according to which Alexander, 'when asked where his treasures were, gave the kindly answer, "in the hands of my friends"'[16]. Here, although the interrogator may have expected to be shown Alexander's treasure-house, Alexander does not present his friends; rather, he confines himself to giving a witty answer, almost as if citing a standard expression. Indeed, the statement had already currency as a proverb in Plautus and other writers[17]. Furthermore, the element of charity is characteristically absent.

3. Heavenly palaces

a. As the abode of celestial beings

Heavenly palaces are a normal feature of Greek myth. Hephaestus built these on Mount Olympus and the gods dwell there in their bliss. On the highest peak is Zeus' palace, where the other gods assemble to make merry and to deliberate. Mulciber (Hephaestus) also built the palace of the Sun painted in Ovid's *Metamorphoses* 2.1-30[18]. Poseidon has his magnificent palace in the depths of the sea, at Aegae, where he is surrounded by his own marine gods. Hades' palace, on the other hand, is in no way attractive, although he and his wife Persephone do not seem to be bothered by this. There is no place for

---

[15] For the passage in the *ATh* and the *Lausiac History*, cf. R. Reitzenstein, *Hellenistische Wundererzählungen* (Leipzig, 1906 = Stuttgart, 1963) 77, and Bornkamm (n. 7) 22. To these examples G.J.M. Bartelink, *Palladio, La Storia Lausiaca* (s.l., 1974) 316-17, adds the story about St Laurence.

[16] Ammianus Marcellinus 25.4.15.

[17] C.G.A. Erfurdt (ed), *Ammianus Marcellinus, Opera quae supersunt* II (Leipzig and London, 1808 = Hildesheim and New York, 1975) 104; A. Otto, *Die Sprichwörter und sprichwörtlichen Redensarten der Römer* (Leipzig, 1890 = Hildesheim, 1964) 20-1; I.B. Pighi, 'De studiis Iacobi Lumbroso Ammianeis', *Aegyptus* 13 (1933) 275-93 at 291.

[18] R. Brown, 'The Palace of the Sun in Ovid's *Metamorphoses*', in M. Whitby *et al.* (eds), *Homo Viator: Classical Essays for John Bramble* (Bristol and Oak Park, 1987) 211–20.

mortals in these palaces, apart from those who have been carried off
to heaven like Ganymedes or deified like Heracles[19]. But even these
do not join the heavenly company as a reward for a righteous life[20].
The Isles of the Blest are reserved for them. However, Elysium is not
heaven and no gods dwell there.

In the Old Testament, God 'has built his high dwelling place in
the heavens' (Amos 9.6); there he 'has fixed his throne' (Ps. 103.19),
residing as a king surrounded by his heavenly army of angels[21]. This
heavenly palace is no more intended for mortals than it is in Greek
myth. As a rule, the abode of the dead is the underworld, Sheol, and
there are only two men to have 'vanished and be taken by God'
(Enoch: Gen. 5.24) or 'gone by a whirlwind into heaven' (Elijah: 2
Kings 2.11).

b. *As accessible to human beings*

In the deuterocanonical works Wisdom (3.1-9; 4.7; 5.15-16) and 2
Maccabees (7.36), we meet for the first time the idea of heaven as the
place of the blessed deceased, which also appears in the New Testament and afterwards[22]. A curious representation of this idea, which
has come to light only recently, is the poem called *The Vision of
Dorotheus*[23]. Dorotheus reports a vision he had and whose scene is

---

[19] I mention in passing Psyche's assumption into heaven in Apuleius'
Metamorphoses 6.23. Earlier in his fairy tale, Apuleius describes Cupid's
mysterious palace; for this cf. S. Brodersen, 'Cupid's Palace – A Roman
Villa (Apul. *Met.* 5,1)', in M. Zimmerman *et al.* (eds), *Aspects of the Golden
Ass* II: *Cupid and Psyche* (Groningen, 1998) 118-25.
[20] But cf. Seneca, *Agam.* 813-14, on Hercules: *bis seno meruit labore /
adlegi caelo / magnus Alcides*.
[21] 1 Kings 22.19; Daniel 7.10. Cf. also Ps. 29.9; Is. 6.1-4; Hab. 2.20; Mic.
1.2; in these passages the term *hêkāl* is used, which may denote either
God's palace in heaven or the temple of Jerusalem. This idea occurs also in
1 Enoch 14.10-23, 71.5-10; the Qumran literature: 1QSb 4.25-6, and the
New Testament: Mt 5.34; 23.22; Acts 7.49; Rev 4.2.
[22] W. Bauer *et al.*, *Griechisch-deutsches Wörterbuch zu den Schriften des
Neuen Testaments und der frühchristlichen Literatur* (Berlin and New York,
1988⁶) s.v. οὐρανός 2d; A. Lumpe and H. Bietenhard, 'Himmel', *RAC* 15
(1991) 173-212 at 201-2.
[23] A.H.M. Kessels and P.W. van der Horst, 'The Vision of Dorotheus
(Pap. Bodmer 29) Edited with Introduction, Translation and Notes',
VigChris 41 (1987) 313-59; J.N. Bremmer, 'The Vision of Dorotheus', in

heaven, represented as an imperial palace. He is adopted into the ranks
of the angels and gets the important function of gatekeeper. His func-
tioning, however, is not always satisfactory and he is punished by
being thrown in prison and whipped. In the end, he is again a gatekeeper of heaven. A heavy accent is put here on the military character
of God's court[24]. More importantly, the equation of the heavenly
palace with the palace of the Roman emperor has been carried here to
such an extent that the members of God's bodyguard are liable to mis-
behaviour and may be punished in heaven. This is a new element, and
a much more radical divergence from the biblical picture than is the
story of Thomas. As for the term used for 'palace', this is the old
poetic word τὰ μέγαρα, not the latinisms πραιτώριον or παλάτιον
used in the ATh 20 and 21, although the Vision of Dorotheus does not
at all shrink from Latin words alongside Homerisms.

c. Heavenly palaces for individual persons

The idea of an abode for men in heaven developed in still another
direction, namely that of personal accomodations in the heavenly
world. In rabbinic as well as in patristic sources, this image will be
used to express a gradation of heavenly bliss in accordance with each
person's merit[25]. Initially, however, we cannot with certainty establish a one-to-one relationship between dwellings and occupants; all
we can say is that the plural is used to denote the dwellings, e.g.
Joseph and Aseneth 12.12: 'For behold, all the funds of my father
Pentephres are transient and obscure, but the houses (δώματα) of
your inheritance, Lord, are incorruptible and eternal'[26]. In some texts,

J. den Boeft and A. Hilhorst (eds), Early Christian Poetry: A Collection of
Essays (Leiden, 1993) 253-61, reprinted in his The Rise and Fall of the
Afterlife (London and New York, 2002) 128-33, 184-6.
[24] For the militarization of the picture of heaven cf. J. Fontaine, Sulpice
Sévère, Vie de saint Martin II (Paris, 1968) 630 n. 1. Add the Coptic fragment of AA, Pap. Utrecht 1 p. 15 l.l. 25-30: Andrew 'turned to the demon
and said [to him], "Now indeed it is time for you to come out of this young
man [a soldier], so that he may enter on (military) service at the heavenly
palace [παλάτιον οὐράνιον]"' (trans. J.K. Elliott).
[25] G. Fischer, Die himmlischen Wohnungen. Untersuchungen zu Joh 14,2f
(Bern and Frankfurt/M., 1975) 72-3, 145-6, 209-14, 232-5, 292.
[26] According to the edition of M. Philonenko, Joseph et Aséneth (Leiden,
1968). C. Burchard prefers the reading δόματα, see J.H. Charlesworth (ed.),

the word σκηνή, 'tent', is used for the dwelling. Clearly the word cannot here have the connotation of a portable and temporary dwelling of canvas or the like, because it often carries the epithet of 'eternal'. There are no unmistakable pre-Christian passages. Examples include[27]: Luke 16.9: 'Make friends for yourselves by means of unrighteous mammon, so that when it fails they may receive you into the eternal tents'; *AA*, Martyrium Prius 13 (Andrew praying to Jesus): 'Receive me into your eternal tents'; *5 Esdras* 2.11: 'I will give them eternal tents, which I had prepared for them'. Of Johannine origin is the use of the word μοναί as it appears in John 14.2: 'In my Father's house are many abodes'[28], unless the Greek of Ethiopic *1 Enoch* 39.4: 'There I saw other dwelling places of the holy ones and their resting places' had made earlier use of the word. Both designations are combined in the long recension of *Testament of Abraham* 20.14: 'Take therefore my friend Abraham to paradise; there are the tents (σκηναί) of my righteous and abodes (μοναί) of my holy ones Isaac and Jacob in his bosom.' These heavenly dwellings are provided with their negative counterparts in Slavonic *2 Enoch* 61.2 (long recension): 'Many shelters have been prepared for people, good ones for the good, but bad ones for the bad, many, without number. Happy is he who enters into the blessed houses; for in the bad ones there is no rest, no returning.' This idea of individual dwellings for the sinners was already present in *1 Enoch* 45.3: 'Their resting places will be without number.' A later occurrence appears in the Ethiopic version of *The Preaching of Saint Andrew and Saint Philemon among the Kurds*. In this text, Andreas raises a boy to life, who reports what he had seen in Gehenna after his death: forty builders with burning torches constructing a house from sulphur and bitumen in which his father will be burned after his death as a punishment for his sins. Upon hearing this, the father repents and is willing to distribute his possessions among the needy[29].

The Old Testament Pseudepigrapha, II (New York, 1985) 222. As far as possible, quotations from 'Old Testament Pseudepigrapha' in the present paper are from Charlesworth's collection.

[27]   Fischer (n. 25) 224-9. Patristic passages are mentioned in G.W.H. Lampe, *A Patristic Greek Lexicon* (Oxford, 1961-1968) s.v. σκηνή 1b.

[28]   Fischer (n. 25) 69-71; Lampe (n. 27) s.v. μονή 1c.

[29]   See E.A.W. Budge, *The Contendings of the Apostles* (London and New York, 1899-1901); English translation of the passage II, 175-7.

Compared with this imagery, the picture in the *ATh* shows the innovation that the dwelling is not just a home but a magnificent residence, a palace. This is also the case in the sixth-century *Life of John the Almsgiver* by Leontius of Neapolis. Ch. 27 of that work narrates the story of a bishop, Troilus, who is cured of his avarice in a dream sent by God:

> 'I saw,' said he [Troilus], 'a house whose beauty and size no human art could imitate, with a gateway all of gold and above the gateway an inscription painted on wood which ran thus: "The eternal home (μονή) and resting-place of bishop Troilus." 'When I read this, I was overjoyed,' he continued, 'for I knew that the king had granted me the enjoyment of this house. But I had scarcely finished reading this inscription when behold, an imperial chamberlain appeared with others of the divine retinue, and as he drew near to the gateway of the radiant house he said to his servants: "Take down that inscription," and when they had taken it down he said again: "Change it and put up the one the King of the World has sent." So they took away the one and fixed up another while I was looking on, and on it was written: "The eternal home and resting-place of John, the Archbishop of Alexandria, bought for thirty pounds."' (trans. E. Dawes)

On John's suggestion, Troilus had given the thirty pounds to the poor, but he was so upset of the 'loss' of his money that John had returned it to him[30].

A comparable version may be found in Jacobus de Voragine's *Golden Legend* 9.41-71. Saint John convinces two young men to sell their possessions and give the proceeds to the poor. When, however, they see their former slaves in wealth while they themselves have but one cloak between them, they begin to have regrets. Then John turns some sticks and pebbles into gold and precious stones for them so that they can buy back their possessions. In the meantime, he raises to life another young man who has died recently and orders him to tell the other two men about his vision of their loss. The man

> did so, speaking at length about the glories of paradise and the pains of hell... He told them they had lost eternal palaces built of shining gems, filled with bankets, abounding in delights and lasting joys. He also spoke about the eight pains of hell. (trans. W.G. Ryan)

[30] For additional material, see L. Rydén, *Bemerkungen zum Leben des heiligen Narren Symeon von Leontios von Neapolis* (Uppsala, 1970) 74f.

The men implore St John to obtain mercy for them. He orders them to do penance and to pray that the sticks and stones may revert to their former nature. Their prayer is answered and the two young men receive 'the grace of all the virtues that had been theirs'.

If we may extend both our geographic and chronological boundaries, a further parallel might be drawn. It is a story told among the Santals, a tribe of the Munda people in India and reads as follows:

> Once upon a time there was a Raja, who had many water reservoirs and tanks, and round the edges he planted trees, mangoes, pipals, palms and banyans; and the banyan trees were bigger than any. Every day after bathing the Raja used to walk about and look at his trees, and one morning, as he did so, he saw a maiden go up to a banyan tree and climb it, and the tree was then carried up to the sky, but when he went in the evening he saw the tree in its place again; the same thing happened three or four days running. The Raja told no one, but one morning he climbed the banyan tree before the maiden appeared, and when she came, he was carried up to the sky along with the tree. Then he saw the maiden descend and go and dance with a crowd of Gupinis (Divine milk maids) and the Raja also got down and joined in the dance.
>
> He was so absorbed in the dance that he took no note of time; so when at last he tore himself away, he found that the banyan tree had disappeared. There was nothing to be done, but stay where he was; so he began to wander about and he soon came to some men building a palace as hard as they could. He asked them for whom the palace was being built, and they named his own name. He asked why it was being built for him, and they said that Thakur [the supreme Being] intended to bring him there, because he was a good ruler, who did not oppress his subjects and gave alms to the poor and to widows and orphans.
>
> There was no difference between night and day up in the sky, but when the Raja came back, he found that the banyan tree was there, and he climbed up it and was carried back to earth by it. Then he went home and told his people that he had been on a visit to a friend. After that the Raja used to visit the banyan tree every day, and when he found that it did not wither although it had been taken up by the roots, he concluded that what he had seen was true and he began to prepare for death. So he distributed all his wealth among his friends and among the poor; and when his officers remonstrated he made them no answer. A few days later he died, and was taken to the palace which he had seen being built[31].

---

[31]   C.H. Bompas, *Folklore of the Santal Parganas* (London, 1909) 240-1.

This story was recorded only a century ago; we do not know its origin, and the plot is very different from the story of St Thomas. Nevertheless, there are interesting points in common: both stories take place in India; under certain conditions it is possible to return to earth after seeing the palace in heaven[32]; the heavenly palace is due to royal persons, who earn it by giving alms to the poor; the palace has not been prepared beforehand but is being erected particularly for individual persons.

4. Conclusion

In the preceding sections we dealt with parallels concerning some features of the story of the palace building in the *ATh*. In our material, alms-giving was so omnipresent that it needed no discussion; manual labour played a role in only one parallel story; some examples of pious fraud could be found in contexts rather different from that in the *ATh*; and the idea of abodes in heaven generated the representation of a palace in heaven for the personal use of those having spent their riches for the benefit of the needy. *ATh* makes use of all these traditional views and images but is, nevertheless, highly original in at least three ways. First of all, the palace is being built during the life of the future occupant from his charitable deeds, whereas in other texts the palace is ready beforehand and can be earned by supporting the poor, but lost by avarice. There are parallels here, but they appear much later: the story about the Raja and the passage from *The Preaching of Saint Andrew and Saint Philemon* (and there an infernal building was intended). Second, the future occupant of the palace does not build it himself by means of his charitable deeds, but it is built from his money without his knowledge. Apparently, the assumption is that the king, once converted, will approve of it. Last but not least, the palace-building is integrated into a conspiracy of pious

---

[32] Returning to earth is envisaged also in Luke 16.27-31.

V. Thomas, the Slave of the Lord

MONIKA PESTHY

It is well known that the whole apocryphal literature related to Thomas is centred around the supposition that Thomas is the twin brother of the Lord. However, the twin motif is in no other document given such importance and made so explicit as in the *ATh*. Here, it appears under two different aspects: Thomas, the twin brother of the Lord on the one side, and the two brothers in the *Hymn of the Pearl* – the one who departs on the quest and the other who remains in their heavenly country – on the other.

As it is generally accepted that the *Hymn of the Pearl* is an independent piece, inserted later in the *ATh*, it has quite often been analysed in itself as an independent entity. Drijvers in his Introduction to the *ATh* argues that whoever inserted the *Hymn of the Pearl* in the *ATh*, did it with good reason because 'The main theme of the Hymn of the Pearl is exactly that of the *ATh*, man's return from the demonic world to that condition in which God created him, and his reunion with his brother Christ, with whom he will be heir in the kingdom' and it was inserted at the right place[1].

In this chapter I shall focus on the relationship between Jesus and Thomas, which received much less attention than the question of the double in the *Hymn of the Pearl*. The idea of a heavenly counterpart as it appears in the *Hymn* has been first of all connected with Gnostic and Iranian sources. As to myself, I shall look for parallels in the field of Jewish-Christian tradition.

---

[1] H.J.W. Drijvers, 'The Acts of Thomas', in *NTA* II, 332.

My objective is:
1. to examine the position of Thomas in *ATh*;
2. to present a Jewish tradition where Jacob plays a similar role to that of Thomas;
3. to draw some conclusions concerning the figure of Thomas as presented in the *ATh* in the light of the above;
4. to show very briefly that on some points Origen's thinking is very much akin to the ideas expressed in the *ATh*.

1. *Thomas and Jesus*

Kuntzmann in his book about twins emphasizes the identity of Thomas and Jesus. According to him, the two personalities are interchangeable and, as the story advances, so the identity grows more perfect, and in the end 'Thomas definitely yields his place to Jesus'[2]. On the other hand, Pieter Lalleman states that 'Thomas is not Jesus himself in another form'[3]. Ménard establishes a parallel between the transfiguration of Christ in Origen's interpretation and the *Hymn of the Pearl*, without mentioning Thomas[4]. Bovon describes the condition of the apostles in the *AAA* as follows: 'Christ, being absent from the terrestrial world, has a lieutenant on earth, the image of his divinity'. He thinks that in addition to this Thomas the twin becomes the spiritual brother of the Saviour[5].

2. *Thomas, the Slave of the Lord*

In the relation between Thomas and Jesus a certain contradiction can be observed. On the one hand they are very close to one another: it is Thomas who received the secret revelation of the Lord, as he

---

[2] R. Kuntzmann, *Le symbolisme des jumeaux au Proche-Orient ancien. Naissance, fonction et évolution d'un symbole* (Paris, 1983) 181.
[3] P.J. Lalleman, 'Polymorphy of Christ', in Bremmer, *Acts of John*, 109.
[4] J.E. Ménard, 'Transfiguration et polymorphie chez Origène', in *Epektasis. Mélanges patristiques offerts au Cardinal Jean Daniélou* (Paris, 1972) 367-72.
[5] F. Bovon, 'La vie des Apôtres. Traditions bibliques et narrations apocrypes', in F. Bovon *et al.*, *Les Actes Apocryphes des Apôtres* (Geneva, 1981) 141-58 at 152).

himself states in a prayer: 'Jesus, …, who did set me apart from all my companions and speak to me three words, wherewith I am inflamed, and tell them to others I cannot'. In certain passages, this closeness is practically already an identity: in c.11, the bridegroom sees Jesus in the likeness of Judas Thomas; here they are really inter-changeable. In c.34 the young man raised from death calls Thomas 'a man that has two forms'. The demon in c.45 says to Thomas: 'For you art altogether like him, as if begotten of him'. The epiclesis in c.50 expresses their perfect equality when it calls the Holy Spirit the 'Holy Dove that bearest the twin young'. On the other hand Thomas himself emphasizes their difference and the distance which separates them: 'I am not Jesus, but a servant of Jesus. I am not Christ, but I am a minister of Christ' (160).

If we want to understand how Thomas can be practically identi-cal with Christ and at the same time separated from him, we only have to pay attention to the words of the ass's colt in the Fourth Act, who addresses Thomas as follows: 'Twin brother of Christ, apostle of the Most High and fellow-initiate into the hidden word of Christ, who doest receive his secret saying, fellow-worker of the son of God, who being free didst become a slave and being sold didst lead many to freedom…'

I think that the position of Thomas could not have been better determined: being the twin brother, the fellow-initiate and the fel-low-worker of Christ, he has become a slave in order to help others.

Throughout the ATh, Thomas is characterized mainly by the fact that he is a slave. Right at the beginning, Jesus sells him as a slave to an Indian merchant: that is how he comes to India. Thus, Thomas is the slave of the Lord both physically and spiritually. He always refers to himself as servant or slave of the Lord (the Greek always has dou-los, the English translation uses either 'slave' or 'servant'): 'I am the servant of Jesus Christ, the eternal king' (139); 'thou who givest mighty works and great wonders by the hands of thy servant Judas' (141). When Misdaios asks him whether he is a slave or a free man, he answers: 'I am a slave'.

In Drijvers' Introduction to the ATh we read that 'the earthly existence of mankind is dominated by ignorance and error', which is true, but, first of all, this earthly existence is slavery. Man in his fallen condition is a slave, and the opposite of being slave is not being lord or master, but being free. This world is a world of slavery, while the other world where Thomas comes from is a world of free-dom. Thomas who was free became a slave and lead many to free-dom (cf. 39, quoted above). In c.167 he says of himself: 'I have become a slave; therefore today I do receive freedom'. Thomas' prayer in prison is almost a hymn of freedom: 'Liberator of my soul from the bondage of many, because I gave myself to be sold... Behold, I am set free from the cares on earth... Behold, I am set free from grief, and put on only joy. Behold, I become carefree and unpained, dwelling in rest. Behold, I am set free from slavery, and called to liberty. Behold, I have served times and seasons, and am lifted above times and seasons' (142). Christ is the liberator, because it is he who is absolutely free: Thomas calls him 'the free man, (scion) of kings' (143).

The leitmotiv of the *Hymn of the pearl* is also the opposition of slavery and freedom. Thus, whereas in c.111.56 Drijvers translates: 'I remembered that I was son of kings / And my noble birth asserted itself', *eleutheria* here really means 'freedom', and Poirier translates it in this way: 'et voilà ma condition libre de se mettre à chercher (ce qui sied à) ma race'[6]. The Syriac is even clearer (and we know that *the Hymn of the pearl* is better conserved in Syriac then in Greek), here we have: 'my freedom longed for its nature' or 'sought its nature'

But there is an important difference between Thomas and the young prince. Both of them are sent on an errand and both become slaves, but while with Thomas this is done to him on his own accord so that he can help others ('I gave myself to be sold' says Thomas in c.142), and remains conscious of his real nature and of his task all the time, the young prince falls in slavery by his own fault, completely forgetting about his origins and the errand he was sent for. It is sig-nificant that Thomas has his price with him: he could buy himself free at any moment, but chooses to remain a slave.

In the other *AAA* the apostles are seen sometimes to overshadow Christ completely. This is especially true for the *AA* where Andrew acts practically on his own: it seems that it is he who gives salvation to others and not Christ through him. The role of Thomas is absolutely different: he never acts on his own, in whatever situation he is, it is Christ who acts through him. Whatever he does, he does it

---

[6]   See also Bremmer, this volume, 86.

only to manifest the glory of Christ. Thus Thomas, twin brother of the Lord consented to become a slave in order to free others from slavery. And throughout the *ATh* he behaves as a real slave: he has no will of his own, but fulfils only the will of his master. We are not very far from the idea of Christ having willingly taken the form of slave as expressed in the ancient hymn of the Letter to the Philippians (2.6-9): 'who, though he was in the form of God, did not count equality with God a thing to be grasped, but emptied himself, taking the form of a servant, being born in the likeness of men. And being found in human form he humbled himself and became obedient unto death, even death on cross. Therefore God has highly exalted him and bestowed on him the name which is above every name'[7].

In his Introduction, Drijvers remarks that Thomas is like Jesus not only in his appearance 'but also in his destiny and his works' (p. 324). But while Jesus acts on behalf of the Godfather (see e. g. Jn 14.10: 'The words that I say to you I do not speak on my own authority, but the Father who dwells in me does his works.') in order to glorify the Father (Jn 14.13: 'Whatever you ask in my name, I will do it, that the Father may be glorified in the son'), Thomas acts on behalf of Jesus: for him Jesus is *the* God. Thus the levels have changed: Christ was sent by God the Father, Thomas was sent by Christ; Christ obeyed God the Father, Thomas obeyed Jesus; in Jesus God the Father is glorified, in Thomas Jesus.

Thomas and Jesus are both heavenly beings who descend to earth and take up the form of slave in order to help others. Jewish and Christian tradition knows about other heavenly beings, too, who put on human bodies for the sake of men. Since these beings retain their heavenly nature while becoming completely human, this can lead to a certain doubling of the personality. This is the case of Jacob – Israel.

3. Jacob – Israel

In the curious apocryphon called the *Prayer of Joseph* (first century AD) of which we possess only three short fragments[8], all three by Origen, we read the following passage:

[7] Quoted according the *Revised Standard Version*.
[8] Transl. with introd. by J.Z. Smith in J.H. Charlesworth (ed), *The Old Testament Pseudepigrapha*, 2 vols (New York, 1985) II.699-714.

I, Jacob, who is speaking to you, am also Israel, an angel of God, and
a ruling spirit. Abraham and Isaac were created before any work. But,
I, Jacob, who men call Jacob but who's name is Israel am he who God
called Israel, which means a man seeing God, because I am the first-
born of every living thing to whom God gives life.

When I was coming up from Syrian Mesopotamia, Uriel, the angel of
God, came forth and said that 'I [Jacob-Israel] had descended to earth
and I had tabernacled among men and that I had been called by the
name of Jacob'. He envied me and fought with me and wrestled with
me saying that his name and the name that is before every angel was to
be above mine. I told him his name and what rank he held among the
sons of God. 'Are you not Uriel, the eighth after me? and I, Israel, the
archangel of the power of the Lord and the chief captain among the
sons of God? Am I not Israel, the first minister before the face of
God?' And I called upon my God by the inextinguishable name[9].

In this fragment Jacob-Israel has a double personality according to
his two names: he is Jacob, a human being, and Israel, a heavenly
being, while we cannot really speak of two persons. In another fragment we have an additional detail which is important for us. According to this fragment Jacob 'was a chief captain of the power of the
Lord and had, from of old, the name of Israel; something which he
recognises while doing service in the body, being reminded of it by
the archangel Uriel'[10]. Thus Jacob the human being had to be
reminded of his heavenly nature, and probably that was the reason
why Uriel attacked him.

The double nature of Jacob-Israel appears more clearly in early
Rabbinical tradition. These writings generally combine Jacob's
wrestling with the angel in Genesis 32 with the ladder-vision of c.28.
As J.Z. Smith states in his introduction to the *Prayer of Joseph* this
'vision supplies the picture of ascending and descending angels so
central to the *Prayer of Joseph* and this motif is used, in both Palestinian Targumim and early Midrashim, as the chief proof-text for
heavenly Jacob-Israel'[11]. These texts give several reasons for the
angels' going up and down the ladder[12], the most important being

---

[9]   Op. cit. 713.
[10] Op. cit. 714.
[11] Op. cit. 710.
[12] Concerning the Rabbinical interpetation of Gen 28 see: J.H.C. Neeb,
'Origen's interpretation of Genesis 28:12 and the rabbis', in *Origeniana
Sexta. Origène et la Bible* (Leuven, 1995) 71-80.

that they do so in order to compare the sleeping patriarch with his image engraved on the throne: 'for thou art a prince together with God, thy features being engraven on high' (*Bereshit Rabba* 78.3), the face of Jacob being like the face of the *chayyah* which is on the Throne of glory in the vision of Ezekiel. Another, somewhat surprising motif for the ascending and descending of the angels is the 'raising up and dragging down' of Jacob, 'dancing on him, leaping on him, abusing him'[13].

According to several sources, the name of the angel who wrestles with Jacob is Israel and he bestows his own name on the patriarch. We have the same idea in Christian tradition, too. In the *Dialogue with Tryphon* Justin states: 'Our Christ touched the thighs of Jacob... Israel was his name from old / from above and he called the blessed Jacob by his own name' (125.5). 'In this tradition, Jacob the man, does battle with his heavenly counterpart, the angel Israel'[14].

3. Conclusions concerning Thomas

Jacob shows several similarities with Thomas on the one hand, and with the hero of the *Hymn of the pearl* on the other hand:
1. Jacob is the earthly manifestation of the angel Israel (identified in early Christian tradition with Christ) – Thomas is the earthly counterpart of the Lord.
2. Though Jacob and Israel are fundamentally identical, Jacob in his human condition is not aware of this identity. In the *Prayer of Joseph* it is stated explicitly, and in the Rabbinical sources it is implicit in the fact that Jacob is always pictured as sleeping, while the angels are comparing him with his image above. He had to be reminded of his divine nature: in the *Prayer of Joseph* it happens with the aid of Uriel, in the *Bereshit Rabba* I would conjecture this is the reason why the angels abuse him: it is to awaken him and make him understand his real nature. Jacob had to be reminded of his real self through a heavenly intervention, just as the hero of the *Hymn of the pearl*.
3. Jacob enters in possession of his divine self (symbolised by the acquiring of the name Israel) only after a trial (the wrestling) – the

---

[13]   Neeb, op. cit. 77.
[14]   Smith, op. cit., 707.

young prince regains his royal identity (symbolised by putting on the royal garment) also after a trial: the battle with the dragon.
4. Jacob does service in the body in the same way as Thomas.

As stated above, the three short fragments of the *Prayer of Joseph* are conserved by Origen. He quotes the first fragment because he wants to prove that John the Baptist was an angel who assumed human form in order to announce the coming of the Lord (*ComJoh* II.31). In other passages he declares that while souls in general enter the human body as a consequence of their fall, there are angelic beings who, without committing any sin, take up bodies to help fallen mankind[15].

In my opinion therefore two conceptions intermingle in the person of Thomas as depicted in the *ATh*: the conception of the twin brother and that of the heavenly helper, and this is why his figure has become somewhat contradictory. The two conceptions are quite different: while the twin motif emphasises the identity of the two, the slave motif emphasises their difference. Even if in certain scenes Thomas has the appearance of Jesus or Jesus that of Thomas, Thomas himself never becomes the Saviour, and he never claims it to be, he is only the helper of the Saviour. While the twin motif is characteristic of Syriac Christianity and is probably connected with the Gnostic idea of the heavenly counterpart, the slave motif is typically Jewish–Christian. In the Thomas-literature it appears only here, which is what distinguishes the Thomas of the *ATh* from other representations.

4. Origen and the Hymn of the Pearl

As Thomas seems akin to Origen's angelic beings doing service in the body, the ideas expressed in the *Hymn of the pearl* are quite similar to Origen's conception of the destiny of the soul: its heavenly origin, its fall, its adventures in the lower world or worlds and its return to its home-country where, at the end of time, it will reign together with Christ. In his *Commentary on Matthew* (Mt 13.45-6 the pearl of great value) he gives a curious description of human fate, almost in the terms of the *Hymn of the pearl*:

[15] See e. g. *De Princ.* I.7.5, II.9.7, III.5.4, IV.3.12(24), etc.

Therefore every soul who comes into infancy and advances toward perfection, until the totality of time will be present for him, needs a teacher, stewards and guardians, in order that after all this he, who earlier did not differ at all from a slave, though lord over everything, after being liberated from his teacher, stewards and guardians should receive his patrimony, that which is analogous with the very precious pearl and with the coming Perfect One.

VI. The *Acts of Thomas*: Place, Date and Women

With the *ATh* we come to the last of the great *AAA*. Where and when
was it written? These simple questions are not easily answered. In
fact, most introductions to the more recent translations give only a
general indication and refrain from a more detailed discussion, as a
representative selection may illustrate. Klijn suggests Syria in the
third century, Drijvers opts for 'the beginning of the 3rd century in
East Syria', Poirier and Tissot go for 'Édesse dans la première moitié
du IIIe siècle' and Keith Hopkins thinks that the author probably was
'a member of Edessene high society'[1]. These answers are clearly on
the right track, but can they be substantiated or can we even improve
upon them?

Let us start with the place of composition. Poirier's and Tissot's
location is of course supported by the tradition that Thomas was
buried in Edessa, but his tomb there only starts to appear in the
fourth-century Ephraem Syrus (*Carmina Nisibena* 42) and the pilgrim Egeria, who visited Edessa in AD 384 (*Itinerarium* 17.1, 19.3).
For earlier indications pointing to Edessa, an important argument
must be the influence of the Edessene philosopher Bardaisan (Greek
Bardesanes: AD 154-222) on the *ATh*[2]. In this connection the name

---

[1] A.F.J. Klijn (ed), *Apokriefen van het Nieuwe Testament* II (Kampen,
1985) 56, 65-6; H.J.W. Drijvers, 'The Acts of Thomas', in *NTA* II, 322-411
at 323; P.-H. Poirier and Y. Tissot, in F. Bovon and P. Geoltrain (eds),
Écrits apocryphes chrétiens I (Paris, 1997) 1324; K. Hopkins, *A World Full
of Gods* (London, 1999) 176.
[2] For Bardesanes and his influence see most recently Drijvers, 'Acts of
Thomas', 327, 336, who compares *cc.* 27, 32, 50, 82, 91 and 148; J. Teixidor,
Bardesane d'Édesse. La première philosophie syriaque (Paris, 1992);
S.K. Ross, *Roman Edessa* (London and New York, 2001) 129-23 and passim.

of one of the protagonists, Mygdonia, the wife of a relative of the king, may also be relevant. In real life it was an extremely unusual name, mentioned only twice in literature, only once in inscriptions and in papyri not at all[3]. As Strabo tells us that Mygdonia was the name given by the Macedonians to the land surrounding Nisibis, which was also called Mygdonian Antioch (11.14.2, 16.1.23), its presence here does seem to point to the area of Osrhoene.

In the Syriac version of the *Hymn of the Pearl* the protagonist is called *pasgriba* (48a)[4]. Although the title also occurs outside Edessa, for example in Hatra, it is important to note that in a recently published Syriac document of the year AD 240 the father of the ruling Edessene king Abgar X (239-242) is called 'Ma'nu the crown-prince' (*pasgriba*)[5]. The same title occurs in an inscription from the Edessan citadel, dating to the first half of the third century, naming 'Šalmath, the queen, daughter of Ma'nu the crown-prince'[6]. The *Hymn* probably already existed separately before the *ATh* and was written, at the latest, at the beginning of the third century in a aristocratic milieu with close Parthian contacts, as is indicated by its many Iranian loan words and titles[7]. The proximity of the *Hymn* to the *Cologne Mani*

[3] Literature: see the discussion of the two fourth-century Eastern Mygdonii by S. Corcoran, *The Empire of the Tetrarchs* (Oxford, 2000[2]) 281-2 (with thanks to Peter van Minnen). Inscription: D. Feissel, *Recueil des inscriptions chrétiennes de Macédoine* (Paris, 1983) no. 60.4 (V/VI AD).
[4] For documents and title see P.-H. Poirier, *L'hymne de la perle des Actes de Thomas* (Louvain-la-Neuve, 1981) 212-23; J. Teixidor, 'Deux documents syriaques du IIIe siècle ap. J.-C., provenant du Moyen Euphrate', *CRAI* 1990, 144-66 at 161; S. Ross, *ZPE* 97 (1993) 192-3; Drijvers and Healey, *Old Syriac Inscriptions*, no. P2; A. Luther, 'Abgar Prahates filius rex (CIL VI, 1797)', *Le Muséon* 111 (1998) 345-57 at 348-52.
[5] For the rule of Ma'nu see now A. Luther, 'Elias of Nisibis und die Chronologie der edessenischen Könige', *Klio* 81 (1999) 180-98 at 193-4; L. Cotta Ramosino, 'Edessa e i Romani fra Augusto e i Severi: aspetti del regno di Abgar V e di Abgar IX', *Aevum* 73 (1999) 107-43.
[6] H.J.W. Drijvers and J.F. Healey, *The Old Syriac Inscriptions of Edessa and Osrhoene* (Leiden, 1999) no. As1, tr. F. Millar, *The Roman Near East, 31 BC – AD 337* (Cambridge MA, 1993) 477.
[7] The strong Parthian influence in the area is well documented by G. Widengren, *Iranisch-semitische Kulturbegegnung in parthischer Zeit* (Cologne and Opladen, 1960); see also Luttikhuizen, this volume, Ch. IX.

Codex (*CMC*) suggests that it was interpolated by Manichaeans in the course of the third century[8]. The Manichaeans had also been influenced by Bardaisan[9], and Mani himself wrote letters to Edessa (*CMC* 63.16.22), a strong indication of the importance of the city for the movement.

The social hierarchy of the *ATh* also suggests an eastern origin. The French classicist Suzanne Saïd has argued that with the last great pagan novel, the *Aethiopica* of Heliodorus, one enters the world of late antiquity, as the palace now supersedes the agora[10]. This can hardly be true. In Heliodorus' time, that is the period around AD 230[11], cities in the Greek East were still flourishing, witness the somewhat later *Martyrdom of Pionius* of AD 250. It is much more likely that at this point Heliodorus reflects the political realities of the East where local dynasties maintained themselves much longer than in Asia Minor. Whereas the earlier *AAA* all derive from Asia Minor and their non-apostolic characters are firmly situated among the local aristocrats, the 'firsts of the cities'[12], the *ATh* and Heliodorus clearly reflect the situation of Edessa and Emesa, where political structures lacked the Greek tradition. Admittedly, individually none of these arguments is conclusive, but cumulatively they do indeed seem to point to eastern Syria, in particular Edessa, as the place of composition.

---

[8]   Poirier, *L'Hymne*, 310-7.
[9]   See most recently, with extensive bibliographies, S.N.C. Lieu, *Manichaeism in the Later Roman Empire and Medieval China* (Tübingen, 1992²) 55-9, and *Manichaeism in Mesopotamia and the Roman East* (Leiden, 1994) 38-44.
[10]   S. Saïd, 'The City in the Greek Novel', in J. Tatum (ed), *The Search for the Ancient Novel* (Baltimore, 1994) 216-36 at 223.
[11]   For this much discussed problem, which is not yet definitively settled (some scholars still prefer the fourth century AD), see now the bibliography in J.N. Bremmer, 'The Novel and the Apocryphal Acts: Place, Time and Readership', in H. Hofmann and M. Zimmerman (eds), *Groningen Colloquia on the Novel* IX (Groningen, 1998) 157-80 at 165; more elaborately, Bremmer, 'Achilles Tatius and Heliodorus in Christian East Syria', in H.L.J. Vanstiphout (ed), *All Those Nations... Cultural Encounters within and with the Near East* (Groningen, 1999) 21-9.
[12]   Bremmer, 'The Novel', 165-70.

If the *ATh* was indeed written in Edessa, when did that happen? A *terminus post quem* is AD 212/213 when King Abgar was deposed[13]. Moreover, the *ATh* already betrays Roman influence: the royal palace is called *praitôrion* (3, 17-19: the normal term for the headquarters of a Roman governor), the name of King Misdaeus' wife is Tertia (134), and that of Mygdonia's nurse Marcia (120). In fact, in real life the Edessene kings started to assume Roman names around AD 200[14]. *ATh*'s interest in India suggests a date not long after the reign of Elagabalus (AD 218-22) when Bardaisan met an Indian embassy to the Emperor and composed a book about India and its customs[15]. This points to the 220s or 230s as the date of composition, the very time when Edessa no longer had a king, but a close relative of king Abgar still called himself 'crown prince' (above)[16]. Such a date also fits an observation by Carl Schmidt, on the basis of both Eusebius' quotation from the third book of Origen's commentary on Genesis (*HE*. 3.1) and the mention of *AAA* elsewhere in his work, that from the *AAA* Origen knew only those of John, Peter, Paul, Andrew and Thomas[17]. Finally, the date also fits the *ATh*, since it is the decade just before Shapur I was to cast his formidable shadow over the region; it is also just before the Romans definitively abolished the briefly restored monarchy by turning Edessa into a *colonia* in AD 241[18].

Can we say something about the author of the *ATh*? Drijvers has noted that he belonged to 'a learned milieu, to which symbolism and typology were familiar and in which a certain form of biblical exegesis had already developed'[19]. We may add that our author was also

---

[13] Luther, 'Elias von Nisibis', 193
[14] Luther, 'Abgar Prahates', 355-6.
[15] Bardesanes *FGrH* 719 F 1 (= Porphyrius, fr. 376F1 Smith) and 2 (= *De abst.* 4.17; Hier. *Adv. Jov.* 2.14); O. de Beauvoir Priaulx, 'On the Indian Embassies to Rome from the Reign of Claudius to the Death of Justinian', *JRAsS* 19 (1862) 274-98; J. Ryckmans, *Bibl. Or.* 21 (1964) 282; F. Winter, *Bardesanes von Edessa über Indien* (Thaur, 1999), to be read with the review by A. Dihle, *JAC* 43 (2000) 221-4.
[16] Millar, *The Roman Near East*, 476-7; Luther, 'Elias von Nisibis', 193.
[17] C. Schmidt, *Die alten Petrusakten im Zusammenhang der apokryphen Apostelliteratur* (Leipzig, 1903) 63-4, 130 n. 1, accepted by A. Harnack, *Geschichte der altchristlichen Literatur bis Eusebius* II (Leipzig, 1958²) 172.
[18] Millar, *The Roman Near East*, 152; Ross, *Roman Edessa*, 57-64.
[19] Drijvers, 'Acts of Thomas', 327.

well versed in the *AAA*. He had certainly read the *AJ* and the *AA*[20], and most likely also the *APt* and the *AP*[21], although his acquaintance with the last has repeatedly been denied[22]. Since in recent years it has become increasingly clear that eastern Syria was highly hellenized, Greek literary influence should not surprise us[23]. And indeed, considering the many parallels with motifs from pagan novels, there can be little doubt that our author had read some of those as well, particularly Achilles Tatius, whose popularity in Edessa is confirmed by his being used in the *Book of the Laws of Countries*[24]. Ephraem Syrus tells us in his commentary on the *Third Letter of Paul to the Corinthians*, which is preserved only in Armenian, that the *AAA* had been written by the followers of Bardaisan. As the influence of the latter philosopher on the *ATh* is clear, we may perhaps look for the author in the same milieu as the great Edessene philosopher, if not in the circle of his pupils.

    After its composition in Syriac, the *ATh* was soon translated into Greek and subsequently appropriated by various groups, which have left their imprint on the text[25]. Unfortunately, it is impossible to trace this process in great detail and we will therefore look at the text as a whole. Given that until now the interest in our text has been mainly theological and liturgical, it might be useful to take a look at the social aspects as well. In line with my earlier investigations I will discuss here the role of women in the *ATh* (§1), except those who are

---

[20]   *AJ*: E. Junod and J.-D. Kaestli, *Acta Iohannis*, 2 vls (Turnhout, 1983) 517 n. 2; *eidem, L'histoire des actes apocryphes des apôtres du IIIe au IXe siècle: le cas des Actes de Jean* (Geneva, 1982) 38-9; P.J. Lalleman, *The Acts of John* (Leuven, 1998) 108. *AA*: J.-M. Prieur, *Acta Andreae*, 2 vols (Turnhout, 1991) I.393.

[21]   *APt*: Klijn, *Acts of Thomas*, 23f. *AP*: E. Peterson, *Frühkirche, Judentum und Gnosis* (Freiburg, 1958) 183-208 (although Peterson still maintains the priority of the *ATh*); Klijn, *ibidem*, 24f.

[22]   For example by P. Devos, 'Actes de Thomas et Actes de Paul', *Anal. Boll.* 69 (1951) 119-30; Drijvers, 'Acts of Thomas', 323.

[23]   For an overview of this influence see G. Bowersock, *Hellenism in Late Antiquity* (Ann Arbor, 1990) 29-40; add now *SEG* 39.1558 (a Greek mosaicist's signature in Nisibis).

[24]   Bremmer, 'Achilles Tatius', 23-5.

[25]   Y. Tissot, 'Les Actes de Thomas, exemple de recueil composite', in F. Bovon, *et al.*, *Les Actes Apocryphes des Apôtres* (Geneva, 1981) 223-32.

clearly allegorical such as the daughter of the king in the wedding hymn (7)[26]. We conclude with a short discussion of two recent studies on the role of women in emerging Christianity (§2).

1. *Women*

The first woman whom we encounter in the *ATh* is the daughter of the king, whose wedding is celebrated (4), when the apostle arrives in Andrapolis. Here the apostle is meant to convert the king, but how will he talk to him in a foreign language? The problem is solved by the introduction of a Jewish flute girl, who apparently had recognised his origin and 'played at his head a long time' (5). The mention of the language problem is somewhat unexpected in such a fictional text, but it may well reflect the situation in Edessa, where aristocrats like Bardaisan could read Greek but wrote in Syriac, the local language of the region[27].

However, the flute girl was not just an interpreter. In the contemporary world her status cannot have been very high. Among the Greeks, flute girls had a particular reputation, which is well reflected in the praise of Phylarchus that in Keos 'neither courtesans nor flute girls' were seen (*FGrH* 81 F42). Flute girls could be auctioned off at a symposium (Persaios *FGrH* 584 F4), but the attractive ones could also make lots of money (Theopompus *FGrH* 115 F248) or become the king's favourite, such as Lamia with Demetrius Poliorcetes (Athenaeus 13.577c). This doubtful status was still prevalent in the times of the *ATh*, as appears from the conjunction of flute girls with courtesans in fragments of a gospel of the Synoptic type (*POxy.* 840) and the *Gospel of the Nazareans* (18)[28]. In fact, Syrian flute girls enjoyed a special fame in this respect[29].

---

[26] H. Kruse, 'Das Brautlied der syrischen Thomas-Akten', *Or. Christ. Per.* 50 (1984) 291-330; Drijvers, 'Acts of Thomas', 329f.
[27] For Syriac and Greek see R. MacMullen, *Changes in the Roman Empire* (Princeton, 1990) 32-6.
[28] See also Klijn, *Acts of Thomas*, 167-8; J. Davidson, *Courtesans and Fishcakes* (London, 1997) 81-2; B. Stumpp, *Prostitution in der römischen Antike* (Berlin, 1998) 45f.
[29] M. Eichenauer, *Untersuchungen zur Arbeitswelt der Frau in der römischen Antike* (Frankfurt, 1988) 64f.

Despite her status, the girl is the only person who understands the apostle and through her we hear that he is the 'most handsome among those present' (8). She continuously gazes at him, like Thecla at Paul, but he does not respond and keeps staring at the ground, apparently to avoid the suspicion of being sexually attracted. And it is she who reveals the true nature of the stranger to those present, after a dog has brought back the hand of a wine pourer who had struck the apostle. She throws away her flute, the symbol of her trade, and exclaims: 'This man is either a god or an apostle of God' (9) – an interesting illustration of the widely attested belief in antiquity that people with special powers had to be gods[30]. Although Thomas does disappoint the girl by not taking her along to India, she is eventually allowed to instruct the king (16). The incident shows the power of the apostle, but also already sounds the theme of chastity, which is of cardinal importance in the *ATh*.

Some women receive much less emphasis than the flute girl, as when Thomas confronts a serpent who confesses to have killed a handsome youth: he had intercourse with a woman of a neighbouring village, with whom he also did other 'shameful things' (31), presumably of a sexual nature. More interesting is another anonymous woman. When a young man took the Eucharist with his mouth, 'his two hands withered up'. A similar case occurs in the *APt* where the adulterous woman Rufina is paralysed the moment she wants to take the Eucharist from Paul (2). Both passages are very interesting, since they show the high esteem in which the early Christians held the Eucharist[31]; they may also be an additional argument for the knowledge of the *APt* by the author of the *ATh*. We find the same esteem in the West where Cyprian (*De lapsis* 25-6) relates that a pagan woman who secretly participated in the Eucharist had terrible pains, as if she had taken poison.

The reason for the punitive miracle was a murder by the youth. Having seen a beautiful girl in an inn, the youth had fallen in love with her and, after having heard Thomas, he had tried to persuade her

[30] Bremmer, *Acts of Peter*, 10.
[31] For the Eucharist in the *ATh* see G. Rouwhorst, 'La célébration de l'eucharistie selon les Actes de Thomas', in Ch. Caspers and M. Schneiders (eds), *Omnes circumadstantes. Contributions Towards a History of the Role of the People in the Liturgy* (Kampen, 1990) 51-77.

THE ACTS OF THOMAS AND WOMEN

to live with him in chastity. When she declined, he 'took a sword and slew her'. The scene gives us a glimpse of the low life in Edessa, as a girl living in an inn surely was a prostitute. Another example would be Mary, the niece of the hermit Abraham of Qidun, a village near Edessa, who for two years lived as a prostitute in an inn[32]. The inn itself was situated outside the city (51) and had a courtyard (53). A chance find two decades ago has actually given us a view of such a *pandocheion*. Some 17 kilometers outside Edessa, excavations have brought to light an inn of about AD 260 which consisted of three caves, probably used as stables, and a platform for the travellers. As an inscription above the central cave mentions, there was also a well. The inn had been built by the governor of Osrhoene, Dasius, which shows the importance of the institution for an area where travelling must have often been a gruelling activity[33].

After Thomas had let the youth wash his hands and had sealed him with the cross, he charged the youth to resurrect the girl with the very hand with which he had killed her (54), a kind of reversed *ius talionis*. This is of course symbolic, but the act also is one more testimony of the healing function of the hand, which is often attested[34]. Whereas pagan magicians always seem to resurrect the dead by themselves, Thomas let somebody else do it. This is a specific feature of the *AAA* where the recently converted personally resurrect others (*AJ* 24, 47, 82-3; *AAla* 19). Naturally, the girl 'immediately' sat up: such an instant effect is a standing element of miracle healings[35]. As is usual in the novel and the *AAA*, the miracle is also witnessed by a 'great crowd that stood by'[36].

---

[32] T.J. Lamy, *Sancti Ephraem Syri hymni et sermones* IV (Malines, 1902) 1-84, tr. S.P. Brock and S.A. Harvey, *Holy Women of the Syrian Orient* (Berkeley, Los Angeles, London, 1998[2]) 27-39.

[33] H. Petersen, 'A Roman prefect in Osrhoene', *Tr. Am. Philol. Ass.* 107 (1977) 265-82; C. Mango, 'A Late Roman Inn in Eastern Turkey', *Oxford J. Arch.* 5 (1986) 223-31 (= *SEG* 36.1277).

[34] O. Weinreich, *Antike Heilungswunder* (Giessen, 1909) 14-62, 127 n. 3.

[35] Add this example to Weinreich, *Antike Heilungswunder*, 197f.

[36] For the role of the crowd see R. Söder, *Die apokryphen Apostelgeschichten und die romanhafte Literatur der Antike* (Stuttgart, 1932 [repr. 1969]) 158-62; note also G. Theissen, *Urchristliche Wundergeschichten* (Gütersloh, 1974) 78-81; R.I. Pervo, *Profit with Delight* (Philadelphia, 1987) 34-9; Saïd, 'The City in the Greek Novel', 221f.

Of even greater interest, perhaps, is the experience of the woman
during her period of death (55-7). As she relates, a black man led her
to a place that is clearly a kind of hell[37]. It cannot be here the place
to discuss in detail the genre of the 'tours of hell' or the penalties[38],
but we may make a few observations. There are important differences here between the Greek and the Syriac versions. In the Greek
version there is a variety of sins, whereas the Syriac version concen-
trates solely on sexual transgressions. Regarding women, the Greek
version mentions adulterous-females and reports that 'those that are
hung by the hair are the shameless who have no modesty at all and
go about in the world bare-headed' (56)[39]. The Syriac version equally
mentions adulterous women but, in addition, 'maidens, who have not
kept their state of virginity'. Klijn has argued that the Syriac version
is the original, but this is not immediately persuasive. One could also
argue that the Syriac version has been simplified[40], since the references to penalties for greed in the description fit the general stress in
the *ATh* on the relative value of worldly possessions (83).

   Naturally after this impressive report the people believed. For us
it is interesting to note that as an effect of their faith they contributed
much money in order to support the widows, whom Thomas 'had
gathered in the cities' (59). This sudden appearance of widows is
somewhat surprising. Klijn thinks of an influence from the New Testament[41], but it seems more persuasive to think of the prominence of
widows in the early Church, which also in Syria was not negligible,
witness the Syriac *Didascalia Apostolorum*[42].

---

[37] For the negative valuation of black, note also the black dog (8) and the
black men (64); Bremmer, *Acts of Peter*, 8; add to his bibliography P. Frost,
'Attitudes Towards Blacks in the Early Christian Era', *Second Century* 8
(1991) 1-11; P. Habermehl, *Perpetua und der Ägypter* (Berlin, 1992) 148-60.
[38] See M. Himmelfarb, *Tours of Hell* (Philadelphia, 1983).
[39] For the penalties see S. Lieberman, *Texts and Studies* (New York, 1974) 43f.
[40] Himmelfarb, *Tours of Hell*, 12 n18.
[41] Klijn, *Acts of Thomas*, 254 compares Rom 15.25-6; 2 Cor 8-9.
[42] For early Christian widows see most recently R. Bruno Siola, '*Viduae* e
coetus viduarum nella Chiesa primitiva e nella normazione dei primi imper-
atori cristiani', in *Atti dell' Accademia Romanistica Constantiniana: VIII
convegno internazionale* (Naples, 1990) 367-426; C. Methuen, 'Widows,
Bishops, and the Struggle for Authority in the *Didascalia Apostolorum*',
J. Eccl. Hist. 46 (1995) 197-213; Bremmer, 'Pauper or Patroness? The

After these anonymous women in the first half of the *ATh*, we meet more specific ones in the second half. Mygdonia, whose name we have already discussed, is the wife of Charisius, a close kinsman of king Misdaeus (134). She is represented as rather young, since she has no children as yet and has been married less than a year (100). We may compare the wife of Vazan, the son of king Misdaeus, who married his wife when he was fourteen years old, his wife therefore surely younger[43]. The moment she appears on stage, she is carried in a litter. Cassius Dio, a perhaps somewhat older contemporary of our author, briefly discusses the history of the Roman habit of being carried around in a covered chair. He notes that some Romans were also carried in litters 'such as women still affect even at the present day' (60.2, tr. E. Cary). In the case of Mygdonia she is portrayed as a *grande dame*, who is impatient and not loath to use her worldly power: when the litter makes insufficient progress, she asks her husband to send officers to repulse the crowd and beat them (82).

When the apostle saw the people carrying her, he started a long oration, in which he exhorted his audience to abstain from sins like adultery and murder and to indulge Christian virtues like holiness, friendliness and goodness (84-5). The culmination of the oration is an exhortation to gentleness (86). The term used, *praotês*, fits the circumstances of the oration much better than the Syriac 'humility', since the servants of Mygdonia had just demonstrated harshness, such as will be typical of her husband Charisius (92) and king Misdaeus (138). The quality of 'gentleness' is a virtue that is often extolled in Greek civic inscriptions, but from a civic virtue it gradually evolved into a personal quality, as is the case in this passage[44].

Having descended from her litter, Mygdonia prostrated herself in front of the apostle and entreated him to pray for her (87). The apostle commanded her: 'rise up from the ground and compose thyself'.

Widow in the Early Christian Church', in J. Bremmer and L. van den Bosch (eds), *Between Poverty and the Pyre: Moments in the History of Widowhood* (London, 1995) 31-57; C. Schlarb, 'Die (un)gebändigte Witwe', in M. Tamcke *et al.* (eds), *Syrisches Christentum weltweit* (Münster, 1995) 36-75.

[43] Add this example to those in Bremmer, *Acts of Peter*, 2. Note also that discussions about the age of marriage do not take into account these literary examples.

[44] J. de Romilly, *La douceur dans la pensée grecque* (Paris, 1979) 269f.

After another apostolic exhortation to sexual abstention, she 'falling
down did him obeisance and departed to her house'. Thus Drijvers,
but Festugière and Poirier/Tissot translate with 'adora', like Klijn's
'bad... aan'. This comes close to the Syriac 'she bowed down and
prostrated herself before him, because she thought that he was Jesus'.
The latter explanatory version seems clearly later, since Mygdonia in
the beginning of *c*.87 invokes the apostle as 'pupil of the living God',
not as Jesus himself. It seems better therefore to stick to Drijvers'
translation which is supported by *c*.129 where Mygdonia stands up
from a sitting position and performs a *proskynêsis* for the apostle,
just like Mnesara in *c*.155. This makes Charisius say to Thomas: 'Do
you see how she fears and honours you, and willingly does everything that you command?' The Greek term used, *prosekynêse*, refers
to the Persian custom of *proskynêsis*, which, in cases of a great social
distance, consisted of prostrating oneself and, perhaps, throwing a
kiss towards the social superior[45]. This Persian custom is also attested
among the Parthians and Sassanians, and thus seems to be a local
detail[46].

After Mygdonia had came home, her husband Charisius returned
from the baths (89). When his wife did not show up for dinner, he
went to her bedroom. It is interesting to note that the couple apparently slept in separate bedrooms, as was also the case with Maximilla
and Aegeates in the *AA* (13, 15) – perhaps a custom in the upper
classes? Charisius reproached his wife for having left the house and
thus forsaken her status as a free woman. There can be little doubt
that in Asia Minor upper-class women were frequently visible in
public, but this may have been different in Syria. In fact, a passage
from Heliodorus suggests that girls were not used to walking long
distances (2.19).

The confrontation between Charisius and Mygdonia now gradually reaches a climax. At first, the husband is afraid to deal with her
directly, since she was 'superior both in wealth and in understanding'

---

[45] E. Bickerman, 'A propos d'un passage de Chares de Mytilène', *Parola
del Passato* 18 (1963) 241-55; P. Briant, *Histoire de l'empire perse de
Cyrus à Alexandre* I (Leiden, 1997) 234f.
[46] W. Sundermann, 'Zur Proskynesis im sasanidischen Iran', *Mitt. Inst.
Orientf.* 10 (1964) 275-86; H. Gabelmann, *Antike Audienz- und Tribunal-
szenen* (Darmstadt, 1984) 172-4.

(95)[47]. He therefore slanders Thomas as a poor person, who has only one garment (96) – probably a reflection of Jesus' commandment to his disciples to dress in such a way (Mt 10.10; Mk 6.9), but also typical of the ancient philosopher, pagan or Christian[48]. When her husband tries to sleep with her, she flees the bed naked and dressed only in a curtain, a typically novel-type saucy detail[49]. She takes refuge with her nurse, who slept in the court (120), and spends the night there. The trusted nurse is of course already a familiar figure from tragedy and it is impossible to decide whether she owes her existence here to literature or to life – or to both[50]. The name of the nurse is in Syriac Narqia, but in Latin Marcia, which is perhaps a calque on the Syriac. Considering that the *AAA* regularly use names of historical persons, the name could conceivably also refer to Marcia, the concubine of Commodus, who had Christian sympathies[51].

After another confrontation with her husband, Mygdonia left for the prison where king Misdaeus had locked up Thomas after an intervention by Charisius. She took ten denarii to bribe the gaolers, a practice well attested in antiquity[52]. However, on her way to the prison, she met Thomas, who has already left the prison in order to baptise Mygdonia (120-1), just as he will do with Vazan and various women (150-8). Similarly, Paul left the prison to baptise Artemilla (*AP* 7 [PHeid. 3]): one more testimony to the dependence of the *ATh* on the *AP*. Thomas shone like a light in the dark, which made Mygdonia think he was a noble (118). According to Klijn (*ad loc.*), the

---

[47]   For such unequal marriages see M.-Th. Raepsaet-Charlier, 'Tertullien et la législation des mariages inégaux', *Rev. Int. Droits Ant.* 29 (1982) 254-63.
[48]   Bremmer, 'Symbols of Marginality from Early Pythagoreans to Late Antique Monks', *Greece & Rome* 39 (1992) 205-14.
[49]   For such details see the reflections of E. Castelli, 'Visions and Voyeurism: Holy Women and the Politics of Sight in Early Christianity' = *Protocol of the Colloquy of the Center for Hermeneutical Studies* NS 2 (1995).
[50]   For nurses note L. Robert, *Ant. Class.* 37 (1968) 441-4; K. Bradley, *Discovering the Roman Family* (New York and Oxford, 1991) 13-36; A. Capomacchia, 'Nutrice di eroi: ruolo e valenza di un personaggio 'minore' della tragedia greca', *St. Mat. Storia Rel.* 60 (1994) 11-24.
[51]   Hippolytus, *Ref.* 9.12.10f; Cassius Dio 72.4.7.
[52]   Add this example to Bremmer, *Acts of Paul*, 48 note 45; J.-U. Krause, *Gefängnisse im Römischen Reich* (Stuttgart, 1996) 306-8.

man is 'obviously the leader of the keepers of the prisoners', but why is this obvious? More likely, it is an interesting testimony to the splendour of the local aristocrats, who could afford torch bearers to go in front of them.

After the conversion and baptism of Mygdonia there is room for another woman of the highest circles. Enter Tertia, the queen. When sent by her husband to Mygdonia to advise her to keep away from Thomas, she is instead converted by the apostle (136). When she came home, the king reproached her for going on foot, 'which is not fitting for free-born women like thee' (137). Charisius made a similar reproach to his wife that she did not have regard 'for her position as a free woman' by leaving the house (89).

The king touches here upon one of the sub-themes of the *ATh*: the difference between the earthly status of a (surely high-born) free woman and the real liberty of the Christian, even if a slave on earth. The theme is sounded first when the ass's colt addresses the apostle with the words: 'fellow-worker of the Son of God, who being free didst become a slave and being sold didst lead many to freedom' (39)[53]. We find this 'freedom' when Mygdonia is anointed and the apostle says: 'Let thy power come; let it be established upon thy slave (*doulên*) Mygdonia and heal her through this freedom' (121). Following a suggestion by Bonnet, Drijvers emends 'freedom' (*eleutherias*) to 'unction' (*elaiothêsia*), but the emendation not only neglects the force of the opposition slave/freedom in this passage. It also neglects Mygdonia's request to Marcia to bring her bread and a mixture of water and wine for the Eucharist, 'having regard for my freedom' (120), which here surely means 'spiritual freedom', not 'free birth' (Drijvers and the Syriac translation)[54]. Thomas himself sounds the theme three more times towards the end of his life. In prison he tells Vazan, the son of the king, and Siphor with his family: 'behold, I am set free from slavery, and called to liberty' (142). Held by his executioners, he exhorts them to conversion and 'to conduct your lives in all freedom' (166), and in his final prayer, he says: 'I have been a slave; therefore today do I receive freedom' (167). For the author of the *ATh*, then, freedom is primarily a spiritual matter,

---

[53] For the prominence of animals in the period, also in the *AAA*, see Weinreich, *Antike Heilungswunder*, 126-9 at 127 n. 2.
[54] See also Klijn, *Acts of Thomas*, 284; Pesthy, this volume, Ch. V.2.

not a matter of earthly status.

The last important woman is Mnasara, the sickly wife of the son of king Misdaeus. She had been married for seven years to Vazan, but they had not consummated their marriage. Her husband was already Christian, but she herself had not yet converted. When her husband visited Thomas in prison, where also Mygdonia, Tertia and Marcia had bribed their way in (151), Thomas miraculously enabled them to leave through closed doors in order to be baptised (153)[55]. Vazan went ahead to prepare his house, but half way there he met his wife. It is typical of the Christian Vazan that, unlike Misdaeus, he did not reproach his wife for walking, but just inquired how in her unhealthy state she had been able to get up. It was (she said) an invisible 'young man', who had helped her. Klijn and Lalleman identify this youth with Jesus[56], but Mnesara says that Jesus delivered the youth to her. And when she complains that she no longer can walk after the disappearance of the youth, Thomas reassures her that 'Jesus shall lead thee by the hand henceforth' (155). It is the husband, though, who is the most important in this scene since, although Mygdonia is allowed to anoint the women (just as Marcia anoints Mygdonia in the Syriac version: 121), Thomas himself anoints Vazan first (157).

We now approach the end of the apostle's life. He returns to his prison and refuses Tertia, Mygdonia and Marcia – note the descending order of status – to join him (159). They returned home where they resisted their husbands' pressure to defect from Christianity[57], encouraged by Thomas' appearance in a dream.

Once again the interest in women has been considerable. Would women have liked the *ATh*? We don't know, but Edessene women were certainly interested in religion. A century later Ephraem Syrus complains about the ease with which ascetics could impress local women. However this may be, assuming that the final chapter is a later addition, we notice that the last word is not about women but about men: Siphor will be a presbyter and Vazan a deacon. However

---

[55] For the miracle see Bremmer, *Acts of John*, 43.
[56] Klijn, *Acts of Thomas*, 299; P.J. Lalleman, 'Polymorphy of Christ', in Bremmer, *Acts of John*, 97-118 at 109.
[57] For such unions see M. MacDonald, 'Early Christian Women Married to Unbelievers', *Studies in Religion/Sciences religieuses* 19 (1990) 221-34.

valuable women's contributions to the early Church were, for the author of *ATh* men remained more important.

2. *Women and the AAA*

Having studied in successive volumes the role of women in the major *AAA*, we may perhaps conclude our survey of the *ATh* with asking in what way the women of the *AAA* help us to understand the role of women in the Christian victory. The question has become once again relevant, since in recent years a leading ancient historian, Keith Hopkins, and a prominent sociologist of religion, Rodney Stark, have tried to rethink the place of women within the rise of Christianity. Both approaches are new in so far as that they try to work with modern demographic and sociological models.

Stark has summarised his conclusions as follows. Firstly, through their prohibitions against infanticide and abortion the Christians rapidly developed a surplus of females. Secondly, being in the majority women therefore enjoyed a substantially higher status among Christians than the women among their pagan contemporaries. Thirdly, given a surplus of pagan men and Christian women there were many mixed marriages that produced secondary converts. Fourthly, 'the abundance of Christian women resulted in higher birth-rates – that superior fertility contributed to the rise of Christianity'[58]. Hopkins is less clear. Although he recognises that women played an important role in the earliest Christian churches, he suggests that the stress on female presence in Christian sources 'arises precisely from women's social visibility and rarity'. He also states that 'ancient pagan criticisms that Christianity was particularly attractive to women and slaves were a literary cliché, expressing a depreciatory attitude towards women and Christianity more than cool observation'[59].

Let us start with Hopkins, whose observation is hardly supported by the evidence of either pagan texts or the *AAA*. It is of course

---

[58]   R. Stark, *The Rise of Christianity* (Princeton, 1996) 95-128 at 128.
[59]   K. Hopkins, 'Christian Number and Its Implications', *JECS* 6 (1998) 185-226 at 204-5. Note that Hopkins very much seems to write from a Roman perspective and takes the Greek evidence much less into account.

possible to belittle the pagan texts, although it would be hard to find pagan equivalents for the prominence of widows among the Christians as mentioned by Celsus and Lucian[60]. It is even more important to note that a depreciatory attitude is completely absent from the *AAA*. In fact, here we find an astonishing variety of women, from a royal family, 'firsts of the city' and wives of Roman governors, via rich women like Eubola, to those at the lower end of the social scale such as old women, widows and flute-girls. Although women are of course also prominent in the pagan novel, these novels do not contain the same variety as in the *AAA*. Finally, Christian women are not a rarity but appear as soon as we are able to attain a closer look at the ancient social reality[61]. It is surely hard to accept that somebody like Tertullian would write books *De cultu feminarum* or *De virginibus velandis*, when women were no more than exotic spectacles on the Roman scene, like freaks in an American circus at the beginning of last century.

Some of Stark's observations seem more attractive. I am not sure that Christian rejection of abortion and infanticide would soon produce a surplus of females, since the effects of Christian attitudes in this matter are totally invisible in our sources. Neither am I convinced that Christian women were very successful in converting their husbands. We do not find any evidence in this direction in our more documentary sources and the *AAA* certainly do not unequivocally support this idea, witness Thamyris in the *AP* and Charisius and Misdaeus in the *ATh*. On the other hand, Christians may well have had a superior fertility rate and the female majority certainly gave women a more special place in the Christian church. An *ordo viduarum* is unthinkable without a substantial female representation in the early church.

The harvest of the application of modern models to the age-old problem of the reasons for the Christian victory seems relatively small. Still, modern studies of new cults may open our eyes to neglected aspects of the problem. On the basis of modern evidence Hopkins postulates a higher incidence of young adults as possible

---

[60] Lucian, *Peregrinus* 12; Origen, *Contra Celsum* 3.55.
[61] J.N. Bremmer, 'Why did Christianity attract Upper-class Women', in A.A.R. Bastiaensen *et al.* (eds), *Fructus centesimus. Mélanges G.J.M. Bartelink* (Steenbrugge and Dordrecht, 1989) 37-47.

sources of recruitment[62]. Now the everyday life of young adults, their frustrations and aspirations, rarely appears in our sources, but the protagonist of the *Acts of Paul and Thecla* is a young adult and she sees many girls entering the house of Onesiphorus in order to listen to Paul (7). Moreover, in the *Book of the Laws of Countries* Bardaisan rebukes his pupil Awida, who had started to put theological questions to his own friends, by saying 'You should learn from somebody older than them' (p. 5 Drijvers)[63]. However this may be, the fact that the *AAA* point to a considerable presence of women among the emerging Christian church can hardly be seriously doubted[64].

[62] Hopkins, 'Christian Number', 205.
[63] R. Lane Fox, *Pagans and Christians* (Harmondsworth, 1986) 312 concludes, surely wrongly, from the passage that 'age-mates' did not discuss these things amongst each other.
[64] For comments I am most grateful to Glen Bowersock and Ton Hilhorst.

VII. Human Nature and Character as Moving Factors of Plot in the *Acts of Thomas*

JÁNOS BOLYKI

The *Acts of Thomas* (*ATh*) is usually studied from the perspective of religious history[1]. It is thus considered as an important link between Gnostic-Christian and Manichean texts[2]. If, however, its literary character is discussed, such discussion concerns its place within the Hellenistic-Oriental novel[3]. We, on the other hand, are concerned about an issue not yet fully elaborated, notably the mainsprings of the plot of *ATh*. Our hypothesis is that the plot of *ATh* is motivated by human nature and human character as influenced by the Platonist Christians of the period.

We wish to start from the anthropological perspective of the work. This apostolic novel, in accordance with its world-view, sees human nature (*natura, physis*) as contradictory. According to this, man, on the one hand, due to his bodily nature, lives subject to mortality, while on the other hand, due to his spiritual nature, he is connected with God and is therefore called to everlasting life. This provides the mainspring: man is to give up his mortal and sinful bodily nature and put it at the service of his spiritual nature.

But the derivation of its plot from abstract human nature would make *ATh* a mystery drama and not allow for its being considered as

---

[1] G. Bornkamm, 'Thomasakten, Die religionsgeschichtliche Stellung', in *NTA* II, 307-8.
[2] Bornkamm, op. cit., 300-2; P. Nagel, 'Die apokryphen Apostelakten des 2. und 3. Jahrhunderts in der manichäischen Literatur', in K.-W. Troeger (ed), *Gnosis und Neues Testament* (Berlin, 1973) 149-82.
[3] T. Szepessy, 'Az apokrif apostolakták és az antik regény', *Antik Tanulmányok, Studia Antiqua* 38 (1994) 116-39.

a novel. Its novelistic character, and sometimes even its dramatic character, is a result of the fact that its plot is motivated not only by abstract human nature, but also by human character. Here we face not abstract man but the major characters, an apostle, a demon, saved men and impenitent men, in a 'drama' of salvation history as interpreted by Platonist Christians. If ancient drama was reinterpreted myth, then the *ATh* – and generally the *AAA* – were Hellenistic salvation myths reinterpreted by Christianity in dramatic or narrative form. In the following we hope to demonstrate our thesis by analysing the plot and selectively considering the text.

Man subject to mortality: the drama of the body

A.F.J. Klijn begins his introduction to the teaching of the *ATh* by stating: 'The doctrine of these *Acts* is dominated by the contrast between corruptible and incorruptible'[4]. In *c*.37 the apostle preaches to the crowds on how 'the whole body... becomes dust, returning to its own nature.' Two seemingly contradictory modes of action might derive from this: the corruptible body is to be denied and at the same time it is to be put to the service of the incorruptible.

The corruptible and at the same time sinful nature of the body is particularly manifest in three aspects: infatuation with sexuality, debauchery and power. In respect of sexuality, the whole *ATh* is imbued by *enkrateia* – ascetic piety. The author rejects sexual relation in the married lives of the main characters[5]. In *c*.12, he calls wedlock 'filthy intercourse', and even objects to having children. *Cc*.89-103 relate how the wife of King Charisius, Mygdonia, becomes the disciple of the apostle Thomas and tells her husband: 'Henceforth thou hast no place with me' (98). Upon this, the king attributes to Thomas the teaching that 'a man should not live with his own wife, and what the nature requires and the deity has ordained he

[4] A.F.J. Klijn, *The Acts of Thomas* (Leiden, 1962) 34.
[5] If we are justified in maintaining that this was an excess of the Encratic-Christians sect or movement, we should nevertheless take into account the fact that since the *AJ*, *AA* and *ATh* reject marital union only in respect of the main characters this might mean a call to a special mode of life and does not claim to be a universal ethic. It certainly does not appear in the apostolic exhortations to minor characters and crowds.

overthrows' (96). In his sermons to the people and the crowds, the apostle is far more restrained: he only condemns adultery, points to the mortality of the body and praises the virtue of purity (28).

Debauchery and boastfulness also belong to the sins of the body, whether in respect of food and drink or wealth and fame. In his first sermon to them, Thomas exhorts the members of the newly converted and baptised congregation as follows: 'And the service of the belly plunges the soul into cares and anxieties and sorrows, since it becomes anxious lest it come to be in want and reaches out for what is far from it' (28). Outsiders describe Thomas' behaviour by saying 'continually he fasts and prays, and eats only bread and salt, and his drink is water, and he wears one garment whether in fine weather or in foul' (20). As what we gain by debauchery is waste, so it is vain to boast with bodily beauty. 'For it is not beauty that is enduring with men; for those who rely upon it, when old age takes hold of them, shall be suddenly put to shame' (66). Wealth is similarly wasteful, since while seeking possessions we might damage others and fill our souls with vain desires. Therefore 'raise yourselves out of... the wealth which is left here, and the possession which comes from the earth and grows old' (37).

The characters have to give up their bodily oriented lives, and the story of this provides the bulk of the plot. However, it is equally important that they are to put their bodies to the service of their spirit and God, to make them the instruments of the Good. But how can the sinful body become the servant and instrument of God?

First, by being healed from its various diseases through the apostle's miracles, which demonstrate his divine calling and the power of God that sent him, and which help the conversion of those who were healed and were witnesses. Therefore the apostle prays as follows: 'In thy holy name raise thou up by thy power her who lies here, to thy glory and the confirmation of the faith of them that stand by' (53).

Second, the dignity of the body might consist in the fact that it can become the carrier of the spirit. In the Fourth Act, the ass's colt, which carried the apostle to the town but dies before the gate, is a symbol for the body; it carries the body through earthly existence to heaven, but is unable to enter there.

Third, the body becomes a servant of God if it serves its brethren. This is what is called deaconship (*diakonia*) in clerical language, the support of the sick, the poor, the disabled, with financial

means and physical labour. 'But he (Thomas) went about the towns
and the villages round about, distributing it (money) and bestowing
alms on the poor and afflicted, and gave them relief' (19). As crowds
become faithful, one consequence is that 'they brought much money
for the service of the widows' (59).

The fourth opportunity of the body for divine service is martyrdom. Thomas' fate is driven in this direction, this being the mainspring of the plot. How does the apostle, who in the beginning act is
very loath to go on the mission to India, become a martyr of Christ
there? At the conclusion (164-8), the apostle explains the fact that
four soldiers lead him to the place of execution by saying that his
body is composed of the four elements and that these four elements
hold his spirit in captivity. Thus martyrdom for him is liberation from
the captivity of the elements and the reaching of Him whom he
belongs to. This is why he witnesses before his death: 'today do I
receive freedom' (167).

According to the author, however, human nature is constituted
not only of its bodily features and the liberation from them. The other
mainspring in the plot is the aspiration of the soul towards God and
the heavenly world. The heavenly world calls the characters in the
novel in three ways. The man responding to this threefold call is a
Platonic Christian who finally partakes of the heavenly world.

The author of *ATh* sees a metaphor for the heavenly in every
phenomenon of this world. He provides an actual 'hermeneutical
key' to how 'visible things' reflect – though imperfectly, still recog-
nisably – 'the world above', the heavenly realities. When as he
speaks and sees people paying attention to him and 'lifting themselves up that they might see him, and they were going upon high
places' (37), he immediately creates a metaphor out of this very situation by saying: 'Take an example from this and see that unless you
are lifted up you cannot see me ... unless you raise yourselves a little from the earth, how can you see him who dwells in the height ...
unless you first raise yourselves out of your former condition and
your unprofitable deeds ...' (37). Let us mention three particular
metaphors. The first is the building of the earthly and the heavenly
palace. The second one is the comparison between earthly and heavenly marriage. And the third one contrasts heavenly and earthly reality in the language of humour: the king's friend puts the left shoe on
his right foot in the morning. In the middle-Platonist interpretation,

this symbolises the replacement of the wrong earthly orientation by the right heavenly one[6].

Divine revelation may come to man by way of dreams too. These may also call man to an encounter with God, and the seeing and interpretation of such dreams as well as following the admonitions in them are also motives in the plot of the novel. For example, a dream was seen by an ill young woman. In her dream, a youth put his hands on her and told her to go to the place where the 'stranger' (the apostle Thomas) was staying and she would be healed. So she did. The dream literally 'moved' the lame woman, for it was what gave her the strength to go to the place of her healing. The dream thus became a 'mainspring' of the plot.

The characters of the novel also receive divine calling through the words of the New Testament and Christian teaching. At the beginning of the story (3), the apostle Thomas would be happy to go anywhere but India. Upon the word of Jesus, he has second thoughts and says: 'I go whither thou wilt, Lord Jesus; thy will be done!' (Mt 6.10). In c.28, the apostle preaches the Word to those accompanying him. He entreats them not to be anxious for the morrow (Mt 6.34), to receive the yoke of Jesus (Mt 11.29-30). He encourages a converted youth thus: 'But look thou to him (Jesus), and he will not disregard thee; and turn to him, and he will not forsake thee' (36). And he tells the crowd: 'but the merciful and lowly in heart, they shall inherit the kingdom of God' (66; Mt 5.7); 'do not return evil for evil!' (58; Rom 12.17). To the litter-bearers, he quotes the words of Jesus with which he called to himself the heavy laden and those that labour (Mt 11.25-30), and then adds: 'This blessing and this admonition ... is now for you who are heavy laden!' (83). We can say that New Testament quotations as well as apostolic admonitions and exhortations encourage the characters in the *ATh* to plot-motivating conduct: conversion, faith, rectification, and God seeking.

---

[6]   Bornkamm, op. cit., 301. See also Bolyki, 'Head Downwards: The Cross of Peter in the Lights of Apocryphal Acts, of the New Testament and of the Society-Transforming Claims of Early Christianity', in Bremmer, *Acts of Peter*, 111-22. The upside-down crucifixion of Peter also implies that, in this world, 'all has to be turned upside down' for things to get into their proper place, for 'the downwards to become upwards'.

The one who shakes off the dominance of the body, and puts it to the service of God and the spirit, is a Christian of middle-Platonic spirit. The first stage of his journey is enlightenment. The enlightened princess prays thus: 'Thou... didst show me how to seek myself and to recognise who I was and who and how I now am, that I may become again what I was' (15). From enlightenment, faith proceeds. The believer is freed from the body and his former sins, so as to be in communion with the Saviour. The apostle promises one youth that 'If thou art free... thou shalt both see him and be with him forever' (35). Faith and deliverance bring about enormous changes in the life of men. Freed believers are armed against the temptations of life. Such a man may receive the 'mark' of Christians, baptism, and take part in the eucharist[7] (e.g. 26-27). This is how his road from perdition to salvation ends, which is one of the main lines of the plot.

Character and Plot

As yet, we have been studying man in rather abstract terms; we have been speaking not of individual persons but of 'man' as introduced by a third century middle-Platonic Christian author. We shall now consider in further detail human or trans-human individuality. We shall discuss three types of character: the apostle invested with divine calling and power; the personifications of demonic forces; and finally, freed man, the ideal Christian. As a result, we shall see that this novel also demonstrates the validity of the literary rule that human or demonic character strongly influences both narrative and dramatic plot.

The figure of the apostle in these *Acts* differs from those of other *AAA* in that he is a twin brother of Christ (1, 31). The New Testament also knows Thomas to be a twin (Jn 11.16), but does not state whether he is a brother of Jesus or not[8]. With the idea of the twin, the *ATh* expresses how closely the apostle resembles Jesus. In *c*.31, even the demon acknowledges: 'Thou art the twin brother of Christ!' This is why someone says to the apostle: 'For thou art a man that has two

---

[7]   On Gnostic-influenced baptism and eucharist cf. J. Roldanus, 'Die Eucharistie in den Johanesakten', in Bremmer, *Acts of John*, 72-96; Klijn, *Acts of Thomas*, 54-61 (Baptism and Eucharist).
[8]   Mk 6.3 and par.

forms, and wherever thou wilt, there thou art found' (34), which implies the investment of divine omnipresence in the apostle. Thomas is a divine man because he partakes of divine attributes.

However, this apostle, so similar to Jesus, is also Jesus' slave. This turns out so already at the beginning of the novel when Jesus sells him to a merchant. But the Lord gave the purchase-price to Thomas and said to him: 'Let thy price also be with thee, with my grace, whithersoever thou goest!' (3). If a slave had his purchase-money in his purse, he would be able to buy himself freedom from his master at any moment. But Thomas did not do so. This is how the author expresses that the apostle was a voluntary slave of Christ. Later on, this is again what the speaking colt tells Thomas: thou 'who being free didst become a slave and being sold didst lead many to freedom' (39).

The main reason for Thomas' dignity is that he received divine revelations: he is a 'fellow-initiate into the hidden word of Christ, who dost receive his secret sayings, fellow-worker of the Son of God' (39)[9]. This is why he is encouraged by the speaking wild ass: 'Thy teacher wishes to show his mighty works by thy hands... thy master wishes to make known the ineffable things through thee' (78). This means that Thomas is not only a bearer of divine revelations, but is also capable of divine acts (miracles). As a consequence, however, he shares not only the revelations and deeds of his Teacher, Christ, but also his fate. The course of his life points towards martyrdom. This is how the character of the hero becomes the mainspring of events related to him. This is true not only of narrative elements, but also of dramatic dialogues. Thomas' prayers are in fact dramatic dialogues with his Master, Jesus. They are animated, passionate and purposeful. And among the genres employed in the novel, they are the most valuable from a literary point of view. In the exorcism scenes, however, he struggles with Satan. Dauntlessness and explosive anger shine through his words; these are truly dramatic conflicts: clashes of the forces of heaven and hell. Flatly opposed to this is the tender, pastoral care with which Thomas treats his spiritual children, those who have become believing Christians. Interestingly

---

[9]   The original Greek word *symboulos* for 'fellow-worker' here meant the counsellor of the ruler. The term 'fellow-initiate' (*summystês*) derives from mystery religions, cf. Nagel, *op.cit.*, 177.

enough, he makes a deep impression on the crowds as he wants to convince them and justifies his deeds; he is hard on their sins, but he shows them the possibility of repentance and conversion. These dramatic encounters are a consequence of the apostle's character, personality, being mainsprings of action.

The characters of the demons appearing in the novel also contribute to the plot, to their own fate. The first demon appears in the likeness of a serpent. It is characteristic of this serpent that he wants to appear frightening, thus he screams while speaking (31), and takes pride in his ancient descent, in his former evil deeds. He tells the apostle that he killed a youth out of jealousy. The apostle's punishment is that the serpent is it to suck out the poison which he had put into the youth. The serpent is forced to obey the command, but when it draws up all the gall into it and the youth springs to life, it dies of its own poison. This serpent-demon put on clamorous and threatening airs, but proved to be easy to destroy. There is an element of irony in the story. It is somewhat laughable that the serpent who had fallen in love with the beautiful woman is jealous and in the end has to drink his own poison. The ironic conclusion is clearly a consequence of his character.

The other demon has a 'human form' ('a manlike one': 43), and not only is he far more fearful than the first, but his evil nature and power increase in the course of the action. In normal cases, literature calls this – if human beings are concerned – development of character; theologically, however, this motif expresses the growth of evil. This demon appears in various forms[10], either as a youth or as an old man: he is thus very cunning. This is also clear from his resistance to the apostle that questions him. And when he realises he cannot but leave he says: 'I shall go to places where the fame of this man has not been heard' (46). Much later in the course of the plot of the novel, we find him again in a distant region. The apostle meets him in the likeness of a demon tormenting two women. The demon wants to torture and kill his victims by painful diseases. Thomas declares that there is no room for mercy with such a ruthless demon. 'God

---

[10]   In *AJ*, it is not demons, but the polymorphy of Christ that we read of (e.g. 82,6); this is how the author expresses the divine and the human nature of the Saviour; cf. P.J. Lalleman, *The Acts of John: A Two-Stage Initiation into Johanine Gnosticism* (Leuven, 1998) 166-7.

forbid that there be propitiation or sparing for you, for you know not sparing or compassion' (75). The demon and the apostle are involved in a dramatic dialogue. The former describes his own and the apostle's missions in contrasting parallels. 'For even as thou didst come to preach the Gospel, so did I come to destroy. And even as, if thou fulfil not the will of him who sent thee, he brings punishment upon thy head, so I also, if I do not the will of him who sent me, am sent back before the time and appointed season to my nature' (76). It turns out that he is the Anti-apostle, for as the Anti-Christ counteracts Christ, so the demon counteracts the apostle, whose work he wants to destroy. This once exorcised demon is now commanded by Thomas to leave the two women he has possessed and to live nowhere near a human settlement. He has no more chance of resisting the apostle and his work, which is the greatest punishment he can suffer. Thus is the tragedy that derives from his character fulfilled.

The novel characterises male figures with names and thus with individual traits according to their conduct with regard to the doctrine of *enkrateia*. King Gundaphorus puts the apostle in gaol because he cannot accept the apostle's spending the money meant for building a palace on the poor. However, when he learns from the vision of his brother on his death-bed that Thomas built a heavenly palace for him from the money spent on the poor[11], he and his brother become disciples of the apostle and are baptised (21-7). The action is thus about the change in the king's values and the consequential transformation of his whole life. His open and perceptive character leads the action towards a positive dénouement. Captain Siphor's character is much like the various fathers in the Gospels who entreat Jesus to heal one or another close relative of theirs[12]. The moving factor of action is his love for his wife and daughter. This is what leads him to the apostle, and consequently to the story of his turning to faith, therefore to action (62, 81 and 131). Just the contrary is true of Misdaeus and his friend, Charisius. It is their own selves that they love, and when their wives convert to Christianity and this disrupts their life-styles they become die-hard enemies of the apostle and the Gospel. Their hearts harden ever more intensively, which leads to the execution of the apostle. It is only the apostle's martyrdom that somewhat softens

---

[11]   See Hilhorst, this volume, Ch. IV.
[12]   Mt 8.5-13; Jn 4.46-54

them; they first resign to their wives conduct, then, finally, the king is able to heal his sick son with the dust from around the apostle's grave, and, in the epilogue, he himself becomes a believer (131).

Human nature, the characteristics of man seen abstractly, moves the plot of the *ATh* towards a mystery drama, from hearing the divine word calling man out of sin to the initiation received in baptism. On the other hand, the characters of individuals depicted in the *Acts* lead towards dramatic conflict and thus shape the plot. The function of this drama is identical to that of ancient drama, namely the calling into doubt, the relativisation, of official values. Middle-Platonic Christianity of the third century was very keen on casting doubt on the official values of the Roman Empire. The most important message of this for today's reader is probably that 'man is a being who cannot afford to remain the same as he is'[13]. Whether the way just depicted is the only one or not that provides an answer for modern man is another question.

[13]   C.F. v. Weizsäcker, *Die Geschichte der Natur* (Göttingen, 1964) 124.

VIII. The Hymn of Jude Thomas, the Apostle, in the Country of the Indians (*ATh* 108-113)

GERARD P. LUTTIKHUIZEN

The text of the so-called 'Hymn' or 'Song of the Pearl' is preserved in only two manuscripts of the *Acts of Thomas*, one Syriac manuscript (10th century) and one Greek (11th century). In the Syriac manuscript, the text of the song is preceded by a title. It is not called 'The hymn of the pearl' (this modern designation is not fully adequate, as we shall see) but, rather, 'The hymn (*madrasha*) of Jude Thomas, the apostle, when he was in the country of the Indians'. In this manuscript we also find a colophon, a concluding description of the poetic text: 'Conclusion of the hymn of Jude Thomas which he said in prison'[1]. In the Greek manuscript, the title and the colophon are missing. Here, more than in the Syriac manuscript, the hymn of the Apostle is an integral part of the text of the *ATh*[2].

However, the contents and the literary form of the hymn even in the Greek manuscript suggest that originally it was transmitted without its present context and that it was put into the mouth of the apostle by the author of the *ATh* or by an editor. Disconnected from the *ATh*, the poetic story sounds like an eastern fairy tale[3]:

[1] In the Syriac manuscript, the poetic text is followed by a doxology or hymn of praise to the Father and the Son. For a discussion of the possible relations between the 'Song of the Pearl', the doxology and the narrative text of the *ATh* see P.-H. Poirier, *L'Hymne de la Perle des Actes de Thomas* (Louvain-la-Neuve, 1981) 171-84.
[2] In the surviving Greek text, more traces of transformation and revision are found than in the Syriac text. Cf. H.J.W. Drijvers, 'Acts of Thomas', in *NTA* II, 322-39 at 330: 'In contrast to the Wedding Hymn, it is the Syriac version of the Hymn of the Pearl which has best preserved the original.'
[3] The text is written in the traditional style of Semitic poetry. It is composed of more than 100 couplets (double clauses), cf. Poirier, *L'Hymne*, 194-7.

In the first-person style, a Parthian prince tells how, as a young boy, he was sent away by his royal parents to achieve a difficult task: he was charged to go to the far country of Egypt in order to snatch away a precious pearl from a dangerous serpent or dragon. When he left home, he had to leave behind not only the luxurious and safe environment of the royal palace but also the costly robe that gave him his princely identity and dignity. An agreement was made with his parents that if he succeeded in his mission, the garment would be returned to him and he would share with his brother the inheritance of the kingdom.

Accompanied by two guides, he sets off on the long road to Egypt. After his arrival in Egypt, the two men leave him. In the neighbourhood of the serpent, he plans to wait until the serpent sleeps and then to snatch away the pearl. The prince tells how initially he was alone and tried to avoid the Egyptians and their unclean habits. But a noble relative of his, who also stays in Egypt, advises him to adapt himself to the Egyptians so that they will not treat him as a foreigner and frustrate his plan by waking up the serpent. Following this advice, he gradually comes under the influence of the people of that country. He begins to wear Egyptian clothes and tastes Egyptian food. Eventually, he wholly forgets about his mission and falls into a deep sleep.

But his wretched situation comes to the notice of his parents, who remind the boy of the agreement they had made with him. They write him a letter that flies like an eagle all the way to Egypt. Not only can the letter fly, it can also talk. The prince awakens to the voice of the letter. When he reads the letter, he remembers his royal descent and the purpose of his stay in Egypt.

He immediately casts a spell on the dragon-like serpent, snatches away the pearl and takes the shortest way home, guided by the shining letter. On the way, he receives back his royal robe that he had almost forgotten. The garment, which in the meantime had grown with him, is as a mirror to him: when he sees it, he becomes one with it and so fully realizes who he is.

Then he comes home. Finally he had achieved what he was charged to do and he is richly rewarded by his father.

The probability that the poetic story was inserted into the *ATh* could induce us to study it as a separate text[4]. But this is not what I intend

---

[4]   As is done by K. Beyer, 'Das syrische Perlenlied. Ein Erlösungsmythos

to do in this chapter. Rather, I will focus on the question of what the text means when it is read *within the context of the ATh*. In the *Acts*, the poem is said or chanted by the apostle Jude Thomas during his imprisonment in India (108-13). I quote the preceding narrative context:

And as he prayed, all the prisoners looked on him, and asked him to pray for them. And when he had prayed and sat down, he began to say this psalm (in the Syriac manuscript 'this *madrasha*', followed by the title)[5]: "When I was a little child in the palace of my father", etc.

Obviously the person of the speaker (the apostle Thomas), his situation in an Indian prison, and the explicit introduction of the text as a didactic poem or a religious song preclude the readers of the *ATh* from understanding the story as a fairy tale. The context clearly suggests that its language is figurative and that it has some religious meaning. Therefore, the question we will discuss is: What did the poem mean to those hearers and readers who were familiar with – and sympathized with – the overall message of the apostle Jude Thomas?

1. A Gnostic Context?

It would not be difficult to perceive the hymn recited by Jude Thomas as a story with a hidden deeper meaning if we could be sure that the context of the *ATh* presents the apostle as a Gnostic teacher. It may be recalled that until recently this assumption was widespread in scholarship, particularly in German research. Suffice it to refer to studies by Günther Bornkamm and Werner Foerster.

In his introduction to the *ATh* in the third edition of Hennecke-Schneemelcher, *Neutestamentliche Apokryphen* (1964) Bornkamm states: 'Die Erlösungsanschauung, die den Akten (the *ATh*) zugrunde liegt, ist die der Gnosis.' Thereupon Bornkamm summarizes the supposedly Gnostic features of the myth of salvation which he finds in

___

als Märchengedicht', *Zeitschr. der deutschen morgenl. Ges.* 140 (1990) 234-59. Cf. his observation on p.236: 'Da das Gedicht ursprünglich selbständig war, muss es aus sich selbst heraus verstanden werden'.

[5]   Cf. 1 Cor 14.26 for a similar use of the word *psalmos*.

the *ATh*[6]. Not surprisingly, Bornkamm affirms that these allegedly Gnostic features of the *ATh* recur in the Wedding Song of *cc*.6-7 and in the Hymn of the Pearl. Actually, in this third edition of Hennecke-Schneemelcher, the *ATh* stands out against the other *AAA* for its Gnostic character. None of the other apocryphal acts are considered undoubtedly Gnostic (with the exception of *cc*. 94-102 of the *Acts of John*, which are interpreted by Knut Schäferdiek as a Gnostic gospel in Johannine style[7]).

Wholly in line with this view of the *ATh* as a particularly Gnostic writing, Werner Foerster incorporates excerpts from the *ATh* - and only from these *Acts* - in his three-volume edition of Gnostic texts[8]. Note that he does not include *AJ* 94-102[9].

Scholars who, like Bornkamm and Foerster, assume that the religious message of the apostle in the *ATh* is Gnostic have good reasons for interpreting the Hymn of the Pearl as a Gnostic allegory. Actually, two alternative Gnostic interpretations of the Hymn of the Pearl have been proposed. The first interpretation, which has been held ever since Theodor Nöldeke (1871), supposes that the royal child, who was sent from his home to the far and impure country of Egypt, represents the soul (or the *pneuma*, the *nous*) having descended from the divine realm into the dark material world[10]. In the cosmic world, the soul is entangled in the forces of darkness. It forgets about its royal provenance and its true identity until it is awakened by a revelation from above (the letter sent by the parents). The beautiful garment is viewed *inter alia* as the purely spiritual or godlike part of the soul[11]. In this interpretation, the function of the pearl is less obvious. But it should be noted that the pearl plays only a supporting part in the story, just as the serpent does. The letter and the garment, in fact,

---

[6] Ibid., 300. Cf. id., *Mythos und Legende in den apokryphen Thomas-Akten* (Göttingen, 1933) 8: 'Die Anschauungen vom Erlöser und von der Erlösung innerhalb der Akten bewegen sich ganz im Rahmen des gnostischen Erlösermythos'.

[7] In the same volume, 142f.

[8] W. Foerster, *Die Gnosis*, 3 vols (Zürich, 1969).

[9] Cf. G. Luttikhuizen, 'A Gnostic Reading of the Acts of John', in Bremmer, *Acts of John*, 119-152 at 133ff.

[10] Nöldeke in his review of Wright's edition of the Syriac text of the *ATh*. Cf. Poirier, *L'Hymne*, 35ff.

[11] Cf. e.g. Bornkamm, *NTA* [3], 304.

are much more important to the development of the story. This can be concluded from the number of lines devoted to these narrative figures (the precious garment is mentioned in 30 double lines, the pearl occurs in 7 double lines). Moreover, the pearl and the serpent remain silent whereas the letter and the garment speak[12]. For these reasons, the current designation 'Song of the Pearl' is not wholly adequate. Although I do not adopt this Gnostic interpretation, it has much to recommend it. I shall return to aspects of this interpretation later.

According to the other Gnostic interpretation, which is preferred by Bornkamm and Foerster and which was proposed for the first time by Erwin Preuschen[13], the prince is not the soul itself (the *pneuma*, the *nous*) *but the heavenly Redeemer of the soul*: the Saviour who was sent from the divine world into the realm of darkness in order to rescue the soul (the pearl) from its imprisonment by demonic forces. It may seem strange that the prince (the Saviour) eats of the food of the Egyptians, that he falls asleep and forgets his mission so that he has to be reminded of his task and be rescued by his parents; here, however, Bornkamm and Foerster follow Reitzenstein who sees in the Hymn of the Pearl an illustration of the postulated Gnostic myth of the redeemed Redeemer (*Salvator salvandus*)[14].

Recent scholarship is less confident about the Gnostic character of the *ATh*. For non-Gnostic interpretations of these *Acts*, I refer to the commentary by A.F.J. Klijn and to the introduction to the *ATh* by H.J.W. Drijvers in the fifth edition of Schneemelcher[15]. I would like

---

[12] Beyer, 'Das syrische Perlenlied', 239.

[13] E. Preuschen, *Zwei gnostische Hymnen* (Giessen, 1904) 45-58 at 46: 'Das Lied schildert die Fahrt, die der Christus macht, um die in der Materie ruhende Seele, oder gnostisch ausgedrückt, um den Lichtfunken zu retten.' Preuschen's interpretation was accepted by R. Reitzenstein, *Hellenistische Wundererzählungen* (Stuttgart, 1906; repr. Darmstadt 1963) 122. Cf. H. Jonas, *Gnosis und spätantiker Geist* I (Göttingen, 1934) 327: 'Für unseren Zusammenhang vertritt das Lied die legendenhaft vermenschlichte Form der Lehre von dem unerkannt in die Tiefe hinabfahrenden und dort die "Seele" befreienden Erlösergotte.'

[14] Cf. e.g. Bornkamm, *Mythos und Legende*, 112: 'Das weitverbreitete mythologische Grundmotiv der Dichtung und die Bildersprache im Einzelnen lassen keinen Zweifel darüber, dass hier der Mythos von dem göttlichen Gesandten, der vom Himmel in das Reich des Bösen ausgesandt, den Mächten verfällt und selbst erlöst wird, dichterisch verarbeitet ist.'

[15] A.F.J. Klijn, *The Acts of Thomas* (Leiden, 1962); Drijvers, 'Thomasakten', *NTA* II (1989), 289-303; English transl. 322-39.

to support this non-Gnostic interpretation of the *ATh* by an examination of the way in which, in these *Acts*, reference is made to biblical traditions. I propose that the evaluation of biblical traditions is a useful gauge or criterion for determining the extent to which a given early Christian writing can be considered Gnostic[16]. My hypothesis is that the readers of the *ATh* are not likely to have interpreted the hymn of *cc*.108-13 in a Gnostic sense, if these *Acts* do not contain a particularly Gnostic soteriology.

I begin with the use of Old Testament traditions. The apostle Jude Thomas emphasizes that world and man were created by God. It was God's enemy, the Devil, who, in the shape of a serpent, incited Adam and Eve to be disobedient to their creator (cf. *c*.32). And it is a consequence of their siding with God's enemy that human beings live a sexual life and produce mortal and ungodly children (*c*.12). The task of the apostle is to persuade people to turn from their allegiance to the Devil – an allegiance which becomes manifest above all in their indulgence in sexual and other passions and pleasures – and to live a fully spiritual life in agreement with what is believed to be God's true purpose for his creation.

The present – supposedly wretched – situation of human beings is seen as the result of their being deluded by the Devil. This view is much more in agreement with the Genesis accounts of the creation and the fall of Adam and Eve as they were interpreted in emerging mainstream Christianity than with the revisionistic rewriting of these biblical traditions in such mythological Gnostic texts as *The Secret Book of John*, *The True Nature of the Archons*, and *The Testimony of Truth*.

In these Gnostic writings, the Genesis accounts are rejected and replaced by the allegedly true story of the creation and the earliest history of humankind. The unorthodox interpretation of the biblical stories is caused by the fact that Hellenistic Gnostic ideas about God, the created world, and man conflicted with the information of the Genesis text. The Gnostics behind *The Secret Book of John* and related writings were convinced that all material and perishable

---

[16]   In my definition of ancient gnosis, I start from those groups and their writings and ideas which, in the ancient sources, are characterized as Gnostic. A central place, then, is due to the group behind *The Secret Book of John*, cf. my 'A Gnostic Reading' (see note 9).

things, the human body included, were not created by their fully transcendent and unknowable highest God but by an ignorant and evil demiurge. They recognized in the biblical creator-God not their supreme Godhead but the inferior demiurge (who, with the help of biblical texts, is depicted as a jealous, ignorant and even malicious god).

How far the *ATh* are removed from the Genesis interpretation of the above texts can be illustrated with the description of the serpent and its role in the Paradise story. In *The Secret Book of John, The True Nature of the Archons, On the Origin of the World*, and *The Testimony of Truth*, the serpent in Paradise is viewed as an ambassador of the true God and even as an early manifestation of Jesus Christ, the Saviour of spiritual humanity. The serpent is glorified because it encouraged the first human beings to violate the commandment of the creator forbidding them to eat from the tree of knowledge. This commandment of the creator-God is interpreted as his attempt to prevent Adam and Eve from attaining the truth about their divine descent and nature[17].

The Gnostic *Testimony of Truth* contains an anthology of 'serpent texts' in which the serpent in Paradise is equated *inter alia* with serpents mentioned in the Moses stories in *Exod* 7 (the rod in Moses' hand which became a serpent) and *Num* 21 (the serpent of bronze which Moses hung on a pole to protect and heal the people)[18]. The obvious intention of this anthology of positive serpent texts is to suggest that, just like the other serpents, the serpent in Paradise acted to the benefit of humankind. The contrast with the enumeration of the wicked deeds of the serpent in *ATh c.*32 is conspicuous.

In *ATh c.*49, Jesus Christ is mentioned as the one who was proclaimed in the Scriptures. The reference to the Old Testament as 'the Scriptures' and the statement that Jesus Christ was proclaimed in the Scriptures bear witness to a high esteem of the biblical text. This view is evidently much more in agreement with the emphasis given to the continuity of the two Testaments in emerging mainstream

---

[17]   See my article 'A Resistant Interpretation of the Paradise Story in the Gnostic *Testimony of Truth*' in G.P.Luttikhuizen (ed), *Paradise Interpreted* = Themes in Biblical Narrative 2 (Leiden, 1998) 140-52.
[18]   Nag Hamm. Cod. IX,3, pp. 48,13-49,9.

Christianity than it is with the critical attitude towards the Old Testament expressed or presupposed in the above Gnostic writings[19].

I now turn to the use of New Testament traditions in the *ATh*. In these Acts, we find a great diversity of allusions to New Testament texts and traditions. I confine my remarks to the life and the mission of Jesus Christ. I have already pointed to *c*.59, where it is said that Jesus was proclaimed in the Scriptures. Several statements lay stress on Jesus' incarnation and on his physical sufferings. In *c*.72, for instance, Jude Thomas affirms that Jesus put on a body and became man and (as such) appeared to all. In *c*.79, he repeats that Jesus was born and he adds that Jesus was reared as a child. The apostle addresses Jesus as the one who was slain, who was dead and buried (47). He praises Jesus' manhood or humanity (*anthropôtês*) that died in order to give us life (80). Jesus gave himself for us (*huper hêmôn*) and with his blood purchased us (72). *C*.158, the last chapter before the martyrdom, contains detailed reminiscences of the humiliations suffered by Jesus before and during his crucifixion. In the long Greek version of *c*.19, Jude Thomas thanks the Lord for his having been dead for a short time in order that he (the apostle) might live for ever. He also praises Jesus' resurrection from the dead, by which rising and rest were given to 'our souls' (80).

This affirmation of the true humanity of Jesus, of his physical sufferings, and his death and resurrection contrasts sharply with the radical reinterpretation of early Christian traditions about Jesus' suffering in Christian Gnostic literature. An interesting case is the revelatory teaching of Jesus about his suffering in *cc*.94-102 of the *AJ*. These Gnostic chapters tell how on Good Friday the Lord shows John, his beloved disciple, the true cross, which is a cross of light. He explains to John that his suffering is of a quite different nature from what the multitude, which at that moment is gathered around the wooden cross in Jerusalem, believes. In his esoteric teaching, the Lord denies that he was ever submitted to physical suffering. After this revelation, John laughs at the multitude of believers who do not understand the true meaning of Jesus' coming into the world. The Christological teaching of these chapters of the *AJ* is in basic agreement with many other Christian Gnostic texts known to us from the Nag Hammadi library, *e.g. The Gospel of Philip, The Letter of Peter*

[19]   Cf. Irenaeus, *Adv. Haer.* IV *passim*.

to Philip, *The Apocalypse of Peter*, and *The first Apocalypse of James*[20]. This comparison of references to Old and New Testament traditions in the *ATh*, on the one hand, and in undoubtedly Gnostic texts, *cc*.94-102 of the *AJ* included, on the other, leads to the conclusion that the *ATh* represents a non-Gnostic realm of thought. It may be the case that, in the course of the transmission of the text, this writing experienced one or more orthodox revisions. But it is difficult to believe that an earlier text of the *ATh* attributed to the apostle basically different ideas about God's creation, about the origin of evil, and about the person and the mission of Jesus Christ[21].

If we wish to understand the Hymn of the Pearl within its present context – as a didactic poem, that is, recited by the apostle Jude Thomas – this conclusion makes a Gnostic interpretation of the song implausible. If it is interpeted in a Gnostic sense, it is bound to remain a *corpus alienum* within the *ATh*[22].

2. A Thomasine Context?

We will now briefly consider the extent to which the *ATh* represent distinctly 'Thomasine' views (views, that is, which this work shares with other texts connected with the name of the apostle Thomas: *The Gospel of Thomas* and and *The Book of Thomas the Contender*, both from the Nag Hammadi collection). A positive conclusion should encourage us to see the text of the song recited by the apostle in light of such ideas.

---

[20] D. Voorgang, *Die Passion Jesu und Christi in der Gnosis* (Frankfurt, 1991).
[21] A.F.J. Klijn, 'Early Syriac Christianity – Gnostic?', in U. Bianchi (ed), *Le Origini dello Gnosticismo* (Leiden, 1970) 575-9 at 577 acknowledges that the text of the *ATh* was corrected in the course of time, but he adds: 'these corrections were not made in Christological passages'.
[22] In the *AJ*, we find a clearly Gnostic revelation (*cc*.94-102) within a non-Gnostic context. But, as P.J. Lalleman, *The Acts of John* (Leuven, 1998) has demonstrated, in the *AJ* the combination of non-Gnostic and Gnostic texts makes perfect sense: the Gnostic chapters are meant as a further, more advanced account of the beliefs of the Johannine community which produced these texts. Lalleman speaks of a two-stage initiation into Johannine

Several recent studies deal with the question of what the Thomas writings have in common[23]. The results, however, are rather negative. Of course, Thomas is a central figure in each of these writings but the roles he plays are quite different. For instance, it is only in the *ATh* that Jude Thomas is depicted as a missionary representative of Jesus' teaching. Only here do we find an elaboration of the twin symbolism. The ideological views these writings have in common (notably: the renunciation of the material world and the preference for an ascetic lifestyle, the disinterest in the resurrection of the body, the emphasis on self-knowledge) are also found in many other writings of Late Antiquity.

3. The Hellenistic Anthropology of the ATh

This brings me to my main point. I propose that we give more explicit attention to the Greek-Hellenistic thought-world underlying and expressing itself in the religious message of the *ATh*, and particularly in its anthropological ideas. If we take into account the basically Hellenistic dualistic character of the religious message of the *ATh*, it makes sense to understand the Hymn of the Pearl as a poetic imagination of these ideas[24].

Gnosticism. There can be no doubt that 'Johannine Gnostics' were able to recognize the Gnostic message of these chapters, however enigmatic and cryptic they may have been to 'the multitude' of non-enlightened Christians. But whereas the Gnostic section of the *AJ* contains clear signs of its being meant as an esoteric Gnostic revelation, similar clues are virtually absent in the *Hymn of the Pearl* and in its preceding context.

[23]   G.J. Riley, 'Thomas Tradition and the Acts of Thomas', *SBL Seminar Papers* 30 (1991) 533-42; P.-H. Poirier, 'The Writings Ascribed to Thomas and the Thomas Tradition', in J.D. Turner and A. McGuire (eds), *The Nag Hammadi Library after Fifty Years* (Leiden, 1997) 295-307; Ph. Sellew, this volume, Ch. II.

[24]   Note that my approach to the texts is different from that formulated by Poirier, *L'Hymne*, 308: 'il faut se demander s'il n'y aurait pas, entre l'HP et les AcTh, une parenté de thème ou de contenu qui aurait suggéré d'y inclure celui-là dans ceux-ci.' My interest is not in the composers of the *ATh* and their possible motives for inserting the hymn but in the interpretation of the hymn by the hearers and readers intended by the authors of the Acts.

The apostle Jude Thomas claims – in his preaching and prayers – that it is the soul which will be saved and will live for ever. He refers to the resurrection of the body only in one passage (the eucharistic ceremony reported in *c*.158)[25]. For the rest there is total silence about the resurrection and the future life of the body. I have already mentioned that in *c*.80 the apostle thanks the Lord for his having offered resurrection and rest 'to our souls' (cf. *c*.36: as long as we are in the body we are not able to express what God will give 'to our souls').

Frequently the worthlessness and corruptibility or mutability of the body is emphasized (cf. esp. 37 and 88). The body is just a temporary dwelling-place of the soul. Death is seen as deliverance and release of the soul from the body (ἀπαλλαγὴ καὶ τοῦ σώματος λύσις: 160). The body grows old and becomes dust and so returns to its true nature (37)[26]. I consider the apostle's reference to God as 'the Saviour of my soul and the one who restores it (the soul) to its own nature' (141) a very significant passage. Apparently the expression 'the restoration of the soul to its own nature' means that after its release from the body, the soul will be restored to the state it was in before it was clothed with a body (cf. 43).

The strict division between soul and body, the idea of the pre-existence and the immortality of the soul and the contempt for the body as a temporary and perishable dwelling-place of the soul, are anthropological ideas which belong to the Platonic *koine* of Late Antiquity[27]. Indeed, several of these ideas were inherited in some form by Christians – by diverse groups of mainstream Christians as well as by Gnostic Christians – and to an extent even by Jews. But this does not alter the fact that we are dealing with a basically Hellenistic dualistic view of man.

I observed above that, in his preaching, the apostle often refers to biblical traditions. First of all, the allegedly wretched situation of

[25]   Here the apostle prays: 'let us receive renewal of soul *and body*'.
[26]   In the last lines of *c*.37, the apostle speaks about the help and guidance of Jesus in the present world (ἡ χώρα τῆς πλάνης). In this connection, he is called 'physician even of the bodies' (ἰατρὸς δὲ καὶ τῶν σωμάτων).
[27]   Very similar ideas about the soul and its fate can be found in *The Tractate of the Soul* (Nag Hamm. cod. II,6), in *Corp. Herm.* X, and in Plotinus, *Enneads*, 5.1. Cf. also Origen, *Comment. in Mt* 13:45-46 (the parable of the precious pearl). The last two texts were brought to my attention by M. Pesthy.

human beings and their inclination to shameful – i.e. sexual – deeds are traced back to the influence of God's enemy, the Devil. Furthermore, the real humanity and the physical suffering of Jesus are emphasized. I suspect that these biblical traditions were used to underscore and further substantiate a teaching which was based, first of all, on a widespread Greek philosophical view of man. The biblical tradition concerning the origin of evil, for instance, served to warn more emphatically against the needs and passions of the body. By renouncing sexuality, the apostle affirms, Christians make themselves immune to the malicious tricks of the Devil. It is made clear that even Jesus had to fight the Devil.

In this connection, it should be noticed that the *ATh* does not contain a soteriology in the sense of a teaching about a Saviour[28]. In these *Acts*, every individual has to achieve his or her own redemption from the bonds and the tricks of the Devil, first of all, indeed, by renouncing sexuality. In this process, Jesus is merely a guide and a model[29].

4. *The Hymn as a Poetic Imagination of the Teaching of the Apostle*

Theological issues are not involved (at least not overtly) in the story of the Parthian prince recited by Jude Thomas. We may take it for granted, therefore, that this text was less exposed to orthodox revisions than other speeches of the apostle. In so far as we can detect traces of editorial interpretation in the poem, they quite probably have a different background. In this respect lines 76-78, 88, and 98 (*cc.*112-3, where the prince describes what happened when, on the way home, he saw his royal garment) are an interesting case[30].

---

[28] Drijvers, in his introduction to the *ATh, NTA* II, 295; English transl. 329.
[29] Cf. *cc.* 10, 80, 37, 39, 60, 66, 81. Also for this reason the readers of the *ATh* are not likely to have found in the *Hymn of the Pearl* a poetic illustration of the mission and the fate of the Saviour.
[30] In these lines, the Greek text does not differ substantially from the Syriac version which is rendered here.

76. When suddenly I saw my garment
it became a mirror image to me.
77. I saw in it my whole self
and I knew and saw myself through it.
78. For although being one, we were divided
and again we were one in a single form.

88. Again I saw throughout it
Motions of knowledge being sent forth.

98. When I had put it on
I ascended to the land of peace and honour[31].

In these passages, the poetic story is interlarded with references to the religious meaning of self-knowledge (which the prince attains when he is reunited with his precious garment, apparently a metaphor for his better half or heavenly twin). They provide the reader with a key for decoding the story and for understanding it as an allegory. As Bentley Layton alleges, 'Starting from this clue, an ancient reader could work back through the story at another level, retelling it as an account or model of the quest for self-knowledge and salvation'[32]. But I doubt that this clue to a specific meaning is an original element of the text. It might, instead, reflect an early attempt to interpret the story as an allegory about redemption through self-knowledge[33]. As such, it would belong to the history of the reception of the poem rather than to its traditional content[34].

I argued above that the readers of the *ATh* are likely to have understood the story recited by the apostle as a poetic expression or illustration of his teaching[35]. They must have been particularly

[31] In 98b I follow the Greek text (Syriac: 'to the gate of hail and adoration').
[32] B. Layton, *The Gnostic Scriptures* (New York, 1987) 366.
[33] This particular allegorical interpretation could have developed in diverse Gnostic, Manichaean, and Catholic environments. Readers will turn to allegorical interpretation when they no longer understand the logic of the story in question or when this logic does not satisfy them.
[34] In the case of an apocryphal text like this, which was constantly re-told and re-written and which is known to us from comparatively late manuscripts, it is quite difficult to distinguish later from earlier recensions (let alone from the original text). But this should not induce us to give up this distinction.
[35] Or also as a metaphor of the missionary travel of the apostle in India which, in its turn, can be read as an image of the dangerous travel of man or

susceptible to words, phrases, narrative sequences, etc. that might illustrate this message. They could be tempted to understand the poem in a typically allegorical way (as the above quoted lines of the surviving versions suggest) but the literary elegance of the text – its poetic form and the alluring plot – may just as likely have prevented them from immediately decoding the story in order to find its supposed referential meaning.

I propose that an adequate way to understand this poetic text was – and still is – to read it as a coherent story provoking a network of allusions e.g. to the dignity of the soul and to the danger of losing this dignity and nobility here on earth. If we bear in mind that the poem speaks about a young boy, it also makes sense to see his fate in the light of the Greek philosophical idea that the soul is tested or educated during this life.

When the boy gets himself into trouble, his parents care for him and remind him of his royal descent and of the mission he is to achieve in Egypt. This part of the story can easily be associated with the Christian message represented and proclaimed by the apostle Jude Thomas. As the preceding chapters of the *Acts* have demonstrated, the apostle reminded people of the dignity of their soul and called upon them to free themselves from the passions and low desires that prevent them from recovering their true spiritual identity. Read in this way, the poetic story may convey a much broader range of possible meanings than when we approach it as an elaborate allegory (with virtually each narrative detail having its one and only referential meaning).

the soul in the world – the area of hostile powers. Cf. J.M. Lafargue, *Language and Gnosis* (Philadelphia, 1985).

IX. The Serpent in the *Acts of Thomas*

TAMÁS ADAMIK

1. The third act of the *ATh* speaks of a serpent. The Lord commanded
Thomas to go out on a road. So he went out, and near the second
milestone he saw lying there 'the body of a comely youth.' After
having seen the body he began to pray in such a way: 'O Lord, *judge
of living and dead* ... come in this hour in which I call upon thee, and
show thy glory toward this man who lies (here)' (30). After that he
turned to those who followed him and said: '... the enemy has been
at work, ...he has made use of no other form and wrought through no
other creature than that which is his subject' (30).

When he had said this a great serpent came out of a hole and said
to the apostle loudly that he slew the young man because he had seen
him making love to a beautiful woman. He, too, fell in love with her,
and so he killed the young man. The apostle asked him: 'Tell me of
what seed and what race thou art?' (31.) The serpent introduced itself
to the apostle in detail. I cite its whole speech because its words are
meaningful and special:

'I am a reptile of reptile nature, the baleful son of a baleful
father; I am son of him who hurt and smote the four standing brothers; I am son of him who sits upon the throne <and has power over
the creation (Syriac)> which is under heaven, who takes his own
from those who borrow; I am son of him who girds the sphere about;
and I am a kinsman of him who is outside the ocean, whose tail is set
in his own mouth; I am he who entered through the fence into Paradise and said to Eve all the things my father charged me to say to
her; I am he who kindled and inflamed Cain to slay his own brother;
and because of me thorns and thistles sprang up on the earth; I am he
who hurled the angels down from above, and bound them in lusts for
women, that earth-born children might come from them and I fulfil
my will in them; I am he who hardened Pharaoh's heart, that
he might slay the children of Israel and enslave them in a yoke of

cruelty; I am he who led the multitude astray in the wilderness, when they made the calf; I am he who inflamed Herod and kindled Caiaphas to the false accusation of the lie before Pilate; for this was fitting for me; I am he who kindled Judas and bribed him to betray Christ to death; I am he who inhabits and possesses the abyss of Tartarus, but the Son of God did me wrong against my will, and chose out his own from me; I am a kinsman of him who is to come from the east, to whom also is given power to do what he will on the earth' (32).

When the serpent had said this, the apostle answered angrily: 'Cease now, most shameless one, and be thou put to shame and entirely done to death! For thine end, destruction, is come. And do not dare to say what thou hast wrought through those who have become subject to thee. I command thee in the name of that Jesus who contends with you until now for the men who are his own, that thou suck out thy poison which thou didst put into this man, and draw out and take it from him' (33).

But the serpent said: 'Not yet is the time of our end come, as thou hast said. Why dost thou compel me to take what I have put into this man and die before the time? For indeed if my father draw forth and suck out what he cast into the creation, then is his end!' (33)

But the apostle said to him: 'Show now the nature of thy father!' (33) And the serpent set his mouth against the young man's wound and sucked the gall out of it. The young man revived, sprang up and fell at the apostle's feet. But the serpent burst and died, and his poison and gall poured out. In the place where his poison poured out there came a great chasm. The apostle said to the king: 'Send workmen and fill up that place, and lay foundations and build houses on top, that it may become a dwelling place for the strangers' (33).

2. This passage caught my attention because it is a perfect drama. R. Merkelbach emphasizes that in primitive times the killing of dragons was performed as a cult drama[1]. There are four protagonists: Thomas (the twin brother of Christ), the serpent (the son of Evil), the handsome young man and the beautiful woman. And there is also a chorus: the followers of Thomas, among them the king and his brother.

---

[1] Cp. R. Merkelbach, 'Drache', in *RAC* IV (Stuttgart, 1959) 229: 'In ältester Zeit war der D.kampf ein zentraler Kultmythos vieler heidnischer

According to Aristotle: '... tragedy is the representation of a complete i.e. whole action which has some magnitude (for there can be a whole with no magnitude' (7, 2) [2]. That is, the unity of plot, place and time is important in a tragedy, and plots are either simple or complex... 'By "complex", I mean an action as a result of which the transformation is accompanied by a recognition, a reversal or both' (10, 2). 'A reversal is a change of the actions to their opposite, as we said, and that, as we are arguing, in accordance with probability or necessity' (11, 1). 'A recognition, as the word itself indicates, is a change from ignorance to knowledge, and so to either friendship or enmity, among people defined in relation to good fortune or misfortune' (11, 2).

In a drama there is always a motive that is the source of the conflict which assures the cohesion of the plot. In this passage this motive is beauty. According to Plato (*Phaedrus* 250), beauty attracts everything to itself, that is, it is the source and cause of temptation. Not far from the road lay the corpse of a comely youth. The woman, too, was beautiful and both the young man and the serpent fell in love with her. The handsome young man and the beautiful woman were attracted to each other and made love to each other. The serpent fell in love with her at first sight. The serpent, as the son of Evil, is envious and jealous, and kills the young man out of jealousy. The real protagonists of the drama are Thomas and the serpent. The serpent is the Evil, who kills; Thomas is the Good, who revives. The structure of this drama is as follows:

a. Thomas finds the corpse, then begins to pray to God, and asks him: 'show thy glory toward this man who lies here'. After this he states that 'this thing has not happened to no purpose', 'the enemy has been at work', and he used 'no other creature than that which is his subject' (30). By these words the apostle points to the fact that he knows who the murderer was – the serpent.

b. In order to prove that the apostle knows and says the truth, God sends the serpent who confesses that he killed the young man, and explains why. It is not without interest that the serpent was afraid

Religionen u. ist vielfach regelmässig im Kult repräsentiert worden, bei Kosmogonie u. Stadtgründung, Neujahrsfest, Thronbesteigung u. Kriegerinitiation'.
[2] For the text and translation of the *Poetics* I use R. Janko, *Poetics I* (Indianapolis and Cambridge, 1987).

of Thomas: 'Now it would be easy for me to disclose them before thee, <but I dare not do it (Syriac)>. For I know that thou art the twin brother of Christ, and dost ever abolish our nature.'

c. Then the apostle orders him to say of what race he is. The serpent answered that he is the son of Evil and enumerated the works of Evil.

d. After having heard the works of Evil, the apostle grew angry, and said to the serpent that he would be done to death entirely. Then he bade him to suck out the poison from the young man. But the serpent protested, and said that Thomas could not compel his father, Evil, to draw forth and suck out 'what he cast into the creation'.

e. But Thomas said to him: 'Show now the nature of thy father!' Thereupon the serpent sucked the gall out of the wound of the dead young man who revived, but the serpent, having swelled, burst and died. In the place where his poison poured out a great chasm came into being (33).

Thus the story of the serpent consists of five acts, like a real drama. In its plot there is a Reversal: the killed young man revives, the killer serpent dies. But there is a Recognition, as well: the followers of Thomas recognize that God is more powerful than Evil. Evil's work is death, but life belongs to God.

3. The speech of the serpent, in which it introduces itself and enumerates its deeds, is remarkable in itself because it is a complex treatise on the serpent. Some ingredients of it are well known from the Old and New Testaments. These stories belong to the second part of the speech. For example, when the serpent says that it 'entered through the fence into Paradise and said to Eve all the things' it refers to Genesis 3.1: 'Now the serpent was more subtle than any beast of the field which the Lord God had made. And he said unto the woman, Ye, hath God said, Ye shall not eat of every tree of the garden' (King James translation). But in the Bible, Paradise has not yet a fence. The motif of the fence of Paradise is to be found first in the apocryphal *Life of Adam and Eve* (*Apocalypse of Moses*): 'And immediately he suspended himself from the walls of Paradise about the time when the angels of God went up to worship' (17)[3]. When the

---

[3]   J.H. Charlesworth, *The Old Testament Pseudepigrapha*, 2 vols (New York, 1983-85) II.277.

serpent says, that it is the one who 'inflamed Cain to slay his own brother' (32), it hints at Genesis 4.5. By stressing that 'thorns and thistles sprang up on the earth', he again points to the consequences of Eve's sin (Genesis 3.18). The words 'He hurled the angels down from above, and bound them in lusts for women', hint at Genesis 6.1-4. 'He hardened Pharaoh's heart', alludes to Exodus 1. 'He led the multitude astray, when they made the golden calf', refers to Exodus 32. 'He enflamed Herod and kindled Caiaphas to the false accusation', alludes to Matthew 27 and Luke 23.6-16. 'He bribed Judas to betray Christ to death', points to Matthew 26.14-6. The words 'he possesses the abyss of Tartarus', allude to Revelations 9.11 (32). Now in the Bible it is not said that the Satan accomplished all these deeds, but this enumeration is well known in rabbinic tradition.

The first part of the speech of the serpent has some statements that are not easy to explain. The first sentence of the serpent 'I am a reptile of reptile nature, the baleful son of a baleful father' perhaps hints at Genesis 3.14: 'And the Lord God said unto the serpent, Because thou hast done this, thou art cursed above all cattle, and above every beast of the field; upon thy belly shalt thou go, and dust shalt thou eat all the days of thy life'. That is, according to Genesis the serpent became a *reptile* because he misled the first woman, and so he caused the fall of mankind. According to an age-old tradition: 'Il (sc. the serpent) n'est qu'une ligne, mais une ligne vivante; une abstraction, mais, selon le mot d'André Virel, une abstraction incarnée. On ne voit de la ligne que sa partie proche, présente, manifeste.... Rapide comme l'éclair, le serpent visible jaillit toujours d'une bouche d'ombre, faille ou crevasse, pour cracher la mort ou la vie, avant de retourner à l'invisible'[4]. The serpent is baleful because God cursed him in such a way: 'And I will put enmity between thee and the woman, and between thy seed and her seed; it shall bruise thy head, and thou shalt bruise her heel' (Genesis 3.15).

Even more difficult to explain is the following sentence: 'I am son of him who hurt and smote the four standing brothers' (32). Who are these four standing brothers? According to H.J.W. Drijvers there are two possibilities: 'The four standing brothers are the four archangels who stand before God's throne (cf. Job 1.6; Lk 1.19; Jn.

---

[4] J. Chevalier and A. Cheerbrant, *Dictionnaire des symboles* (Paris, 1982²; repr. 1992) 867.

8. 44; *2 Enoch* 29, 4-5 [...]). They could also be identified with the four elements (*stoicheia*) (*2 Enoch* 15, 16.7 [...]). Then we must assume in addition to early Jewish and Christian angelology the influence of Bardaisan's cosmology (Drijvers, *Bardaisan of Edessa*, 1966, 96ff.), according to which darkness through chance destroys the harmony of the other elements, as a result of which the origin of the world comes about. Angelology and Bardaisan's cosmology lead to the idea of the four standing brothers, who are injured by the fifth'[5].

In order to demonstrate the possibility of the first interpretation Drijvers gives the following passages: Job 1.6; Luke 1.19; John 8.44; *2 Enoch* 29.4-5. In Job at the given place we can find the sons of God and Satan. In Luke there is the angel Gabriel, 'who stands in the presence of God'. In John there is a sentence of Jesus: 'Ye are of your father the devil, and the lusts of your father ye will do'. In *Enoch* we read: 'And from the rock I cut off a great fire, and from the fire I created the ranks of the bodiless armies – ten myriad angels – and their weapons are fiery and their clothes are burning flames. And I gave orders that each should stand in his own rank. [Here Satanail was hurled from the height, together with his angels.] But one from the order of the archangels deviated, together with the division that was under his authority. He thought up the impossible idea, that he might place his throne higher than the clouds that are above the earth, and that he might become equal to my power. And I hurled him out from the height, together with his angels. And he was flying around in the air, ceaselessly, above the Bottomless'[6].

Now the following motifs occur in these texts: sons of God, the angel Gabriel who stands, the father the devil, the fallen angels, and their leader, but we do not find the number 'four' and 'the four archangels' together. Therefore I would add to these places two other passages of Revelation: a) in which the number four is to be found: 'and round about the throne, were four beasts full of eyes before and behind. And the first beast was like a lion, and the second beast like a calf, and the third beast had a face as a man, and the fourth beast was like a flying eagle. And the four beasts had each of them six

---

[5] H.J.W. Drijvers, in *NTA* II, 328-9.
[6] I quote the English translation of *Enoch* from Charlesworth, *Old Testament Pseudepigrapha* I, 148.

wings about him; and they were full of eyes within: and they rest not day and night, saying, Holy, holy, holy, Lord God Almighty, which was, and is, and is to come' (4.6-8). b) 'And after these things I saw four angels standing on the four corners of the earth, holding the four winds of the earth, that the wind should not blow on the earth, nor on the sea, nor on any tree' (7.1). Even more precisely we can find the four archangels by name in the *Life of Adam and Eve* (*Apocalypse of Moses*): 'And God said to Michael, Gabriel, Uriel, and Raphael, "Cover Adam's body with the cloths and bring oil from the oil of fragrance and pour it on him"' (40). These places of Revelation and the *Life of Adam and Eve* contributed to Christian tradition according to which there developed the idea of the four archangels: Michael, leader of God's armies and conqueror of Satan; Gabriel, who brought the news of Christ's incarnation to Mary; Raphael, 'God's healer', mentioned in *Tobit*[7], and Uriel who is over the world and Tartarus[8].

The second interpretation, that the four standing brothers are the four elements, is also possible, since Thomas, before his martyrdom, says: 'For behold, how four have laid hold of me, since from the four elements I came into being! And one leads me, since I belong to one, to whom I depart <...> But now I learn that my Lord, since he was of one, to whom I depart and who is ever invisibly with me, was smitten by one; but I, since I am of four, I am smitten by four' (165). Here Thomas refers to John 19.34: 'But one of the soldiers with a spear pierced his side, and forthwith came there out blood and water', and to his own death, which will be caused by the four soldiers in such a way: 'And when he had prayed, he said to the soldiers: "Come and fulfil <the command> of him who sent you!" And at once the four smote him and slew him' (168).

The symbolism 'is a fundamental artistic process, which may be formalized ... or more often arises spontaneously, or is created within an individual context, at once conveying to the reader its explicit meaning and affecting him by the range and force of its suggestions'[9]. Therefore a symbolical description has not only this one explicit meaning but a lot of other meanings, too. So the image of the 'four standing brothers', hurt and smitten by the serpent, can allude

---

[7]   J. Summerscale (ed), *The Penguin Encyclopedia* (Baltimore, 1965) 25.
[8]   *1 Enoch* 19-20, in Charlesworth, *Old Testament Pseudepigrapha* I, 23.
[9]   *The Penguin Encyclopedia*, 577.

to the four rivers of Paradise, as well: 'And a river went out of Eden
to water the garden; and from thence it was parted, and became into
four heads. The name of the first is Pison.... And the name of the
second river is Gihon.... And the name of the third river is Hid-
dekel.... And the fourth river is Euphrates' (Genesis 2.10-4). These
rivers occur in *Ecclesiasticus* as the symbols of divine wisdom
(24.23-7). The four rivers of Paradise are well known in apocryphal
Christian literature, such as, for example, in the *Apocalypse of Paul*
(23). The four rivers of Paradise are represented in the iconography
by four men[10], so they can be named 'four brothers', as well. That is,
the serpent's statement can mean, too, that the serpent fights against
the wisdom of God.

The statement of the serpent: 'I am a kinsman of him who is outside the ocean' expresses an ancient conception: the serpent symbolizes the outside ocean that surrounds the earth. The continuation of
the sentence: 'whose tail is set in his own mouth' describes the serpent as the symbol of the infinite. According to R. Merkelbach: 'Er
symbolisiert das Unendliche, sich ewig Erneuernde, das Jahr (Mart.
Cap. 1, 70), den nach vorn und hinten blickenden Ianus, der selber ein
Bild der sich immer verjüngenden Welt ist (Macr. *Sat.* 1, 9, 9, 12),
die Sonne (Pistis Soph. 136) und vor allem den äusseren Ozean, der
sich rund um die Erde schlingt, den grossen Drachen der äusseren
Finsternis.... Hier berührt sich die Vorstellung des kreisförmigen
Drachen mit der vom Drachen als dem Vertreter des Wassers, des
amorphen, chaotischen, lebensfeindlichen Elements'[11].

Thus, from the speech of the serpent we can conclude that an
unknown author took over motifs not only from the Bible but also
from rabbinic sources. It is remarkable that the same deeds of the serpent are enumerated in the prayer of Ciliacus according to R. Merkelbach and A. J. Festugière[12].

4. R. Merkelbach writes about the battle against the serpent as follows: 'Über die ganze Welt verbreitet ist der Mythos vom

---

[10] G. de Champeaux and S. Sterckx, *Introduction au monde des symboles*
(Saint-Leger-Vauban, 1972) 226.
[11] Merkelbach, *Drache* 227f.
[12] Merkelbach, *Drache* 236; A.-J. Festugière, *Les Actes apocryphes de
Jean et de Thomas* (Geneva, 1983) 60 note 12.

Drachenkampf. Der Drache verkörpert die Mächte des Chaos und des Bösen, welche das Leben der Menschheit zu vernichten drohen. Ein Gott oder göttlicher Held besiegt den Drachen und stellt die Ordnung der Welt wieder her'[13]. According to C. H. Gordon, in Sumerian literature Gilgamesh and Enkidu already fight against the evil dragon Humbaba. The dragon is well known from the Old Testament, as well: the crooked serpent is Leviathan (Job 3.8, 40.25); he is actually named as such in Ugaritic texts, too[14]. We know the parallel myth of the Greeks: Python killed by Apollo and the seven-headed Hydra slain by Heracles. Lucian (AD 120-180) tells a story about serpents in his work *Philopseudes*. A man was stung by a serpent, but a Chaldean cured him by incantation. After that he went out to the fields and by magic formulas and acts he collected all the serpents, and he blew on them, and they were burnt (11-12). Merkelbach mentions that in the myth of the serpent the virgins play a big part: they are either rubbed by serpents or sacrificed to him[15]. In Christian literature the struggle against the serpent is described for the first time in Revelation and is connected to the woman clothed with the sun: 'And there was a war in heaven: Michael and his angels fought against the dragon; and the dragon fought and his angels. And prevailed not; neither was their place found any more in heaven. And the great dragon was cast out, that old serpent, called the Devil, and Satan, which deceiveth the whole world: he was cast out into the earth, and his angels were cast out with him' (12, 7-9)[16]. In the *AJ*, in the love story of Drusiana and Callimachus, a serpent kills Fortunatus (63-86). It was easy for the unknown author to combine these two descriptions with the story of God's sons who married the daughters of men (Genesis 6.2) and with Hellenistic wander tales on serpents. Utilizing these stories he constructed his own story of the serpent who fell in love with the beautiful woman, in order to illustrate his encratic ideas. According to Merkelbach[17], in the *AAA* the serpent is

[13] Merkelbach, *Drache*, 229.
[14] C.H. Gordon, *The common background of Greek and Hebrew civilizations* (New York, 1965) 190f.
[15] Merkelbach, *Drache*, 229.
[16] H. Bietenhard, *Die himmlische Welt im Urchristentum und Spätjudentum* (Tübingen, 1951) 214.
[17] Merkelbach, *Drache*, 247.

the symbol of sexual desire. On the basis of the above I think that his function is more complex[18].

5. From the *AAA* the image of the serpent passed into Christian hagiography. Jerome, who knew well both Christian and pagan literature, describes the deeds of a big serpent in his *Life of Hilarion*. When Hilarion wanted to hide himself in Dalmatia, he failed because a big dragon (*draco mirae magnitudinis*) appeared in the countryside and began to devastate the animals and the people. He was so big that he swallowed the cattle and the herdsmen. Hilarion prayed to Christ and had the people build a big pyre, then he ordered the dragon to climb on the pyre, and so he burnt the beast: *tum itaque cuncta spectante plebe immanem bestiam concremavit*[19]. R. Reitzenstein thinks that Jerome imitated only Lucian[20], but in my opinion Jerome emulated both Lucian and the *Acts of Thomas*.

[18] Ph. Vielhauer, *Geschichte der urchristlichen Literatur* (Berlin and New York, 1978) 712: 'Der Drache in der dritten Praxis stellt sich selbst in einer langen Rede als Sohn Satans und Repräsentanten der bösen kosmischen Macht vor; seine Vernichtung und die Rettung des Jünglings werden so zum Bild der Erlösung.'

[19] Hieronymus, *Vita S. Hilarionis eremitae*, 28 Bastiaensen and Smit (*PL* 23, 50).

[20] R. Reitzenstein, *Hellenistische Wundererzählungen* (Leipzig, 1906) 4: 'Lukian hat den Schluss für seine Zwecke umgestaltet und übertrumpft, anders und doch ähnlich wie Hieronymus in dem Bericht über die Wundertaten des heiligen Hilarion.'

X. India and the Apostolate of St. Thomas

LOURENS P. VAN DEN BOSCH

From olden times the apostle Thomas has occupied an important
place in the imagination of Christianity in India, which is reflected in
many local traditions in south India. He is regarded as the disciple
who preached the gospel on the Indian subcontinent and converted
many Christians on the Malabar coast. According to local narratives,
he had moved his missionary activities subsequently to the Coromandel coast, where he shed his life as a martyr. He found his last
resting place near a city called Mylapore (Madras), where a holy
shrine was built, which was rediscovered by the Portuguese at the
beginning of the sixteenth century. A church was erected to house the
apostle's remains, which was enlarged in 1893 and is nowadays
known as the Roman Catholic San Thome Cathedral in Madras. The
bones of the saint in the church function as symbolic evidence of the
apostolic origin of Christianity in south India and testify as it were to
its antiquity. Thus, unto this day Thomas Christians of south India
firmly hold on to their conviction that their church is founded directly
by the apostle Thomas who brought the gospel to them[1]. The historical reliability of these traditions is not unproblematic since both local
and Portuguese records are not much older than the sixteenth century,
and ancient Indian traditions on the apostle Thomas have not yet

---

[1]   A.K. Mundadan, *History of Christianity in India. From the Beginning up
to the Middle of the Sixteenth Century* I (Bangalore, 1984) 9-66 at 29ff. Cf.
also M. Gielen, *St. Thomas, the Apostle of India* (Kottayam, 1990). See further J.N. Farquhar, 'The Apostle Thomas in South India', *Bulletin of the
John Rylands Library* 11 (Manchester, 1927) 20-50, which is based on the
local traditions of the Syrian Church in South India and interprets the *ATh*
on the basis of these late traditions in a speculative and sometimes phantastic manner.

been found. For this very reason we are thrown back on ancient western sources which might inform us on the apostolate of St. Thomas. The apocryphal *ATh*, probably to be dated to the beginning of the third century and originating from an east Syrian milieu, functions in this context as the most important source to enforce the claim of his missions to India[2]. The *ATh* were, in all probability, written in Syriac, but may have been translated into Greek simultaneously or somewhat later. They relate the journey of the apostle Thomas and his missionary activities in India in a 'romantic' way, like many other hagiographies of the period. According to some scholars, the description has been the result of a rich imagination of the author[3]. This makes the claim of Thomas Christians that their oldest communities were founded by the apostle more problematic. In this context one may ask how one should evaluate the relationship between early Indian Christianity and traditions in the *ATh* and other ancient sources[4]. I shall

---

[2] H.J.W. Drijvers, 'Thomasakten', in W. Schneemelcher (ed.), *Neutestamentliche Apokryphen* II (Tübingen, 1989[5]) 289-367 at 291-2, transl. R. McL. Wilson, in *NTA* II with an abridged introduction; A.F.J. Klijn, *The Acts of Thomas* (Leiden, 1962) 26, 30-3; see also Mundadan, *History of Christianity in India*, 23f.

[3] See e.g. Drijvers, 'Thomasakten', 292 with references to secondary literature.

[4] For a recent, but totally unconvincing, attempt to support the historical reliability of Thomas' visit to India see H. Waldmann, *Das Christentum in Indien und der Königsweg der Apostel in Edessa, Indien und Rom* (Tübingen, 1996). The author wrongly states that the dates of Gundophoros and his brother have now been established between 19 and 46 AD (p. 10, 35-42), although the numismatic and other archeological and historical material do not allow such a conclusion. Raschke (see note 13), to which Waldmann refers, mentions the older literature, but does not offer any hard evidence with respect to this matter. But even if Gundophoros would have lived at that time it does not follow that Thomas would have met him personally. Secondly, the supposition seems highly improbable that the tradition of Bartholomew's visit to India originated in a wrong understanding of Mar-Thoma (via Bar-thoma to Bartho(lo)ma: pp. 13-7). Thirdly, the supposition (pp. 48-9) that Andrapolis should be identified with a city Andronpolis in Egypt is highly speculative and evokes more questions than it offers solutions. Fourthly, Waldmann's supposition (pp. 50-2) that Thomas would have gone twice to India, the second time to South India (after 52 AD), is not substantiated by any ancient source, while the much later Indian traditions are unreliable from a historical point of view. Fifthly, the author incor-

first focus in my paper on the tradition of the apostle Thomas and India according to the *ATh* and discuss the actual information about India. Then I shall deal with some other ancient sources that contain information on missionary activities of the apostles to India and, in line with this, with the existence of Christian communities on the Indian subcontinent. Finally, I shall try to reconstruct the outlines of Christian missions in India in the first four centuries AD and return to the question as to why the *ATh* acquired such an important place in the perception of Indian Christians.

1. *India in the Acts of Thomas*

The *ATh* starts with the meeting of the apostles in Jerusalem after Jesus' death and relates that they divide the various regions of the world for their missionary activities[5]. The result is that India falls by lot and division to Judas Thomas, who is also described as the brother of Jesus and the twin brother of the Messiah[6]. Yet Thomas does not feel competent for this task and explicitly refuses to go (1). The next day he is sold by the risen Lord as a slave to a certain Indian merchant Abbanes (Habbân) who searches for a skilled carpenter by order of a king named Gundophoros (Gûdnaphar) (2). The two embark in an unspecified port and sail to a town called Andrapolis in Greek, and Sandarûk in the Syrian text (3). During his stay in the city the apostle gets involved in all kinds of meetings and festivities and testifies to his faith amidst a partly hostile assembly which

rectly suggests that names as Mazdai, Mygdonia, Tertia, etc. might be conceived as Greek or Latin translations of Indian names originating in south India (Mylapure); they all seem to refer to Parthian regions. Sixthly, the author fails to deal adequately with the genre of the text, its audience and its intentions. Seventhly, the author does not seem to know the important contributions by A. Dihle on India in antiquity (see note 10, 12, etc.) and by others (see various notes). In other words, facts and fictions are mixed up in this phantastic book, which pretends to be highly scientific.

[5]   Klijn, *Acts of Thomas*, 157f. Cf. also E. Junod, 'Origine, Eusèbe et la tradition sur la répartition des champs de mission des apôtres', in F. Bovon *et al.*, *Les Actes apocryphes des apôtres* (Paris, 1981) 233-48.

[6]   Klijn, *Acts of Thomas*, 192 with references to *ATh*. 11, 31 (Greek version) and 39; Drijvers, 'Thomasakten', 291.

is surprised by his wonderful powers. The local king invites Thomas to apply his powers for the well-being of his only daughter who will be married. The apostle's prayer leads to the appearance of the risen Lord Jesus who teaches both bride and bridegroom to preserve themselves from filthy intercourse, a deed of corruption. The bride is impressed and testifies in front of her father to the meeting with her true heavenly Husband who will give her later the taste of life eternal. The king is enraged and instructs to search for Thomas, but the apostle has left the town and has entered the realm of India. There he is commissioned by king Gundophoros to build a palace, but uses the money he receives for the propagation of the gospel. When the king invites him to account for his behaviour, he defends himself by saying that he has built a heavenly palace. As a consequence of this, he is accused of sorcery and thrown in jail, but is freed after the intercession of the brother of the king, a certain Gad, who dies but is resurrected to life and testifies to the heavenly palace which he has seen in the hereafter (22-24). The king is baptised and preaches the Christian faith throughout the country[7].

According to the next part of the story, Judas Thomas passes during his missionary tour throughout India (62) on to another country with a king called Mysdaios (Mazdai) (87) and makes many converts, even among the royal family. In spite of this, he is imprisoned because he is suspected of sorcery and bewitchment of people. The martyrium in the concluding section of the *ATh* relates how the apostle Thomas is stabbed to death outside the town at the top of a hill where he is also buried (159-69). The final chapter reports that Mysdaios decides to exhume the bones of Thomas in order to exorcise a devil who tortures one of his sons, but he does not find the remains as they have been transported secretly to the West (170). Yet, the king is converted and the son is healed.

As can be seen from this outline, the concrete information about India in the *ATh* is extremely poor[8]. Toponyms are almost lacking,

---

[7] Cf. also L. Leloir, 'Le baptême du Roi Gundaphor', *Le Muséon* 100 (1987) 225-35 with an analysis of the Armenian traditions about the baptism of King Gundophoros.

[8] For a description of the boundaries of India in the works of Roman geographers of the Imperial period and the changes in the perception of Christian authors, see H. Gregor, *Das Indienbild des Abendlandes (bis zum Ende des 13. Jahrhunderts)* (Vienna, 1964) 11-5.

and material descriptions of everyday life with references to climate, flora and fauna are as good as absent, while the records of concrete persons are concealed in a legendary halo. The references to India are vague and do not convey the impression that the author is well acquainted with its location and with the situation at the spot. India functions as an imaginary landscape in which the acts of the apostle are sketched, but it remains unclear how this imaginary landscape relates to the reality of India as it was known in various circles at that time[9]. Yet many attempts have been made to identify the kings in the *ATh* and to situate at least the few mentioned places in order to reconstruct the beginnings of Christianity in this subcontinent. In this section I shall first deal with the name of the port of disembarkment, Sandarûk, and discuss whether the names of the kings offer us any clues to situate the story of the apostle in space and time.

As is mentioned before, Thomas embarks at an unspecified place - Jerusalem seems to be suggested, but this is impossible - and sails by boat to a place called Sandarûk, c.q. Andrapolis in the Greek version. Some Greek manuscripts of the *ATh* relate that the name Andrapolis is not the correct name and add the toponym ENADROX, probably a slight corruption of the Syrian Sandarûk, as Albrecht Dihle has shown[10]. The addition of the term *polis* to the incomplete Greek form Andra may have led to a further corruption of the Syrian name. Ernst Herzfeld has suggested to regard the Syrian expression Sandarûk as an imitation of the Persian name Sind(a)rûd, i.e. Indus river[11]. If this is correct, the port of Thomas' disembarkment has to

[9] For the place of imagination in the description of India by Greek travellers see F. Javier Gómez Espelosín, 'L'Inde dans les récits grecs de voyage', in J.C. Carrière *et al.* (eds), *Inde, Grèce ancienne. Regards croisés en anthropologie de l'espace* (Paris, 1995) 21-37 at 23-4; *ibidem*, C. Jacob, 'L'Inde imaginaire des géographes alexandrins', 61-80 at 72ff.
[10] A. Dihle, 'Neues zur Thomas-Tradition' (1963), in his *Antike und Orient* (Heidelberg, 1984) 66 note 22.
[11] Cf. Dihle, 'Neues zur Thomas-Tradition', 66 note 24 with a reference to also J. Duchesne Guillemin, *La religion de l'Iran ancien* (Paris, 1962) 242, who in turn refers to E. Herzfeld, *Archeological History of Iran* (London, 1935) 62: 'the apostle landed in India, the kingdom of Gundophar, at the port Sandrôkh, a slight clerical error for Sindrôdh, the "river Sindh", hence modern Karachi, old Daibul'.

be located somewhere near the mouth of the river Indus in the Sindh, although he does not specify the name of the port.

The above mentioned hypothesis gains probability in the light of the sea-routes then existing between the Persian Gulf and the region of Sindh, which gradually developed since the fourth century BC[12]. It was by far the most convenient trading route between the Mesopotamian region with the port of Charax Spasinu at the mouth of the Tigris and the region of the Sindh in northwest India[13]. The sea route was well-known since the days of Alexander the Great who collected his army in 325 BC at the mouth of the Indus and sailed back with a part of his army to a port near the Euphrates. This enabled merchants to transport more goods through the regions of Parthia and Bactria (Afghanistan) in a shorter time than the often dangerous roads by land. After the discovery of the regularities underlying the monsoon winds in the first century BC new trading routes came into existence between the red Sea region and various ports along the coast of India, *inter alia*, with a port called Barbarikon at the mouth of the river Sindh.[14]

After the decline of the Mauryan empire in north India at the beginning of the second century BC the Greeks of Bactria invaded the northwestern parts of India (the Punjab and Sindh). In the course of time they acquired the control of the coastal regions as becomes clear from the existence of two Greek cities called Demetrias-Patala and Theophila near the mouth of the Indus, which functioned as important ports in the trade between India and the West[15]. The

[12] Dihle, *Antike und Orient*, 109-18 ('Der Seeweg nach Indien' [1974]).
[13] W.W. Tarn, *The Greeks in Bactria and India* (Cambridge, 1951^2) 53; M.G. Raschke, 'New Studies in Roman Commerce with the East', *ANRW* II.9.2 (Berlin, 1978) 604-1361 at 643. Charax Spasinu was a trading port with a motley population of many races and languages. In earlier texts the city is also called Antioch or Alexandria. See further Gregor, *Indienbild*, 20-1 and 86 with references to the *Commonitorium Palladii* by bishop Palladius from Helenopolis of Bithynia (about AD 400) with a description of the most important trade routes to and in India in the fourth century AD.
[14] L. Casson, *The Periplus Maris Erythraei. Text with Introduction, Translation and Commentary* (Princeton, 1989) 11-44, 188ff and appendix III, 283-91.
[15] Tarn, *The Greeks in Bactria and India*, 171, 356-7, 362, 368, 371-3; Raschke, 'New Studies in Roman Commerce with the East', 657 and 663.

increase of trade by sea between these two regions in the first century AD thus seems to have created a more international atmosphere in these ports where people with various cultural backgrounds met.[16] If this is correct, the author of the *ATh* may have referred to an unspecified port near the mouth of the Indus river. He evokes its multicultural character by referring to a Hebrew woman who plays the flute (5). When the rather cryptic name Sandarûk as designation for the Indus river was no longer understandable, it was replaced in the Greek text by the more conceivable name Andrapolis, 'city of people'. The later added gloss, 'royal city', explains the town as a royal residence as is evident from the story.[17]

In this context mention should also be made of a different theory which identifies the name Sandarûk with the trading city Hatra in the desert between the Tigris and the Euphrates.[18] The full name of this town would have run Hatre de Sanatrûk. The last part of the name, thus it is suggested, refers to a king of Parthian origin who founded the city in the second century AD. Yet it remains then unclear why the author of the *ATh* would have used this name Sandarûk in stead of its common name Hatra and why the translators of the text did not use the common and well-known Greek name Atrai in order to explain which city was intended instead of appealing to the vague expression Andrapolis. Moreover, this interpretation is at odds with the story of the *ATh*, which suggests that Thomas was sailing directly to a port in India and disembarked in the city of Sandarûk (2-4).

Cf. also Casson, *Periplus Maris Erythraei*, 16, 75 with the commentary at 188f). The author of the *Periplus* (middle of the first century AD) who was well-acqainted with the trade between Egypt, the Red Sea region and India, mentions the city of Barbarikon (*Periplus* 39: 13.10-12) at the mouth of the river and Minnagara (*Periplus* 38: 13.3-4) as the former Skythian capital of the region. For the trade see now also F. de Romanis and A. Tchernia (eds), *Early Mediterranean Contacts with India* (New Delhi, 1997), to be read with the review by C.R. Whittaker, *J. Rom. Arch.* 13 (2000) 691f.

[16]   For the stark increase in trade between India and the Red Sea region see Casson, *Periplus Maris Erythraei*, 21ff.

[17]   Farquhar, 'The Apostle Thomas in North India', incorrectly suggests that the capital of Gundophoros, Taxila, would have been meant on account of the qualification 'royal city'.

[18]   G. Huxley, 'Geography in the *Acts of Thomas*', *Greek, Roman, and Byzantine Studies* 24 (1983) 71-80 at 72f.

132   LOURENS P. VAN DEN BOSCH

A double transfer is not likely, since the text does not offer any clue for this hypothesis.

The name Gundophoros (Gûdnaphar) which is mentioned several times to designate the Indian king at whose court the apostle stayed (e.g. 2; 17) is not unknown to historians from other sources. It is equated with the name Gondophernes which occurs on ancient Indian coins and on the inscriptions from Takht-Bah in the district of Peshawar (Pakistan)[19], which are nowadays stored in the museum of Lahore. The name is of Parthian origin and may have corresponded to the Persian Vindipharnah, i.e. 'winner of victory'[20]. On coins, Gondophernes is sometimes also denoted by the name Orthagna, a corruption of the Sanskrit expression Verethraghna, 'remover of obstructions'[21]. The Nike figure on his coins may be regarded as an iconographic symbol expressive of this qualification. Gondophernes is described by historians of the region as an Indo-Parthian king, who started his career as a governor (*suren*) of Arachosia, presently situated in modern south Afghanistan. He conquered the central part of the Shaka kingdom, which roughly coincided with parts of the Punjab and Sindh, while the Saurashtra region and the region around Mathura remained outside his control[22]. Thus, he became one of the most powerful kings in the northwestern parts of India at the time. He appealed to the Western imagination which preserved his name as one of the three kings in the Christmas story, though in a mutated form, namely as Gathaspar or Casper[23]. After his death the Indo-Parthian kingdom rapidly declined and became incorporated in new political and geographical configurations. In the first century AD Indo-Parthians, Shakas, c.q. Scythians, and the remnants of the Indo-Greeks

[19] D.C. Sircar, *Indian Epigraphy* (New Delhi, 1965), 245.
[20] Klijn, *Acts of Thomas*, 160 with a reference to F. Justi, *Iranisches Namenbuch* (Marburg, 1895) 368f. See also J. Filiozat, 'La Valeur des Connaissances Gréco-Romaines sur l'Inde', *Journal des Savants* 1981, 97-135 at 133 note 83.
[21] For the numismatic evidence and the dating of various foreign kings beween the Bactrian period and period of the Kushanas see now O. Bopearachchi, *Ancient Indian Coins* II (Turnhout, 1998), 177-273 at pp. 219-23 (with a survey of recent literature).
[22] Tarn, *Greeks in Bactria and India*, 341, 344-5, 346-7, 352-4.
[23] Herzfeld, *Archeological History of Iran*, 63-6.

frequently fought each other, while yet another wave of invaders from Central Asia made their entrance, the Kushanas[24]. The complex situation in northwest India between the first century BC and AD makes it very difficult to date its various kings. Various attempts have been made, but none of them gained general assent. Recent studies suggest to place the reign of Gondophernes between 20 and 46 AD, although some scholars argued to date him earlier, somewhere between 30 and 10 BC[25]. The first hypothesis does not exclude the possibility that Thomas visited the kingdom of Gondophernes, but the second one implicitly suggests that the name of this king only functioned as a means to provide the story in the *ATh* with a kind of authenticity by referring to an historical well-known personage. In any case, also the later dating of king Gondophernes does not furnish us with sufficient historical proof that Thomas actually went to India and met him[26].

It has been argued that the record of a certain Gad (21), a brother of King Gundophoros, might strengthen the argument of historical reliability, if he could be traced in the numismatic material[27]. In this context Gad is equated with a certain Gudana, a name which appears on some Indo-Parthian coins, while on the reverse the name Orthagna

---

[24] H. Kulke and D. Rotermund, *A History of India* (London, 1986) 75-83. See also M.A.R. Colledge, *The Parthian Period* (Leiden, 1986) 1-4.
[25] For a discussion of the chronology of the Indo-Parthian kings see D. Mac Dowell, 'The Dynasty of the later Indo-Parthians', *Numismatic Chronicle* (1965) 137-148; A. Bivar, *Cambridge History of Iran* III (Cambridge, 1983) 197; G. Fussman, 'Chroniques et études bibliographiques: Chroniques des études Kouchanes (1978-1987)', *Journal Asiatique* 275 (1987), 333-57 at 338; Bopearachchi, *Ancient Indian Coins* II, 208-223. For the older (controversial) view suggesting a dating somewhere between 30 and 10 B.C. see J.E. van Lohuizen-de Leeuw, *The Scythian Period. An Approach to the History, Art, Epigraphy and Paleography of North India from the 1st Century B.C. to the 3rd century A.D.* (Leiden, 1949), at pp. 349-61; cf. J. Festugière, *Les Actes Apocryphes de Jean et de Thomas* (Genève, 1983), 45f note 1 with critical remarks by J. Filiozat on Van Lohuizen's proposal.
[26] Klijn, *Acts of Thomas*, 27; Huxley, 'Geography in the Acts of Thomas', 75
[27] A Väth, *Der hl. Thomas, der Apostel Indiens, eine Untersuchung über den historischen Gehalt der Thomas-Legende* (Aachen, 1925) 29, 77; Gielen, *St. Thomas*, 127.

is mentioned. Thus, Gad is closely associated with Gondophernes by the Gudana-Orthagna coins and it is even suggested that he might have reigned after the death of Gondophernes. Their common title Orthagna, 'remover of resistance', might then be interpreted as an indication of their close relationship[28]. Be this as it may, also another and more likely interpretation has been offered, which proposes to regard the expression Gudana on the Indo-Parthian coins as an adjective derived from Guda, just as Kushana is derived from Kusha. Gudana is then regarded as a pedigree-indication of Gondophernes, in the style of Kushana[29]. If this is correct, the coins with Gudana on the one side and the title Orthagna on the other one can not refer to two persons, c.q. the king and a close relation (brother or brother-in-law), but to only one person, namely king Gondophernes, who in the last years of his reign introduced this kind of minting. This view seems to be corroborated by the fact that not Gudana (Gad) was the successor of Gondophernes, but most likely a certain Pakores. Nevertheless, the whole reconstruction remains doubtful due to the lack of substantial evidence[30].

This leads us to the question as to how to evaluate the historical references in the *ATh*. The answer, in as far as Gad is concerned, seems to point to an invention, which may have been based on a

[28]   See also E. Herzfeld, *Sâkastân = Archäologische Mitteilungen aus Iran* 4 (1931-2) 79-80.
[29]   Van Lohuizen-de Leeuw, *Scythian Period*, 357 with references to the literature by S. Konow, *Corpus Inscriptionum Indicarum*, XLVI and J.F. Fleet, 'St. Thomas and Gondophernes', *J. Royal Asiatic Soc.* 1905, 223-36.
[30]   Van Lohuizen-de Leeuw, *Scythian Period*, 359f. enumerates various (older) theories. For the recent numismatic evidence see Bopearachchi, *Acient Indian Coins*, 219ff and 267-9, who on the basis of this numismatic material distinguishes four or five Indo-Parthian kings, Gondophares, Abdagases, Pakores, Orthagnes and possibly a certain Gondophares II. Yet Abdagases proclaims himself on some coins as the son of the brother of Guduphares, c.q. Gondophares, which seems to suggest that he acknowledges the authority of Gondophares. The Orthagnes coins refer on the reverse to Gudapharasa/Gadanasa or to Gadanasa, thus suggesting that Gondophares belonged to the pedigree of the Gadanas and was further qualified by the title Orthagna, 'remover of obstruction'. Most of these rulers remain highly elusive due to the lack of concrete historical information which goes beyond the numismatic evidence.

wrong interpretation of coins. But also the other references to possibly historical persons in the *ATh* are so elusive that they do not strengthen the hypothesis that Thomas ever visited India. This concerns Thomas' visit to the realm of king Mysdaios (Mazdai) after his departure from the kingdom of Gundophoros. According to the story, he meets some relations of the king and makes new converts. Indian tradition, as we have mentioned before, situates this realm in south India and locates the martyrium of the apostle near Mylapore[31]. Yet, a closer inspection of the names of the king and his relations suggests another direction. Names as Charisios (Kharish), Mysdaios (Mazdai) (89), and Mygdonia (82, 89, etc.) do not seem to point to south India at all, but may at best refer to the northwestern part of India with its Greek, Parthian and Persian influences. The same applies for the name of a general called Sifur (Sapor) and also for the name of a son of Mysdaios (Mazdai), a certain Ouzanes or Vazân, which might go back to Persian name Wij'en[32].

In spite of these indications which point to the Parthian sphere of influence in the northwestern part of India, three Greek manuscripts seem to locate the kingdom of Mysdaios in a different continent and suggest a Himyarite India in south Arabia, across the Red Sea from Aksum[33]. The presence of Indians in this region between the first century BC and AD is well known due to the discovery of new sea routes between the south India and the Red Sea.[34] Yet this location hardly seems probable, because the *ATh* does not suggest that Thomas travelled by ship to the kingdom of Mysdaios. Moreover, it is stated that the bones of the apostle were secretly conveyed to the West. If the tomb of the apostle had been located somewhere in south Arabia, it would have been more natural to suppose that the remains of the apostle had been transported to the eastern or northeastern

[31] Mundadan, *History of Christianity in India*, 25f.
[32] Klijn, *Acts of Thomas*, 264, 267-8, 272, 290. Cf. also Huxley, 'Geography', 77-78 with note 39. Herzfeld, *Archeological History of Iran*, 64 suggests that these names might refer to historical persons who became the heroes of the love romance of the Shâhnâme. See also Farquhar, 'The Apostle Thomas in South India', 33.
[33] Huxley, 'Geography', 76f.
[34] Casson, *Periplus Maris Erythraei*, 12ff; R. Salomon, 'Epigraphic remains of Indian traders in Egypt', *JAOS* 111 (1991) 731-6.

direction, because the tomb of the apostle was also situated in
Edessa, at least according to ancient traditions from the fourth century AD[35]. For this reason it seems probable that the author of the
ATh imagined the kingdom of Mysdaios somewhere in the neighbourhood of the kingdom of Gundophoros, which explains why the
bones of the apostle were carried westwards. The Greek manuscripts
may offer therefore a reinterpretation of the place of the martyrium
and testify to a further elaboration, convenient to certain Christians in
south Arabia and Ethiopia, who had connections with the gnostic
milieu of Syrian Christianity[36].

In a nutshell: the data in the *ATh* which might provide us with
some historical and geographical information about Thomas' journey
are so elusive that there is insufficient evidence to corroborate the
hypothesis that the apostle actually went to India. The record of the
name Gundophoros and the description of Thomas' sea journey to his
kingdom show at best that the author of the *ATh* had a vague general
knowledge of India and its former kings. The question may now arise
as to how he had acquired this knowledge, and the answer should at
least allow for the fact that the author to all probability lived in
Edessa or its surroundings. For this very reason it has been suggested
that he may have derived his knowledge about north India from local
Edessan traditions in the first two centuries AD. These traditions may
have been rooted in brisk trade connections between the two regions
and subsequent cultural relations. Porphyry relates that the Edessan
philosopher Bardesanes wrote a book on India and its customs[37].

[35] Cf. also N. Tajadod, *Les porteurs de lumière. Péripéties de l'église
chrétienne de Perse IIIe - VIIe siècle* (Paris, 1993), 158f. He suggests that a
pupil of Bardesanes edited the *ATh* and dates the transport of the reliques of
Thomas to Edessa in the year 232 AD. From this time onwards, Edessa
would have been the centre of the cult of St. Thomas. Yet this author does
not mention the sources on which he bases himself, but it might be supposed
that he refers to later (Latin) manuscripts which mention Edessa as the place
of the tomb; see K. Zelser (ed.), *Die alten Lateinischen Thomasakten* (Texte
und Untersuchungen, vol. 122) (Berlin 1977) 41 and 76; *idem*, p. VI with a
reference to Gregory of Tours.
[36] Huxley, 'Geography', 78f.
[37] See H.J.W. Drijvers, 'Hatra, Palmyra und Edessa. Die Städte der
syrisch-mesopotamischen Wüste in politischer, kultur-historischer und reli-
gionsgeschichtlicher Bedeutung', *ANRW* II.8 (Berlin, 1978) 799-906 at 894;
idem, 'Thomasakten', 292 with reference to Porphyry, *FGrHist* 719 F 1.

The author of *ATh* may therefore have used existing local knowledge of India in order to construct his legendary frame story of Thomas' journey to India. Yet facts and fictions were mixed in order to realise the aims the author probably had in mind, namely the foundation of the claim that not only Parthia but also India was the exclusive domain of Thomas' missionary activities. He thus suggested that with his missions to India the apostle Thomas had preached his gospel unto the ends of the earth[38].

2. Ancient traditions on Christianity in India

The view propounded in the *ATh* that Thomas went to India to preach the gospel seems to be an innovation with respect to older traditions. Pre-Nicaean authors such as, for instance, Clement of Alexandria (*-215) and Origen (185-254) link the apostolate of Thomas with Parthia[39]. Origen relates: 'When the holy apostles and disciples of our Saviour were scattered over the world, Thomas, so the tradition has it, obtained as his portion Parthia'[40]. Yet it is not clear whether these two authors meant to say that Thomas traversed the whole of Parthia including the northwestern region of India. They only refer to a tradition which suggests a connection of Thomas with Parthia. This tradition may have been based on the close bonds of the apostle with Edessa which formed a part of the Parthian empire during the first two centuries AD and was sometimes described as 'the daughter of Parthia'[41].

Eusebius relates that Thomas was divinely moved to send Thaddeus as an herald and evangelist of the teachings about Christ to

---

[38] For a general view on the imagination of the ends of the earth see also J.S. Romm, *The Edges of the Earth in Ancient Thought. Geography, Exploration and Fiction* (Princeton, 1992).
[39] See Klijn, *Acts of Thomas*, 27 and 158 with reference to the relevant places. Cf. A. Mignana, 'The early spread of Christianity in India', *Bulletin of the John Ryland Library* X (1926), 435-514, particularly at 443-447.
[40] Eusebius, *HE* 3.1.1: 'Thomas obtained Parthia by lot'. Cf. also Junod, 'Origine, Eusèbe et la tradition sur la répartition des champs de mission des apôtres', 233-48; Mundadan, *History of Christianity in India*, 27.
[41] Klijn, *Acts of Thomas*, 30-3; Drijvers, 'Thomasakten', 290 with a reference to his 'Hatra, Palmytra und Edessa', 885ff.

138   LOURENS P. VAN DEN BOSCH

Edessa[42], and the Syrian *Doctrina Addai* reports a similar tradition that Thomas sent the apostle Addai to Edessa[43]. These two statements seem to suggest that Thomas did not visit Edessa, but limited himself to the organisation of the mission to Parthia, which had been assigned to him by lot[44]. Also the other ancient sources preceding the *ATh* do not inform us about his missionary journeys. They only relate that the apostle was forced by lot to take his missionary responsibility. The author of the *ATh* undoubtedly referred to this notion of compulsion when he stated that India fell by lot and division to Judas Thomas. In other words, it seems that, according to tradition, Thomas did not like to travel to remote countries. The *ATh* mentions two main reasons for this reluctance, namely bodily weakness and linguistic problems that complicated the communication. Yet the text makes it also clear that India was assigned to Thomas as his missionary field, and not to any of the other apostles. Thus, it suggests India as the exclusive domain of Judas Thomas and further reinforced this claim by the miraculous intervention of the risen Lord.

Although the most ancient traditions do not describe Thomas as an enthusiastic missionary and traveller, the miraculous story of his sale by the risen Lord to the Indian merchant Habbanes (Abbân) leads him directly from Jerusalem to India where he died[45]. In spite of this, the apostle became clearly connected with Edessa, and two sources from the fourth century testify to this fact. Ephraem Syrus (306-70) relates that the apostle's relics were venerated in a shrine in Edessa. In addition to this, we have the testimony by the female pilgrim Egeria, who visited the city in AD 384 (*Peregrinatio Egeriae*

---

[42]   Eusebius, *HE* 1.13.4. Cf. also J.W. Mc Crindle, *Christian Topography of Cosmas, an Egyptian Monk* (London 1897, repr. New York, 1970) 72 referring to Cosmas Indicopleustes 2.147: 'For it was in the Roman dominions that the preaching of Christianity first became current in the days of the Apostles, and it was immediately afterwards extended to Persia by the apostle Thaddaeus'.

[43]   Cf. Drijvers, 'Thomasakten', 292.

[44]   See note 40.

[45]   Cf. Th. Schermann, *Propheten und apostellegenden* (Texte und Untersuchungen 31.3) (Leipzig, 1907), 274: 'Von einem Märtyrertode des Thomas weiss die älteste Überlieferung noch nichts. Der Gnostiker Herakleon lässt ihn einen natürlichen Todes gestorben sein', with a reference to Clement, *Alex. Strom.* IV 9, 71 and 73 (ed. Stählin 1906) 280f.

17)[46]. The tradition of the tomb of the apostle in Edessa may have older roots in the third century AD and be at the basis of the report in the *ATh* that the apostle's bones were secretly removed from the kingdom of Mysdaios in India and transported to the West (170). With this transport from the periphery to the centre the author may have indirectly indicated that Christians in Mesopotamia, and particularly in Edessa, at that time regarded their region, c.q. their city, as the centre of Thomas' apostolate. Thus, Edessan Christianity propagated itself as the centre from where the gospel of Thomas was preached unto the most remote parts of the Parthian Empire, namely the northwestern regions of India. India was then seen as belonging to the outer sphere of influence of Edessan Christianity due to the fact that small communities of Christians came into existence in the northern and western regions of India on account of trade and commerce between Mesopotamia and Indian cities along the sea coast of the Sindh.

In this context the question may arise as to why the author of the *ATh* describes the apostle's journey directly from Jerusalem to India, and not from Jerusalem to Edessa, and from there to India, for this would have stressed the position of Edessa. As we have seen, the *ATh* suggests that from the very beginning of the missions in Jerusalem India be allotted to St. Thomas. Its author thus seems to accentuate the primacy and the authority of Judas Thomas over India. He makes it implicitly clear that missionary traditions which might connect other apostles with India had at least to acknowledge the claim of Thomas and his inheritors.

The stressing of this opinion makes sense if we consider the ancient testimonies that mention the apostolate of Bartholomew to India. Eusebius of Caesarea mentions that Pantaenus from Alexandria, the teacher of Clement[47], went as far as India to proclaim the gospel of Christ to the heathens in the East. In this context he relates: 'It is said that he [Pantaenus] went to the Indians and the tradition is that he found that among some of those there who had known Christ the gospel according to Matthew had preceded his coming; for Bartholomew, one of the apostles, had preached to them and left

---

[46]   See also H.J.W. Drijvers, 'Abgar Legend', in *NTA* I, 492f.
[47]   Eusebius, *HE* 6.6.1. Cf. also Dihle, 'Neues zur Thomas-Tradition', 68-71.

them the writings of Matthew in Hebrew letters'[48]. This tradition may go back to the second half of the second century AD and suggests connections between Alexandria and India which are confirmed by some other reports[49]. Yet it remains unclear where exactly we should locate the India of this tradition[50]. According to some authorities, the India of Bartholomew mentioned by Eusebius should be situated in Ethiopia or Arabia Felix and referred to Indian traders who lived along the coast of the Red Sea and on the island Socotra in the first two centuries[51]. They had settled in this region after the discovery of the monsoon by Hippalos (second half of the first century BC) had enabled them to make the long sea journey. Their presence is confirmed by other sources, for instance, in Berenice at the Red Sea, a main port for the trade with India[52]. But it should also be noted that Egyptian ships sailed along the southern monsoon route to south India during the first two centuries AD[53]. Many Graeco-Egyptian coins of the imperial period have been found on the Malabar and Coromandel coasts and attest to the presence of Graeco-Egyptian settlements of traders[54]. It has been suggested that these contacts diminished at the beginning of the third century AD, after the Roman

[48]   Eusebius, *HE* 5.10.1-4, transl. K. Lake (Loeb).

[49]   See also Dihle, 'Neues zur Thomas-Tradition', 68-71, 74 with note 72 referring to Philostorgios 18.15f; Mundadan, *History of Christianity in India*, 65 note 92.

[50]   See also Gregor, *Indienbild*, 86-7 with note 153 who refers to some later sources.

[51]   Mundadan, *History of Christianity in India*, 65; cf. Dihle, 'Neues zur Thomas-Tradition', 68.

[52]   Casson, *The Periplus Maris Erythraei*, 20f. For the epigraphical material see R. Salomon, 'Epigraphic remains of Indian traders in Egypt', *JAOS* 111 (1991), 731-6.

[53]   Dihle, 'Der Seeweg nach Indien', and 'Die entdeckungs-geschichtlichen Voraussetzungen des Indienhandels der Römischen Kaiserzeit', in *Antike und Orient*, 109-18 and 118-152, at 119-123 (with a description of the monsoon-passage); Gregor, *Indienbild*, 21 and Klijn, *Acts of Thomas*, 158.

[54]   Dihle, 'Neues zur Thomas-Tradition', 69 note 38 and 72 note 54; idem, 'Indienhandel der römischen Kaiserzeit', 141f. Cf. also M. Wheeler, *Rome beyond the Imperial Frontiers* (London, 1954), 170ff with a description of the archeological remains of Arikamedu (near Pondicherry), a trade colony from the Roman period between the second century BC unto the second century AD. For a recent study on South India, see R.Krishnamurti, *Late*

Empire lost control over the Red Sea region, and instability increased[55]. Anyhow, it does not seem very plausible to situate India somewhere in Ethiopia or Arabia Felix, when Indian and Western traders in this region could easily point to a country at the other side of the ocean. Moreover, Eusebius did not have Ethiopia in mind, because he clearly spoke about the heathens in the east, thus suggesting a different direction and certainly not the south. For these very reasons, it seems more probable to me to situate the India in Eusebius' report on Pantaenus and Bartholemew on the Indian subcontinent itself.[56]

The presence of Graeco-Egyptian settlements, as attested by coins and other artefacts, along the west and south coast of India and their very absence along the northern coast seems to indicate that in particular connections existed between Alexandria, the Red Sea and south India. Dihle has suggested that Christians from Alexandria and

Roman Copper Coins from South India: Karur and Madurai (Madras, 1994) 3f.

[55]   Dihle, 'Neues zur Thomas-Tradition', 71-3 with note 56; Mundadan, *History of Christianity in India*, 69.

[56]   Dihle, 'Neues zur Thomas-Tradition', 68f; Mundadan, *History of Christianity in India*, 65f with references to G.M. Moraes, *A History of Christianity in India AD 52-1542* (Bombay, 1964) 35-45 and A.C. Perumalil, *The Apostles in India* (Patna, 1971). However, one still might argue that Eusebius incorrectly associated Pantaenus' trip (to the Indians) with the Indian subcontinent, while Pantaenus actually referred to the Indians in Ethiopia and Arabia Felix when he was writing about Bartholomew's mission to the Indians. According to Eusebius, some Indians knew Christ and had been acquainted with the gospel according to Matthew in Hebrew letters, which had been brought to them by Bartholomew. Later traditions seem to confirm a connection between Bartholomew and Egypt, so that it is not impossible that Bartholomew and his disciples expanded their missionary activities in Egypt (and abroad) along the trading routes. If these observations are correct, the small Christian communities as far as Arabia Felix and Ethiopia might have come into existence in the second century AD. Moreover, it is not impossible that Indian traders there might have been converted, as Pantaenus suggests. In line with this, it does not seem implausible to me that these Christians may have transported their religion in the course of time to India along these sea routes, where they spread it in small pockets along the coast of Kerala and Malabar, but additional evidence of Indian Christians communities along the Red Sea (and also in India) during this early period is for the time being virtually absent.

Egypt regularly travelled during the first two centuries AD to Ethiopia and Arabia Felix, and from there to south India where they settled in seaports. They may have formed small Christian communities with customs and beliefs which somewhat differed from their Christian brothers and sisters originating from the Mesopotamian region.[57]

The tradition of the missionary activities of Bartholomew in India also occurs in the *Passio Bartholomaei* of the fourth/fifth century. This highly legendary text presupposes the same geographical frame of India as is sketched above and may indicate that the Bartholomew tradition originates from Graeco-Roman Egypt of the High imperial period[58]. In spite of this, we do not hear about the existence of Christian communities in India that appealed to Bartholomew as their founder. The Alexandrian merchant and traveller Cosmas Indicopleustes who visited India in the first half of the sixth century AD does not tell us anything about Bartholomew traditions in his *Christian Topography*[59]. He found churches with Christians in Taprobane (Ceylon) with a clergy and a body of believers, and also along the coast of Male (the Malabar Coast) and in another place called Calliana, which had a bishop appointed from Persia[60]. The same Cosmas relates elsewhere that a church of Persian Christians existed in one of the trading ports of Ceylon with a presbyter appointed from Persia and a deacon, which was in the possession of a complete ecclesiastical ritual. He further describes the Sindhu river as the boundary between Persia and India and also mentions the most notable places of trade in India: Sindhu, Orrotha (Saurastra), Calliana, Sibor, and the five markets of Male (Malabar) which export pepper[61]. The town Calliana has been identified by some scholars

---

[57]   Dihle, 'Neues zur Thomas-Tradition', 68ff.

[58]   Ibidem, 69-71.

[59]   I quote from the new edition by W. Wolska-Conus, *Cosmas Indicopleustès: Topographie Chrétienne*, 3 vols (Paris, 1968-73). See also Mc Crindle, *Christian Topography of Cosmas*, IV-VIII; X-XI; E.O. Winstedt (ed), *The Indian Topography of Cosmas Indicopleustes* (Cambridge, 1909).

[60]   Cosmas Indicopleustes 3.65, cf. Mc Crindle, *Christian Topography of Cosmas*, 119.

[61]   Cosmas Indicopleustes 11.16, cf. Mc Crindle, *Christian Topography of Cosmas*, 336f.

with the ancient Indian town Kalyan(a) which is situated at the north-eastern end of the Thana creek near present-day Bombay. The town was an ancient port and its name actually means 'happy' or 'felix'. By extension the region and its inhabitants came to be known as India Felix.

The facts mentioned by Cosmas indicate that Christians originating from Persia - the region northwest of the Indus - came to dominate the Christian communities along the west coast of south India and on the island Taprobane. Persian bishops, presbyters and deacons were consecrated and the religious orientation had shifted from Egypt and Alexandria to the region of Parthia, which according to more ancient traditions was connected with Thomas. Be that as it may, the tradition of Bartholomew's mission to south India was not totally lost. According to the seventh-century Pseudo-Sophronius, Bartholomew had preached to the Indians who are called 'Happy'. With these words he seems to have referred to a Greek tradition which related that the apostle went to India Felix.[62] Thus, until early medieval times the tradition of Bartholomew's mission to India remained known in western tradition.

3. A reconstruction of the beginnings of Christianity in India

It may be clear that a reconstruction of the early history of Christianity in India is a problematic affair due to the paucity of reliable reports in the relevant sources. The *ATh* does not inform us about the real situation of Thomas' mission in India, but describes the apostle's appearance in an imaginative Indian landscape reconstructed with the help of local traditions, known in Edessa and surroundings. Its author did not direct himself to Indians, but to kindred spirits in the region and made the apostle to a mouthpiece of his gnostic teachings. Yet, by connecting Thomas with India, instead of with Parthia, he introduced an innovation in the tradition. By claiming India as the missionary field for Thomas, he implicitly made his readers responsible for a successful follow up of the missions in the region. This suggests at least the presence of some Christian communities in north India at the time that the author wrote his *ATh*.

---

[62]   See Mundadan, *History of Christianity in India*, 66 for the reference to Farquhar, 'The Apostle Thomas in North India'.

In line with this claim, one may view Syrian Christianity as successor to the apostolate of St. Thomas, which implied the pastoral care for Christian communities in India, for whom the brother of Jesus had given his life. Thus, the author of the *ATh* not only focused the attention of his readers on the lofty message of Judas Thomas, but also on an imaginary India for whom they were responsible. In summary: the meeting between Judas Thomas and the various persons mentioned in the *ATh* was a creation of the author, in which he expounded his deep gnostic truths in the imaginary historical landscape of northwest India which he only knew from local traditions.

A reconstruction of Christianity in the Indian subcontinent in the first five centuries AD provides us with the following schematic picture. Small Christian communities may have been founded by missionaries from the Syrian and Mesopotamian region along the northwestern coast of India as a consequence of the brisk trading between the Persian Gulf and region of the Sindh. Similar communities were probably founded by Egyptian missionaries in trading towns along the Malabar and Coromandel coast. Dihle has soundly argued that in the course of time the connections between these south Indian communities and Egypt (Alexandria) became more problematic due to the diminishing influence of the Roman Empire in the Red Sea. This led to instability in the region with local conflicts between Arab and Abessinian potentates. As a consequence of this, the commerce along the sea routes between south India and the Red Sea sharply dropped at the beginning of the third century[63]. Thus, the Christian communities in south India became cut off from their mother church in Alexandria and reoriented themselves towards the Mesopotamian and Persian region with its existing traditions of Thomas.

The *ATh* which actually envisioned the northwestern part of India as the imaginary landscape of Thomas' apostolate subsequently became instrumental to a broader missionary goal, in which India was redefined. In the course of time, this India also came to include the regions in south India, where the apostle Bartholomew, according to tradition, once had preached his gospel. In any case, informal knowledge of south India seems to have been virtually absent in Edessa during the second century. With the loss of direct trading

---

[63]   Dihle, 'Neues zur Thomas-Tradition', 71-7.

routes between the Red Sea and south India, other alternatives in the Mesopotamian region became intensified. Thus, the monsoon routes between Charax Spasinu (Basra) at the mouth of the Euphrates and the northern and western ports in the Indian subcontinent became the most busy trade connections of the time[64]. These routes enjoyed the special interest of the Sasanid kings in their endeavour to extend their sphere of influence. The intensive trade between Charax Spasinu and various ports along the coast of north and west India from the beginning of the third century seems to have led to more intensive contacts between the churches in the Mesopotamian and Persian region and Indian Christian communities. Dihle refers in this context to an early medieval Nestorian report of the journey of the metropolitan David of Charax (Basra) in 296/97 to India and suggests that this trip may have led him not only to north India which was already in touch with the Syro-Persian Church, but also to south India in order to include the deserted Christian communities in south and west India into his flock[65].

In any case, it is obvious that the influence of the Syro-Persian church in west and south India increased in the following centuries as becomes clear from various later reports. The tradition of Bartholomew went into oblivion and was replaced by the missions of Thomas to India, as proclaimed by the *ATh*. This tradition provided Indian Christianity with another direct claim to its apostolic origin and seems to have been an important means in the missionary policy of the Syro-Persian church.

When the Portuguese landed on the Malabar coast in the sixteenth century they found Christians communities in Kerala who had kept the East Syrian traditions of St. Thomas alive in their folksongs[66]. These folk traditions seem to have older roots, because we also learn from the Venetian traveller Marco Polo (1254-1325) about the 'burial place of Messer St. Thomas, the Apostle'. Marco Polo visited some parts of Ceylon and the Malabar coast during his passage

---

[64] Cf. also Drijvers, 'Hatra, Palmyra und Edessa', 893ff.
[65] Herzfeld, *Archeological History of Iran*, 103-4; Farquhar, 'The Apostle Thomas in South India', 42-3; Dihle, 'Neues zur Thomas Tradition', 73 with note 63.
[66] Mundadan, *History of Christianity in India*, 29ff; idem, *Sixteenth-Century Traditions of St. Thomas Christians in India* (Bangalore, 1970) 60-7. See also M.N. Pearson, *The Portuguese in India* (Cambridge, 1987) 119.

from China to Italy in 1293, but did not go on pilgrimage to the shrine[67]. His report is rather incoherent and runs as follows: 'The body of St. Thomas lies in the province of Maabar in a little town. There are few inhabitants, and merchants do not visit the place; for there is nothing in the way of merchandise that could be got from it, and it is a very out-of-the-way spot. But it is a great place of pilgrimage both for Christians and Saracens. For I assure you that the Saracens of this country have great faith in him and declare that he was a Saracen and a great prophet and call him *aviarun*, that is to say "holy man"'[68].

It is not exactly clear which region is meant by Maabar, but Marco Polo distinguished it from the Malabar coast[69]. Yet, he gives us a clear hint when he states that the kingdom of Maabar is the same as Chola[70], thus referring to the kingdom of the Cholas who reigned between 850-1279 with varying success in the regions of the Coromandel coast, north of the river Cauvery[71]. The name Maabar may have been a corruption of the name of Mahabali(puram), an important Hindu town in this region with a port, and by extension he may have referred to the surrounding regions[72]. In this connection Marco Polo also speaks about ships which sailed between Maabar and Madagascar and Zanzibar. If the identification of Maabar with Mahabalipuram and its surroundings is correct, it is in harmony with the indigenous tradition which localises the burial place of Thomas in the neighbourhood of present day Madras, 60 km north of Mahabalipuram.

[67]   For Marco Polo see W. Th. Elwert, s.v. 'Marco Polo', *RGG* IV (Tübingen, 1960[3]) 742f. Cf. also A.L. Basham, *The Wonder That Was India* (London, 1963 revised edition) 346 with the wrong suggestion that Polo saw the tomb.
[68]   Marco Polo, *The Travels of Marco Polo. Translated and with an Introduction by Ronald Latam* (Harmondsworth, 1958) 274.
[69]   Marco Polo, *Travels*, 289f.
[70]   Marco Polo, *Travels*, 277.
[71]   Cf. W. Haig (ed), *The Cambridge History of India: Turks and Afghans* III (London, 1928[1], reprint New Delhi), chapter XVIII (W. Haig): 'Hindu States in Southern India, AD 1000-1565', pp. 467-99.
[72]   Marco Polo, *Travels*, 287: this localization is in accordance with Polo's statement that the realm of Quilon lays about 500 miles southwest of Maabar.

Yet it remains unclear why the Saracens would have paid their homage to St. Thomas who has no special place in the Islam, unless one suggests that the practice refers to popular Islam with its veneration of saints and their burial places. A closer investigation of Marco Polo's description of India shows that facts and fictions are often mixed up and that his story about Thomas is from hearsay, probably from Thomas Christians on the Malabar coast[73]. We do not have any other data of that period that the grave of the apostle would have been a great place of pilgrimage for Saracens and Christians. Nevertheless, it should be acknowledged that a tradition might have existed among the Thomas Christians of the Malabar coast which localised the burial place of the apostle Thomas on the Coromandal coast. This tradition was incorporated by Marco Polo and connected with various other legendary stories in his travel report.

The tradition of Thomas' burial place somewhere in the kingdom of Maabar suits with the custom of the East Syrian church to connect the apostolate of Thomas with all the places where this church in the imagination of its followers had been influential at one time or other, and even made him preach in China. The first Portuguese informant who wrote about the existence of the tomb of St. Thomas in Mylapore was Diego Fernandes. In a letter of 1517, he reported that he had rediscovered the tomb of the apostle and brought about an official inquiry by the Portuguese king in 1533, in which he also functioned as the main witness. He stated that his testimony was based on the information he had gathered from the oldest inhabitants of Mylapore: brahmins and other people. Yet he was silent on the question whether the tomb was venerated at the time by local Thomas Christians and whether it functioned as a real place of pilgrimage. In this context one may ask oneself why brahmins and other old people of the village would pass down this tradition? It seems not besides the mark to suggest that Fernandes may have been inspired by the itinerary of Marco Polo which was printed for the first time in Portuguese in 1502[74]. Anyhow, the leader of the royal investigation, a certain

[73] Marco Polo, *Travels*, 274f. The story of the earth of the burial place with its beneficial effects seems to have been derived from the last chapter of the *ATh*.
[74] Elwert, 'Marco Polo', 739: first edition in German 1477, Latin 1484, Italian 1496, Portuguese 1502, Spanish, 1503, French 1556 and English, 1579. See also Pearson, *The Portuguese in India*, 83-4, who mentions that

Miguel Ferreira, concluded that the oldest people of the land, Muslims and Hindus, Indians and foreigners all testified to the same thing 'as if they were speaking with one mouth'[75]. The Portuguese thus 'rediscovered' the tomb of St. Thomas in what once seems to have been the grave of a nameless saint and returned the holy spot to the Thomas Christians in south India. They renamed Mylapure in 1545 in Sao Thomé, under which name the place may have been known to Arabian navigators and merchants in the sixteenth century[76].

It falls outside the scope of this paper to deal with the deeper motives of the Portuguese, but one may guess that they hoped to win the support of Thomas Christians in their endeavour of colonial expansion in India. Yet, at another level the discovery of the remains of the apostle proved to be counterproductive. It is true that the Thomas Christians incorporated this innovation of tradition, but they used the material presence of the apostle also as an argument in their opposition to the religious authority of Rome. The remains of St. Thomas testified to the fact that Indian Christians could appeal to an independent apostolic succession which went back to the brother of the Lord. Thus the ancient imagination of Thomas' visit to India became condensed in a visible tomb which acquired new symbolic functions in an age of colonial and religious expansion.

as early as 1507 a preliminary expedition was sent by Viceroy Almeida of Goa to the Coromandel coast in order to investigate the situation at the spot and to look for the tomb of St. Thomas.

[75]   Mundadan, *History of Christianity in India*, 41.

[76]   G.R. Tibbetts, *Arab Navigation in the Indian Ocean before the Coming of the Portuguese* (London, 1971) 467 with a reference to the port of Mylapure, a corruption of the name Mahabalipuram (four miles to the north of Covelong near Madras). Cf. also R. Strasser, *Südindien. Land der Dravidas und Tausend Tempel* (Stuttgart, 1984) 182 with a reference to a certain Sulaiman at-Tajir (the merchant) who in AD 851 mentions a place Batuma (bait Thomas: house of Thomas) in the region. Yet the most ancient manuscripts do not mention this place at all; cf. G. Ferrand, *Voyage du Marchand Arabe Sulayman en Inde et en Chine. Rédigé en 851 suivi de remarques par Abu Zayd Hasan (vers 916)* (Paris, 1921). The reference to Batuma may have been a later interpolation.

XI. The Apocryphal Acts: Authors, Place, Time and Readership

As this volume is the last in our series of discussions of the five major *Apocryphal Acts of the Apostles* (*AAA*), it seems appropriate to conclude our study with a new discussion of the authors, time and place of composition, and the readership of the major *AAA*[1]. The following analysis hopes to demonstrate that such a discussion is especially fruitful when carried out in dialogue with students of the ancient novel. The idea is not totally new, since in 1932 Rosa Söder already pointed to a number of similarities between the ancient novel and the *AAA*[2]. However, later students of the novel have not displayed the same interest. Tomas Hägg and Niklas Holzberg pay some attention to the *AAA* in their well known introductions to the ancient novel, but they are clearly happy to pass on to more congenial subjects[3]. The three recent collections by Jim Tatum, John Morgan and Richard Stoneman, and Gareth Schmeling contain between them only

---

[1]   This chapter is the abbreviated but updated and somewhat revised version of my 'The Novel and the Apocryphal Acts: Place, Time and Readership', in H. Hofmann and M. Zimmerman (eds), *Groningen Colloquia on the Novel* IX (Groningen, 1998) 157-180. For information and comments on the various versions I am grateful to Glen Bowersock, Ewen Bowie, Ken Dowden, who also skilfully corrected my English, Danielle van Mal-Maeder, Peter van Minnen and Klaas Worp. Kind as always, Egbert Forsten immediately granted my request to reprint this piece.
[2]   R. Söder, *Die apokryphen Apostelgeschichten und die romanhafte Literatur der Antike* (Stuttgart, 1932; repr. Darmstadt, 1969); note also the review by K. Kerényi, *Gnomon* 10 (1934) 301-9.
[3]   T. Hägg, *The Novel in Antiquity* (Oxford, 1983) 154-64; N. Holzberg, *The Ancient Novel. An Introduction* (London, 1995) 22-6.

two, not quite satisfactory contributions on the *AAA*[4]. It is only Kate Cooper, in *The Virgin and the Bride*, who has once again discussed both the ancient novel and the *AAA* as manifestations of the same literary genre[5]. Yet a comparison between the *AAA* and the ancient novel can be rewarding as we hope to show in the following discussion of the authorship (§1), chronology and place of composition (§2), and readership (§3) of the *AAA*.

1. Authorship, text and message

What can we say about the authors of the ancient novel and the *AAA*? In an important study on the sociology, production and reception of the ancient novel, John Morgan has observed that the few references to the novel in ancient literature are not very complimentary. Typical is the Emperor Julian's commentary that 'as for those fictions in the form of history that have been narrated alongside events of the past, we should renounce them, love stories and all that sort of stuff' (*Epist.* 89.301b, tr. Morgan). Morgan persuasively concludes from these and similar comments that it is likely that 'the whole exercise of writing and reading novels was somewhat ambiguous, even ever so slightly illicit'[6]. He draws no further consequences from his conclusion, but it fits his characterisation that until now it has been impossible to demonstrate that one author has written more than one novel. It very much looks as if the novel was a one time only affair, which the author did not want to repeat. This impression is supported by the *AAA*, each of which has been written by a separate author. It also may explain the relative obscurity of the authors of the novel, about whom we mostly know very little, often next to nothing, apart from the information supplied by the novels themselves. Even

---

[4] J. Perkins, 'The Social World of the *Acts of Peter*', in J. Tatum (ed), *The Search for the Ancient Novel* (Baltimore and London, 1994) 296-307, repr. in her *The Suffering Self* (London, 1995) 124-41, 223-4; R. Pervo, 'Early Christian Fiction', in J. Morgan and R. Stoneman (eds), *Greek Fiction* (London, 1994) 239-54 and 'The Ancient Novel Becomes Christian', in G. Schmeling (ed), *The Novel in the Ancient World* (Leiden, 1996) 685-711.
[5] K. Cooper, *The Virgin and the Bride* (Cambridge Mass., 1996).
[6] J. Morgan, 'The Greek Novel. Towards a sociology of production and reception', in A. Powell (ed), *The Greek World* (London, 1995) 130-52.

Tertullian, who possessed detailed information about the author of the *Acts of Paul* (§3), does not mention any name.

This relative anonymity of the author may be partly responsible for a striking characteristic of the text of the novel and the *AAA*. Papyri and the study of manuscript traditions have shown that the texts of various novels, in particular those of the Alexander Romance and *Joseph and Asenath*, display a surprising fluidity in variants and scenes. The same situation, even more pronounced, can be found among the *AAA*. The martyrdom of the apostles soon started to circulate independently, large interpolations occurred within decades, and later authors recycled portions of the text into new stories about apostles or other saints. To a certain extent one may perhaps compare the 'translation' by Apuleius of his Greek model, the *Metamorphoseis* of 'Lucius of Patrai'. Apuleius not only happily inserts stories, like the famous *Amor and Psyche*, new episodes and typically Roman details, but in numerous passages he also makes many small changes. Such fluidity was not the case with every ancient text. Alexandrian philologists protected prominent literary authors, and the texts of important philosophers, like Plato and Aristotle, were initially zealously guarded by their followers. The text of the Old Testament, another one-time pluriform text as the Dead Sea scrolls have shown, was even declared sacrosanct, as soon as the temple in Jerusalem was destroyed and the priests who had always preserved some kind of fixity of the text had disappeared[7]. Admittedly, the textual fluidity of some novels and the *AAA* cannot be ascribed only to the anonymity of the authors: the enormous popularity of some texts must have played a role as well. On the other hand, novels were no bestsellers, and the anonymity of the authors may thus have been a contributing factor to the fluidity of their texts[8].

---

[7] A.S. van der Woude, 'Pluriformity and Uniformity. Reflections on the Transmission of the Text of the Old Testament', in J.N. Bremmer and F. García Martínez (eds), *Sacred History and Sacred Texts in Early Judaism. A Symposium in Honour of A.S. van der Woude* (Kampen, 1992) 151-69.

[8] For this fluidity see the excellent observations of C. M. Thomas, 'Stories Without Texts and Without Authors: The Problem of Fluidity in Ancient Novelistic Texts and Early Christian Literature', in R. Hock *et al.* (eds), *New Perspectives on Ancient Fiction and the New Testament* (Atlanta, 1998) 273-91.

If Erwin Rohde (1845-1898) in his classic study still depreciated the novel, in the late 1920s there appeared a book by a Hungarian author, Karl Kerényi (1897-1973), which postulated a connection between the novel and religion, especially Egyptian religion[9]. Kerényi dedicated his book to the memory of Franz Boll (1867-1924), a learned classicist, who had analysed the last book of the New Testament, Revelation[10]. The ancient novels, however, are no apocalypses, books *par excellence* to be decoded, and Kerényi's approach was immediately rejected by Arthur Darby Nock (1902-1963)[11]. This connection with religion became even more strongly argued by Reinhold Merkelbach, who suggested that the true sense of the novels was accessible only to initiates of the mysteries, but his approach has been equally generally rejected[12]. Even if the specific theses of Kerényi and Merkelbach are not accepted, the importance of religion in the novels cannot be denied. Can it be that this religious element had made it easier for the authors of the *AAA* to model their writings partly on the novel? I find it hard to answer the question, but at least it has to be raised.

2. The chronology and place of origin of the AAA

The authoritative translation of the New Testament apocrypha suggests the following dates and places of composition regarding the five major *AAA*: the *Acts of Andrew* (*AA*) were published in perhaps Alexandria about AD 150, the *Acts of Peter* (*APt*) perhaps in Rome

---

[9] K. Kerényi, *Die griechisch-orientalische Romanliteratur in religions-geschichtlicher Beleuchtung. Ein Versuch*, 1927[1] (Darmstadt, 1962[2]) 'mit Nachbetrachtungen'. For Kerényi see especially A. Henrichs, 'Der antike Roman. Kerényi und die Folgen', forthcoming in the proceedings of a conference on Kerényi held in Ascona in 1997.
[10] F. Boll, *Aus der Offenbarung Johannis* (Leipzig and Berlin, 1914; repr. Amsterdam, 1967). For Boll see the obituary by A Rehm, *Biographisches Jahrbuch für Altertumskunde* 47 (1927) 13-43, 111.
[11] A.D. Nock, *Essays on Religion and the Ancient World*, 2 vols (Oxford, 1972) I.169-175 (= *Gnomon* 4, 1928, 485-92).
[12] R. Merkelbach, *Roman und Mysterium in der Antike* (Munich, 1962) repeated in his *Isis regina – Zeus Sarapis* (Stuttgart, 1995) 335-484. His thesis was rejected by Kerényi, *Der antike Roman* (Darmstadt, 1971) 9 ('all zu vereinfachte Vorstellung').

in the decade 180-190, the *Acts of Paul* (*AP*) in Asia Minor in the period between 185 and 195, the *Acts of John* (*AJ*) in East Syria in the first half of the third century, and *the Acts of Thomas* (*ATh*) also in East Syria at the beginning of the third century[13].

Unfortunately, it is very difficult to reach a satisfactory relative, let alone absolute, chronology of the *AAA*. Only in few cases do we have clear indications for an absolute chronology. Tertullian comments on the *AP* around AD 200, and the mention of Falconilla, the daughter of Queen Tryphaena in the *AP*, supplies a *terminus post quem* of about AD 160. This rare name is most likely derived from Pompeia Sosia Falconilla, the wife of the Roman consul of AD 169 (M. Pontius Laelianus), who is known from various contemporary inscriptions[14]. Moreover, both the interest of the *ATh* in India and the clear influence by Bardaisan point to a time of composition in the 220s or 230s[15]. Finally, the *AJ* must have been written in the second half of the second century, witness its pre-Valentinian Gnostic tendency and specific docetic Christology[16].

A second approach to the chronology is the study of the dependence of individual *AAA* on the ancient novel. Although none of the *AAA* has come down to us in its original form, the *AJ* and *AP* seem to have been closest to the ancient novel, since they have protagonists from the social elite, in addition to the traditional motifs outlined below (§3). This seems to indicate an early date for these two *Acts*. In addition to these limited indications, we can also look at the mutual interdependency of the *AAA*, since they regularly display

[13] See *NTA* II, 114-5 (*AA*: J.-M. Prieur and W. Schneemelcher), 166-7 (*AJ*: K. Schäferdiek), 234-5 (*AP*: W. Schneemelcher), 283 (*APt*: W. Schneemelcher) and 323 (*ATh*: H.J.W. Drijvers).
[14] W. Eck, 'Senatorische Familien der Kaiserzeit in der Provinz Sizilien', *ZPE* 113 (1996) 109-28; Bremmer, *Acts of Paul*, 52 and *Acts of Peter*, 17; *Prosopographia Imperii Romani Saec. I.II.III*, vol. VI (Berlin and New York, 1998) 303-4; C. Marek, 'Ein neues Zeugnis aus Kaunos für den Senator Pompeius Falco', *Mus. Helv.* 57 (2000) 88-93.
[15] Bremmer, this volume, Ch. VI.
[16] P.J. Lalleman, *The Acts of John: a two-stage initiation into Johannine Gnosticism* (Louvain, 1998) 270. For a very recent survey of modern studies of the *AJ* see now A. Jakab, '*Actes de Jean*: État de la recherche (1892-1999)', *Rivista di Storia e Letteratura Religiosa* 36 (2000) 299-334.

signs of intertextuality, just like the ancient novels[17]. It is clear that great care is required in this respect, since mistakes made in determining the dependency of one novel on another have been spectacular. One only needs to read again the relevant pages in Rohde's pioneering work on the novel in order to see that arguments can be often used either way[18]. However, we can be reasonably certain that the *APt* has used the *AJ*, including the latter's well known interpolation of *cc*.79-102 about the Cross, and probably even the *AP*[19], as we can see from its less successful version of the famous *Quo vadis?* scene which also occurs in the *AP*[20]. This suggests a somewhat later period for the *APt*, which indeed is generally considered to date from the end of the second century[21]. The *AA* too must have been written around the same time, since they are theologically related to the Syrian Tatian and oppose military service, an opposition that in Christian circles only becomes manifest at the end of the second century[22]. Thus we may provisionally infer the following order: *AJ*, *AP*, *APt*, *AA* and *ATh* within a period stretching from about AD 150-230.

Some parts of the original *APt*, the *AA* and, via a later Irish translation, also of the *AJ* have been preserved only because of a Latin translation of the major five *Acts*. Can we say when this translation was made? The best evidence for determining the date of a text is often an institutional detail[23]. In this case, too, there is a passage in

[17] For the pagan novel this is stressed by S. Stephens, 'Fragments of Lost Novels', in Schmeling, *The Novel*, 655-83 at 683.
[18] E. Rohde, *Der Griechische Roman und seine Vorläufer* (Berlin, 1914[3]).
[19] E. Junod and J.-D. Kaestli, *Acta Iohannis*, 2 vols (Turnhout, 1983) II.698; J.M. Prieur, *Acta Andreae*, 2 vols (Turnhout, 1989) I.385-403 (the *AA* and the other major *AAA*); P.J. Lalleman, 'The Relation between the *Acts of John* and the *Acts of Peter*', in Bremmer, *Acts of Peter*, 161-77.
[20] Rordorf, 'The Relation between the *Acts of Peter* and the *Acts of Paul*: State of the Question', in Bremmer, *Acts of Peter*, 178-91.
[21] Bremmer, *Acts of Peter*, 16-8; for a full-scale study of the *APt* see now C.M. Thomas, *The Acts of Peter and the Ancient Novel: Beyond Fiction* (Oxford, 2001).
[22] Bremmer, *Acts of Andrew*, 20. Add to my collection of terms for 'gentleness' on page 17 the name Prautês, cf. Milner, *An Epigraphical Survey* (n. 40), no. 142.
[23] For another example from Late Antiquity see my dating of the vision of Dorotheus: 'An Imperial Palace Guard in Heaven: The Date of the *Vision of Dorotheüs*', ZPE 75 (1987) 82-8, reprinted in my *The Rise and Fall of the Afterlife* (London and New York, 2002) 128-33, 184-6.

the Latin translation of the *APt* that has not yet received the interest
it deserves. When a demon had kicked a marble statue in his atrium
to pieces, the senator Marcellus called out: *Magnum flagitium factum
est: si enim hoc innotuerit Caesari per aliquem de curiosis, magnis
poenis nos adfliget* (11). Schneemelcher translates as follows:
'A great crime has been committed; if Caesar hears of this through
some busybody, he will punish us severely'[24]. However, his translation overlooks the fact that the *curiosi* were not 'busybodies', but a
nickname for the *agentes in rebus*, a kind of imperial secret police[25].
It is only from AD 359 onwards that they reported directly to the
emperor and, therefore, became feared as spies[26]. Consequently, the
APt was translated into Latin after that date. And indeed, knowledge
of the Latin translation is not attested before St Augustine's *Contra
Adimantum* (17) of AD 394 and its adoption in Priscillianist circles[27].
The Latin version of the *AJ* is also attested first in late fourth-century
Africa in Manichaean and Priscillianist circles[28]. just as usage of the

[24]   Schneemelcher, in *NTA* II, 297.
[25]   As was pointed out by Th. Pekáry, *Das römische Kaiserbildnis* (Berlin,
1985) 139 note 66.
[26]   *Cod. Theod.* VI.29.1,4; VIII.5.50, cf. A.H.M. Jones, *The Later Roman
Empire, 284-602: a social, economic and administrative survey*, 3 vols
(Oxford 1964) II.578-80; J. Triantaphylopoulos, '*Kouríosos* (P. Vindob.
Sijpesteijn 22^v)', in *Atti dell' XI Congresso Internazionale di Papirologia*
(Milano, 1966) 249-59 and '*Kouríosos*', *Ephemeris Hellen. Nomikoon* 32
(1968) 711-2; W. Blum, *Curiosi und Regendarii: Untersuchungen zur
Geheimen Staatspolizei der Spätantike* (Munich, 1969); G. Purpura,
'I *curiosi* e la *schola agentum in rebus*', *Annali del Seminario Giuridico di
Palermo* 34 (1973) 165-273; C. Vogler, *Constance II et l'administration
impériale* (Strasbourg, 1979) 201-9; P.J. Sijpesteijn, 'Another curiosus',
ZPE 70 (1987) 143-6; *SEG* 35.1523.
[27]   Cf. G. Poupon, 'L'Origine Africaine des *Actus Vercellenses*', in Brem-
mer, *Acts of Peter*, 192-9, who establishes its African origin. Poupon's con-
clusion is supported by the typically African credal formulations, see
L.H. Westra, '*Regulae fidei* and Other Credal Formulations in the *Acts of
Peter*', in Bremmer, *Acts of Peter*, 134-47.
[28]   Philaster, *De haer.* 88.6; Faustus *apud* Augustine, *Contra Faustum*
(AD 397-400) 30.4; Augustine, *Contra adversarium legis et prophetarum*
(AD 421) 1.20. For Manichaean interest in the *AJ* see now G. Jenkins,
'Papyrus I from Kellis. A Greek Text with Affinities to the Acts of John', in
Bremmer, *Acts of John*, 197-216; I. Gardner and K.A. Worp, 'Leaves from

complete Latin version of the *AP* is only attested for the so-called *Cena Cypriani*, which dates from about AD 400[29]. The Latin translation of the *AA* appears first in Philaster of Brescia's *Diversarum haereseon liber* (88.6: about AD 390) and was also used by the Priscillianists[30]. The *ATh* survived only in a later, abbreviated *Passio Thomae* and a *Liber de miraculis beati Thomae apostoli*[31], but the analogy with the other translated *AAA* suggests that Augustine still knew a complete Latin translation, since he is its first witness[32].

Around AD 400 both Faustus of Milevis and Philaster refer to a collection of the five major *AAA* by a certain Leucius Charinus, a Manichaean[33]. We therefore conclude that the five major *AAA*, were translated together by a Manichaean in Africa and immediately adopted in Priscillianist circles. The mention of the *curiosi* in the *APt* establishes a *terminus post quem* of AD 359 for this collection, but we can narrow down its period of origin even more, as Priscillian himself already showed acquaintance with the *AAA* in his so-called Würzburg tractates[34]. Since he was executed in AD 385, the five major *AAA* must, consequently, have been translated into Latin between that year and AD 359.

a Manichaean Codex', *ZPE* 117 (1997) 139-55; I. Gardner *et al.*, *Coptic Documentary Texts from Kellis* I (Oxford, 1999) no. 19.62,73; 21.20; 28.31 (the frequent occurrence of the very rare name Drusiana).
[29] For text, translation, date and *AP* see C. Modesto, *Studien zur* Cena Cypriani *und zu deren Rezeption* (Tübingen, 1992).
[30] Prieur, in *NTA* II, 103.
[31] For a fragment of the original Latin translation see now P. Bernard, 'Un passage perdu dans *Acta Thomae* latins conservé dans une anaphore mérovingienne', *Revue Bénédictine* 107 (1997) 24-39.
[32] Augustine, *De sermone domini in monte* 1.20; *Contra Adimantum* 17; *Contra Faustum* 22, 79, cf. K. Zelzer, *Die alten Lateinischen Thomasakten* (Berlin, 1977) xxvi. My reconstruction is the first to take into account the evidence of the Latin translations of the other *AAA* and differs from those by Zelzer, *op. cit.*, and K. Schäferdiek, 'The Manichean Collection of Apocryphal Acts Ascribed to Leucius Charinus', in *NTA* II, 87-100 at 98 note 62.
[33] Schäferdiek, 'The Manichean Collection of Apocryphal Acts'. For the name Leucius see J. Nollé, *Side im Altertum* I (Bonn, 1992) 259; for the combination of two names, R. Merkelbach, 'Über zweite Namen im Griechischen', *ZPE* 22 (1976) 200-2.
[34] H. Chadwick, *Priscillian of Avila* (Oxford, 1976) 77f.

The chronology proposed for the original *AAA* is supported by its close coincidence with the heyday of the ancient novel. This must have been the second half of the second century, to judge by chronological tables of the papyrological fragments[35]. The overall chronology supports the dating of Heliodorus to the third century, since it would mean that the genre had run its course around AD 230[36]; a sudden reappearance in the later fourth century would be hard to explain. It is true that the first *AAA* continued to be 'recycled' in the next centuries, but the creativity and freshness of the first major five was virtually never regained except, to a certain extent, in the fourth-century *Acts of Philip*[37].

Do we find a similar coincidence regarding the location of the *AAA*? The heartland of the ancient novel was Western Asia Minor, where we probably have to locate Xenophon of Ephesus, Longus, Lollianus and Achilles Tatius (below). Within this area the most important centre was Aphrodisias, where certainly Chariton's *Callirhoe* but also, albeit with various degrees of probability, *Ninus*, *Chione*, *Parthenope*, and Antonius Diogenes' *Wonders beyond Thule* were written[38]. This concentration suggests we should look at Aphrodisias and that region for a potential place of birth of the *AAA*. Do we have any indications in that direction?

[35] E. Bowie, 'The Readership of Greek Novels in the Ancient World', in Tatum, *The Search*, 435-59 at 443; G. Cavallo, 'Veicoli materiali della letteratura di consumo. Maniere di scrivere e maniere di leggere', in O. Pecere and A. Stramaglia (eds), *La letteratura di consumo nel mondo greco-latino* (Cassino, 1996) 11-46 at 15f.

[36] For the date of Heliodorus see A. Henrichs, *Die Phoinikika des Lollianus* (Bonn, 1972) 50 note 21; D. Bonneau, 'Les *realia* du paysage égyptien dans le roman grec: remarques lexicographiques', in Baslez 1992, 213-9 (the Egyptian *realia* in the novel point to the end of the third century as a *terminus ante quem*); G. Bowersock, *Fiction as History* (Cambridge Mass, 1994) 149-60; E. Bowie, 'The Ancient Readers of the Greek Novels', in Schmeling, *The Novel*, 87-113 at 93-4; S. Swain, *Hellenism and Empire* (Oxford, 1996) 423-4; Bremmer, 'Achilles Tatius and Heliodorus in Christian East Syria', in H.L.J. Vanstiphout (ed), *All Those Nations...Cultural Encounters within and with the Near East* (Groningen, 1999) 21-9.

[37] F. Bovon *et al.*, *Acta Philippi*, 2 vols (Turnhout, 1999).

[38] Bowie, 'The Readership', 450-2 and 'The Ancient Readers', 90-1; Bowersock, *Fiction as History*, 38-41 (Antonius Diogenes); Stephens, 'Fragments', 660-1 (*Chione*); Swain, *Hellenism and Empire*, 424-25 (for a first-century date of *Ninus* and *Parthenope*); for the *Parthenope* see now

More recently, the origin of the *AJ* has been looked for in East
Syria (above) and Egypt, and in the past I myself have endorsed
Egypt as place of composition. The most important arguments for
Egypt are the theological resemblances between the *AJ* and Clement
of Alexandria and Origen, but such later parallels cannot be deci-
sive[39]. We move onto much firmer ground, when we look at the
social terminology of the *AJ*. Of the protagonists, both Andronicus
(31) and Callimachus (73) are called a 'first of the Ephesians' (31),
and Antipater is 'a first of the Smyrnaeans' (56). The terminology
recurs in other early *AAA*. In the *AP* Thecla's fiancée Thamyris is
called 'a first of the city' (11), her suitor Alexander 'a first of the
Antiochenes' (26) and she herself 'a first of the Iconians' (26) and in
the *AA*, which have survived only very fragmentarily, we find
'Demetrius, a first of the Amasaeans' (3).

The terminology is not unique. In a number of Greek cities a
member of the elite within the elite called himself or herself (or was
called) *prôtos* (*prôtê*) *tês poleôs, ek tôn prôteuontôn* or *ek tou prôtou
tagmatos*. Now we are fortunate in having a relatively large corpus of
Ephesian and Smyrnaean inscriptions, which show that this terminology was not at home in either Ephesus or Smyrna. Although these
terms occasionally occur elsewhere in the Greek world, the centre of
this aristocratic self-designation was Aphrodisias and Northern
Lycia. In addition, it is found in Eastern Phrygia, Bithynia,
and Pisidia where Antiochene Jews stirred up 'the first of the city'
against the apostle Paul (*Acts* 13.50)[40]; on the other hand, the related

also G. Strohmaier, 'Al-Biruni und der griechische Partenoperoman',
Graeco-Arabica 6 (1995) 72-9.
[39] Cf. Bremmer, *Acts of John*, 54-6. For the definitive refutation of East
Syria and Egypt as possible places of composition see now Lalleman, *The
Acts of John*, 256-61.
[40] L. Robert, *Etudes Anatoliennes* (Paris, 1937) 342; P. Franchi de' Cava-
lieri, *Scritti agiografici*, 2 vols (Rome, 1962) II.18 note 4; F. Schindler, *Die
Inschriften von Bubon (Nordlykien)* (Vienna, 1972) no. 8, 12-3; G.E.M. de
Ste Croix, *The Class Struggle in the Ancient Greek World* (London, 1981)
531; M. Wörrle, *Stadt und Fest im kaiserzeitlichen Kleinasien* (Munich,
1988) 56-7, 135 and *Chiron* 29 (1999) 353-4 (Limyra); R. MacMullen,
Changes in the Roman Empire (Princeton, 1990) 342 note 10; F. Quass, *Die
Honoratiorenschicht in den Städten des griechischen Ostens* (Stuttgart,
1993) 51-5; S. Sahin, *Die Inschriften von Arykanda* (Bonn, 1994) no. 42,
49, 50; M. Adak, 'Claudia Anassa – eine Wohltäterin aus Patara',

terminology of *prôtopolitês* is exclusively found in Syria, Palestine and Egypt[41]. The conclusion seems inevitable that the very first *AAA*, *AJ* and *AP*, were written in this particular region, the *AP* perhaps in Iconium[42]. Unfortunately, Aphrodisias does not enter into consideration, since Christianity was a latecomer to Caria in general and Aphrodisias in particular[43].

The place of composition of two of the later *AAA*, the *APt* and *AA*, is perhaps to be looked for in Bithynia. Bithynians receive special attention in the *APt*, and the *AA* starts off in Northern Anatolia. Moreover, a Bithynian origin for the *AA* is supported by the mention of the wife of the pro-consul Lesbios and her estate manager together in the bath (*AAlat* 23). Although it was perfectly normal for a Roman proconsul to take his wife with him to his province[44], it is totally improbable that she would have taken along his steward. On the other hand, an estate manager (*oikonomos* or *pragmateutês*) of wealthy Greek women is epigraphically well attested, especially in areas with large estates such as Central Anatolia and Bithynia. They must have even been sufficiently recognisable for the author of the *Historia Apollonii regis Tyrii* (31 RA, RB) to introduce one into his novel[45].

Epigraphica Anatolica 27 (1996) 127-42; N.P. Milner, *An Epigraphical Survey in the Kibyra-Olbasa Region Conducted by A.S. Hall* (Ankara, 1998) no. 1; *SEG* 31.1316 (Lycian Xanthus); 41.1343, 1345-6, 1353 (Lycian Balboura); 42.1215 (Pisidian Etenna); 44.1162 (Boubon); 46.1524 (Lydian Sardis).

[41] F. Vattioni, 'A proposito di *prôtopolitês*', *Stud. Pap.* 16 (1977) 23-29 (add *SEG* 38.1586); M. Blume, 'A propos de P.Oxy. I, 41', in L. Criscuolo and G. Geraci (eds), *Egitto e Storia Antica dall' Ellenismo all' età Araba. Bilancio di un confronto* (Bologna, 1989) 271-90 at 286.

[42] Bremmer, *Acts of Paul*, 56f.

[43] P.W. van der Horst, *Essays on the Jewish World of Early Christianity* (Freiburg and Göttingen, 1990) 166-81 ('Jews and Christians in Aphrodisias'); F.R. Trombley, *Hellenic Religion & Christianization c. 370-529*, 2 vols (Leiden, 1994) II.52-73.

[44] J. Carlsen, *Villici and Roman Estate Managers until AD 284* (Rome, 1995); M.T. Raepsaet-Charlier, 'Épouses et familles de magistrats dans les provinces romaines aux deux premiers siècles de l'empire', *Historia* 31 (1982) 56-69.

[45] *Oikonomos*: *SEG* 43.441 (*BCH* 1993, 384-94); *I. Iznik* 196, 1062, 1201, 1208; *RECAM* ii.324; L. Robert, *BCH* 103 (1979) 429 note 13; S. Mitchell, *Anatolia*, 2 vols (Oxford, 1993) II.160; R. van Bremen, *The Limits of Participation* (Amsterdam, 1996) 267-9.

3. *Readership*

Having looked at the authorship, dates and places of origin of the *AAA*, let us now turn to the vexed question of the readership of these writings via a reconsideration of the readership of the ancient novel. The latter problem has roused deserved interest in recent times. In the last five years we have had even five contributions on the readership of the ancient novel: one by Hägg, Morgan, and Stephens, and three by Bowie[46]. As we all accept that most upper class male Greeks and Romans could read and write, the problem mainly boils down to the women. I see here three related questions in particular. First, can we suppose that a reasonable amount of women could read? Secondly, can we presuppose such a potential reading public in Asia Minor and Egypt and, finally, do we have any evidence for female readers of the novel, pagan or Christian?

Let us start with the problem of the reading women. In the last two decades we have had various studies devoted to this problem[47]. They clearly show an enormous range of reading women, who have now turned up even in Vindolanda, near Hadrian's wall[48]. None of these general studies, however, pays any attention to Christian reading women[49]. It is as if the ancient world suddenly stops at some

---

[46]   Bowie, 'Les lecteurs du roman grec', in M.-F. Baslez *et al.* (eds), *Le monde du roman grec* (Paris, 1992) 55-61; Bowie, 'The Readership' and 'The Ancient Readers'; T. Hägg, 'Orality, literacy, and the "readership" of the early Greek novel', in R. Eriksen (ed), *Contexts of Pre-Novel Narrative* (Berlin and New York, 1994) 47-81; Stephens, 'Who Read Ancient Novels?', in Tatum, *The Search*, 405-18; Morgan, 'The Greek Novel', 134-9.
[47]   S.G. Cole, 'Could Greek Women Read and Write?', in H. Foley (ed), *Reflections of Women in Antiquity* (New York, 1981) 219-45; W. Harris, *Ancient Literacy* (Cambridge Mass., 1989) passim; G. Cavallo, 'Donne che leggono, donne che scrivono', in R. Raffaelli (ed), *Vicende e figure femminili in Grecia e a Roma* (Ancona, 1995) 517-26 (with extensive bibliography); K. Hopkins, 'Christian Number and Its Implication', *JECS* 6 (1998) 185-226 at 207-13.
[48]   A.K. Bowman and J.D. Thomas, *The Vindolanda Writing-Tablets (Tabulae Vindolandeses II)* (London, 1994) nos. 291-4 (women of the equestrian officer class).
[49]   But see now R. Lane Fox, 'Literacy and power in early Christianity', in A.K. Bowman and G. Woolf (eds), *Literacy and Power in the Ancient World* (Cambridge, 1994) 126-48; Ph. Rousseau, '"Learned Women" and the Development of a Christian Culture in Late Antiquity', *Symb. Osl.* 70 (1995) 116-47.

invisible Iron Curtain behind which one is not allowed to peep. However, in one of the visions in his mid second-century *Shepherd*, Hermas has to make a copy of a book and give it to a woman, Grapte[50], 'to admonish the widows and orphans' (*Vis.* II.4.2); the second-century Dionysius of Corinth wrote a theological letter to Chrysophora, 'a most faithful sister'; the famous gnostic Valentinus had female followers with poetic pretensions; his pupil Marcus wrote a preserved letter to the rich woman Flora; Hippolytus evidently presupposed that women and maidens could read his work; Origen had many female pupils, and a very recently published fourth-century papyrus reads as follows: 'To my dearest lady sister, greetings in the Lord. Lend the Ezra, since I lent you the little Genesis. Farewell in God from us'[51]. It seems as if reading and intellectually interested women immediately become visible, as soon as we have more information about a leading Christian or Gnostic figure. It is therefore not surprising that in the early fourth-century *Martyrdom of Agape, Irene and Chione* the Roman governor asked these women without further ado: 'Do you have in your possession any treatises, parchments or books of the impious Christians' (4.2)[52]?

This Christian evidence may also make us more reticent in putting into doubt Antonius Diogenes' dedication of his *Wonders* to

---

[50] The name Grapte was rare in Greece and Asia Minor but 'one of the favourite names in slave and libertine circles of Rome', where *Shepherd* was written, cf. M. Ricl, *The Inscriptions of Alexandreia Troas* (Bonn, 1997) 124.

[51] *P.Oxy.* 63.4365, cf. D. Hagedorn, *ZPE* 115 (1997) 147-8, who convincingly identifies 'little Genesis' as the only fragmentarily preserved *Book of Jubilees*; see also A. Hilhorst, *ZPE* 130 (2000) 192. For women's letters on papyrus see now R. Cribiore, 'Windows on a Woman's World. Some Letters from Roman Egypt', in A. Lardinois and L. McClure (eds), *Making Silence Speak. Women's Voices in Greek Literature and Society* (Princeton, 2001) 223-39.

[52] For these and more Christian examples, which are all overlooked by the authors mentioned in my note 47, see Bremmer, 'Why did Christianity attract Upper-class Women', in A.A.R. Bastiaensen *et al.* (eds), *Fructus centesimus. Mélanges G.J.M. Bartelink* (Steenbrugge and Dordrecht, 1989) 37-47 at 42-3; P. Brown, *The Body and Society: men, women, and sexual renunciation in early Christianity* (New York, 1988) 151-2, 184, 193; J.A. Sheridan, 'Not at a Loss for Words: The Economic Power of Literate Women in Late Antiquity', *Tr. Am. Philol. Ass.* 128 (1998) 189-203.

162   JAN N. BREMMER

his sister Isidora (Photius, *Bibl.* 111a-b). She must have been an educated woman and it seems a bit far-fetched that Antonius would have
liked us to see his very own sister to stand for, in the words of Bowie,
'the avid but gullible reader'. Actually, if we accept the persuasive
identification of *PSI* 117 as a fragment of his *Wonders*, Antonius
does even mention a reading woman within his own novel[53].

Unfortunately, we cannot always trace the social position of
reading women, but the papyrological evidence of Oxyrhynchus and
Vindolanda strongly suggests that the skill of reading was not limited
to upper-class women[54]. A handicap in our research is that the own-
ers of literary papyri are very rarely known, but we may note that
recently Roger Bagnall has identified a wealthy, third-century lady
from Oxyrhynchus, Aurelia Ptolemais, who owned a *Sikyonika*, the
Iliad and Julius Africanus' *Kestoi*. Even if she inherited these books
from her father, she, surely, was a potential reader of the novel or the
AAA[55]. We are much less informed about Asia Minor from literary
sources, but archaeology has at least furnished us with an ever
increasing stream of names of women who occupied a leading, sometimes *the* leading, position in their community. Highpriestesses,
agonothetae, gymnasiarchs, demiourgoi, eponymous magistrates or
members of boule and gerousia: there can be no doubt that in the
heartland of the novel there was a wealthy and well-educated female
public available which in principle could have read and appreciated
the various romances[56]. But did they actually do so?

---

[53]   *Contra* Bowie, 'The Readership', 437-8 and 'The Ancient Readers',
103, who follows up a suggestion by S. Stephens and J. Winkler, *Ancient
Greek Novels: the fragments* (Princeton, 1995) 102-03; *PSI* 117 has now
been re-edited by Stephens and Winkler, 148-53. The supposed attitude of
Antonius also hardly squares with the general impression we have of the
brother-sister relationship in Greek culture, see my 'Why did Medea kill her
brother Apsyrtus?', in J. Clauss and S.I. Johnston (eds), *Medea* (Princeton,
1997) 83-100.
[54]   E. Kutzner, *Untersuchungen zur Stellung der Frau im römischen
Oxyrhynchos* (Frankfurt, 1989) 149-51; J.N. Adams, 'The Language of the
Vindolanda Writing Tablets: An Interim Report', *J. Roman Stud.* 85 (1995)
86-134 at 130-1.
[55]   R. Bagnall, 'An Owner of Literary papyri', *Class. Philol.* 87 (1992)
137-40.
[56]   See, most recently, the informative discussions by J. Nollé, 'Frauen wie
Omphale', in M. Dettenhofer (ed), *Reine Männersache?* (Cologne, 1994)

The problems and evidence at stake have now been admirably set out by Bowie, partially in reaction to Hägg, who in turn had reacted to Bowie's contribution to the 1989 Dartmouth conference[57]. Bowie usefully distinguishes between intended and actual readership, but his discussion also makes clear that we have very little information about the gender and social status of his actual readers. As the lack of evidence for female readers of the novel has often been pointed out, it is good to realise that there is also very little information about males as readers of the novel, as Hägg has stressed[58]. It is possible, though, to add a few male readers to Bowie's collection, since he draws insufficient attention to the intertextuality of the novels themselves. Admittedly, this aspect of the readership of the novels may not have seemed central to his argument, but it must nevertheless be spelled out to present the full picture of ancient readership. As I have argued in the original version of this chapter, Apuleius, Lucian, Lollianus and Achilles Tatius all had read 'Lucius of Patrai's' *Metamorphoseis*[59]. It is also clear that Chariton was read by Xenophon of Ephesus[60]; the so-called Protagoras novel (Klaus Alpers' splendid recent 'discovery') by Longus[61]; Xenophon of Ephesus by Achilles Tatius and, probably, by the *Antheia* fragment and

229-59; Van Bremen, *The Limits of Participation*; Adak, 'Claudia Anassa'; K. Mantas, 'Independent women in the Roman East: widows, benefactresses, patronesses, office-holders', *Eirene* 33 (1997) 81-95; S.J. Friesen, 'Ephesian Women and Men in Public Office during the Roman Imperial Period' and U. Soldan, 'Frauen als Fuktionsträgerinnen im kaiserzeitlichen Ephesos: Die weiblichen Prytaneis', in H. Friesiner and F. Krinzinger (eds.), *100 Jahre Österreichische Forschungen in Ephesos* (Vienna, 1999) 107-13, 115-9, respectively.
57 See the literature mentioned in note 46.
58 Hägg, 'Orality', 55.
59 Bremmer, 'The Novel', 168f.
60 J. N. O'Sullivan, *Xenophon of Ephesus. His compositional technique and the birth of the novel* (Berlin and New York, 1994) does not seem to me to have proved the reverse, however informative the book is on Xenophon's literary technique; cf. the review by M. Weissenberger, *Gött. Gel. Anz.* 248 (1996) 176-91.
61 K. Alpers, 'Zwischen Athen, Abdera und Samos. Fragmente eines unbekannten Romans aus der Zeit der Zweiten Sophistik', in M. Billerbeck and J. Schamp (eds), *Kainotomia. Die Erneuerung der griechischen Tradition* (Freiburg, 1996) 19-55 at 47-8. Note that Alpers' dating of his novel points to a somewhat earlier date for Longus than is usually accepted, cf.

the *Historia Apollonii*[62]; Longus by Heliodorus[63]; and Achilles Tatius by Bardaisan, the author of the *ATh*, and Heliodorus[64]. Finally, the author of the elusive *Grundschrift* of the Pseudo-Clementine *Homilies* and *Recognitions* had read Chariton, Xenophon of Ephesus and, most likely, Heliodorus[65].

A few more readers can be detected if we take into account the *AAA*, a genre surprisingly neglected by Hägg and Bowie in their discussions of the readership of the novel. As we have seen, Rosa Söder collected motifs shared by the novel and the *AAA*, but she explicitly denied dependence of the latter on the former. Instead, she suggested that the *AAA* derived from 'Zeugen alter im Volke lebender Erzählungen von den Abenteuern, Wundertaten und Liebesaffären grosser Männer'[66]. There is not a shred of evidence for this view. In fact, the intertextuality of the *AAA* with the novel cannot be doubted, if we look at the cumulation of similar motifs, as collected by Söder: shipwrecks, brigands, sale into slavery, putting girls in brothels, unruly crowds, travel around the empire, thinking of suicide[67], sending messages, corrupting a servant, trials, locking up in tombs, endless journeys and loving couples (Platonic or not).

We may add that, as in the novel, young elite couples are the protagonists in the earliest of the *AAA*, the *AJ* and *AP* (§2). In the *AJ* the apostle John is met by Lycomedes, an Ephesian *stratêgos*, who

---

J. Morgan, 'Longus, Daphne and Chloe: 1950-1995', *ANRW* II.34.3 (Berlin and New York, 1997) 2208-76 at 2229.

[62] J. N. O'Sullivan, *Xenophon of Ephesus* (Berlin and New York, 1994) 166-8 (*Antheia* fragment and Achilles Tatius); G. Kortekaas, *Historia Apollonii regis Tyri* (Groningen, 1984) 130.

[63] T. Szepessy, 'Zur Interpretation eines neu entdeckten griechischen Roman', *Acta Ant. Hung.* 26 (1978) 29-36; E. Bowie, 'Names and a Gem: Aspects of Allusion in Heliodorus' *Aethiopica*', in D. Innes *et al.* (eds), *Ethics and Rhetoric. Classical Essays for Donald Russell on his Seventy-fifth Birthday* (Oxford, 1995) 269-80 at 279-80 (Heliodorus and Longus).

[64] K. Plepelits, 'Achilles Tatius', in Schmeling, *The Novel*, 387-416 at 394-8 (Heliodorus and Achilles Tatius); Bremmer, 'Achilles Tatius and Heliodorus' (Bardaisan and *ATh*).

[65] Bremmer, 'Achilles Tatius and Heliodorus'.

[66] Söder, *Die apokryphen Apostelgeschichten*, 187.

[67] Compare, e.g., *AJ* 19f and 49 with Chariton 1.4.7 and 3.1.1; for a discussion of this theme, S. MacAlister, *Dreams & Suicides. The Greek Novel from Antiquity to the Byzantine Empire* (London, 1996).

tells him about the paralysis of his wife Cleopatra, who was, he says, a beauty 'at which all Ephesus was amazed' (20). As for a second elite couple, Andronicus and Drusiana, the wife is so beautiful that Callimachus, a young 'first of the city', tries to commit necrophilia and strips her of her clothes until he arrives at the undergarment, at which point he is fortunately threatened by a snake (70-1). In the *AP*, the immediate infatuation of Thecla with the apostle Paul is described in stock novelistic terms by her mother to Thecla's fiancée, Thamyris: 'For indeed for three days and three nights Thecla has not risen from the window either to eat or to drink, but gazing steadily as if on some joyful spectacle she so devotes herself to a strange man... (she) sticks to the window like a spider, is (moved) by his words (and) gripped by a new desire and a fearful passion' (7, tr. W. Schneemelcher). Sometimes an author of the *AAA* even borrowed a less common motif, as when in both Chariton (1.4.12-5.1) and the *AJ* (48) a kick produces a loss of voice[68]. The conclusion is inevitable: the authors of the *AJ* and *AP*, at least, had read the contemporary novels and taken from them part of their inspiration.

Of course, the similarities should not blind us to the differences. The *AAA* centre on the martyrdom of an apostle, and chastity is the happy end, not marriage. Moreover, unlike most ancient novels, the *AAA* happily admit the Romans and their world into the fictional world, sometimes even in a humiliating manner, as when the *AA* depicts the Roman proconsul with an attack of diarrhoea (13). Taking such differences into account, Christine Thomas has well formulated the relationship between the ancient novel and the *AAA*: 'though motifs do not a genre make, the ideal romances and the Acts are speaking the same narrative language'[69].

But who were the authors of the *AAA* and who were their intended or actual readers? The authors of the *AJ*, *APt*, *AA* and *ATh* are unknown, but a presbyter from Asia Minor wrote the *AP*, as

---

[68]   See the discussion of the similarities in Junod and Kaestli, *Acta Iohannis*, 517-20, 547-51, where they conclude: 'La fréquence et l'étroitesse de ces parallèles confirment de manière décisive que notre auteur connaît la production romanesque de son époque' (550); add now P.J. Lalleman, 'Classical Echoes (Callimachus, Charito) in the *Acta Iohannis*?', *ZPE* 116 (1997) 66.

[69]   Thomas, 'Stories Without Texts', 278.

Tertullian informs us[70]: a clear case, then, of another male reader of the ancient novel. Tertullian's notice also supplies another, very valuable, piece of information. He tells us that the Christian women of Carthage based claims for teaching and baptizing on the *AP*. As Carthage contained a substantial number of Greek-speaking inhabitants[71], the conclusion suggests itself that women were actual readers of the *AAA*. Now we certainly know that fourth-century Christian women must have read the adventures of Thecla[72], but we may perhaps also identify an earlier reader. The young upper-class woman Perpetua prayed for her brother Deinocrates (*Passio Perpetuae* 7-8), just as in the *AP* Thecla prayed for the deceased daughter of Queen Tryphaena (29), the only two such known cases in the first Christian centuries[73]. Moreover, before her martyrdom Perpetua saw in a dream a black Egyptian (10), just as in the *APt* (22) the Roman senator Marcellus saw an awful black woman before Peter's confrontation with Simon Magus. In both cases the black person is killed and thus predicts the favourable outcome of the forthcoming battle. The parallelism is so close that it is hard to avoid the conclusion that Perpetua had also read the *APt*.

If women, then, were actual readers of the *AAA*, were they also intended readers? There can be little doubt that this was indeed the case. First, both in the *AJ* and *AP* women (virgins, widows and old women) dominate the scene, but it is upper-class women who are the most prominent ones. Both *Acts* display various couples, such as Lycomedes and Cleopatra or Andronicus and Drusiana in the *AJ*, and Thecla and Thamyris in the *AP*, but in both cases women are the heroines and clearly the examples to be followed[74]. Secondly, from

[70]   Tert. *De baptismo* 17.5, cf. A. Hilhorst, 'Tertullian on the Acts of Paul', in Bremmer, *Acts of Paul*, 150-63; G. Poupon, 'Encore une fois: Tertullien, *De baptismo* 17.5', in D. Knoepfler (ed), *Nomen Latinum. Mélanges A. Schneider* (Neuchâtel and Geneva, 1997) 199-205.
[71]   J. den Boeft and J. Bremmer, *VigChris* 36 (1982) 391-2; T. Barnes, *Tertullian* (Oxford, 1985²) 67-9.
[72]   Cooper, *The Virgin and the Bride*, 70, 112.
[73]   Cf. Bremmer, *Acts of Paul*, 43-4.
[74]   For the *AJ* see my, 'Women in the Apocryphal *Acts of John*', in Bremmer, *Acts of John*, 37-56; for the *AP*, my 'Magic, martyrdom and women's liberation in the Acts of Paul and Thecla', in Bremmer, *Acts of Paul*, 36-59.

Adolf von Harnack to Robin Lane Fox, scholars of early Christianity have continuously observed that until Constantine women by far constituted the majority of early Christians[75]. Thirdly, whereas we do not hear of the Christians or other religious groups targeting upper-class men, there is plenty of evidence that the early Christians, just like Jews and Gnostics, were popular among wealthy Greek and Roman women, not least because they took women seriously on an intellectual level[76].

It has never been disputed, I think, that at least some of the authors of the *AAA* meant their novels to have a 'missionary' effect. In the upper-class of Asia Minor, their most obvious targets were women; the conversion of upper-class males, on the other hand, would take much longer and did not take off before the conversion of Constantine. This female focus is supported by the fact that in the *AAA* women are never executed for their adhesion to the new faith; in the case of Thecla she did not even have to cut her hair. The conclusion seems inescapable: women must have constituted an important part, perhaps the largest part, of the intended and actual readership of the *AAA*.

This is not the position of Keith Hopkins, who has argued that there were very few Christians until the end of the second century and, consequently, very few reading women. Both Hopkins and Rodney Stark agree that one could postulate about 7,500 Christians around AD 100 by assuming 1,000 Christians in AD 40 and an annual growing rate of 40%[77]. In fact, Hopkins even assumes that around AD 100 most Christian communities did not have 'among them a single sophisticated reader or writer'[78]. Yet such an assumption would hardly explain the familiarity with Christians in Nero's Rome and the fact that Pliny (*Ep.* 10.96) already finds a worrying number of Christians in Bithynia around AD 110. Moreover, it seems hard to accept that early Christianity spread at an amazing rate despite the fact that most Christian communities were unable to read

---

[75] A. von Harnack, *Die Mission und Ausbreitung des Christentums*, 1902[1] (Berlin, 1924[4]) 589-611; Lane Fox, *Pagans and Christians*, 310.
[76] For examples see Bremmer, 'Why did Christianity', 39-40.
[77] R. Stark, *The Rise of Christianity* (Princeton, 1996) 4-13; Hopkins, 'Christian Number', 193.
[78] Hopkins, 'Christian Number', 213.

a single Christian treatise. Surely, Hopkins takes too little into account that the heavy Jewish contribution to early Christianity must have positively influenced the level of early Christian literacy[79].
My own idea would be that the feverish atmosphere in Palestine in the decades after Jesus' execution must have been even more favourable to the spread of his messianic message than modern quantifications seem to realise. Consequently, I would assume more Christians around AD 160 than the about 60,000 which both Stark and Hopkins suggest, and thus more reading women. It is of course true, as Hopkins argues, that there will have been far less reading women than men. Yet, given the female superiority in numbers in the earlier Christian churches (above) and the fact that upper-class women could become Christian with less cost to their career than upper-class males, a number of Christian communities in Asia Minor must have certainly had a small but significant section of reading women. In any case, we are so used to mass circulation of books that most scholars hardly seem to realise that in antiquity authors, like for example Galen[80], sometimes wrote only for their friends or immediate circle. This could also have been the case with the *AAA*, which need not have been intended for a widespread circulation in the beginning.
Unfortunately, we know nothing about the original *Sitz im Leben* of the *AAA*. In addititon to being intended for the immediate environment of the author, one may wonder whether they were perhaps read in the context of worship, like some of the letters of St Paul. Or did the author first give a 'public reading' in his congregation or religious group before publishing them? The latter possibility seems perfectly likely, given the conventions of the time[81]. Yet, even if such cases of oral presentation took place, the majority of the audience would still have been female given the composition of the earliest Christian communities.
Having considered the female readership of the *AAA*, we are now in a better position to solve the problem of women as possible readers of the ancient novel. Whereas Rohde inferred female readers from the

[79]   See the considerations by H.Y. Gamble, *Books and Readers in the Early Church* (New Haven and London, 1995) 1-41.
[80]   T. Dorandi, *Le style et la tablette* (Paris, 2000) 107.
[81]   Gamble, *Books and Readers*, 82-143.

triviality of the novel, modern scholars think female readers unlikely on the basis of its sophistication: in both cases, male prejudice is evident despite the change in appreciation[82]. There are at least three questions that need attention. Firstly, do the novels themselves indicate reading women? Secondly, do we know of actual female readers? And thirdly, does the nature of the protagonists say anything about intended readers?

In an important study, Brigitte Egger has given persuasive answers to all of these questions[83]. She shows that in the second-century novel – Chariton, Xenophon of Ephesus and Longus – women were represented as literate without any thematisation of that aspect. In an eleventh-century Persian romance, which is an important source for our knowledge of *Parthenope*, the heroine is even depicted as a youthful genius. She started studying at the age of two, became an astronomer and a capable scribe at seven, and in her teens, when her father (Polycrates of Samos) 'examined her in the arts, he found the key of eloquence and the treasures of virtue. In deliberation the cultured child became without need of the instruction of the learned'[84]. Unfortunately, the only attested female reader is the already mentioned sister of Antonius Diogenes, Isidora, but as we have seen, male readers are not attested in abundance either.

As regards the protagonists, it is hard to disagree with Hägg when he states: 'Women are the real heroes of the early novels: Callirhoe, Parthenope, Anthia. They are sympathetically drawn and altogether more alive than their pale husbands and lovers. A partly, some would say predominantly female audience thus remains a fair assumption'[85]. This remains true, even if one agrees with Egger that the female protagonists, although 'immensely emotionally powerful and erotically ravishing', at the same time appear as socially 'restricted and disempowered'[86]; the latter characteristics may well

[82]   Cf. B. Egger, 'Looking at Chariton's Callirhoe', in Morgan and Stoneman, *Greek Fiction*, 31-48 at 32-33 (with bibliography).
[83]   B. Egger, 'Zu den Frauenrollen im griechischen Roman. Die Frau als Heldin und Leserin', in H. Hofmann (ed), *Groningen Colloquia on the Novel* I (Groningen, 1988) 33-66.
[84]   Hägg, 'Orality', 56, quoting from the as yet unpublished translation by Bo Utas.
[85]   Hägg, 'Orality', 59.
[86]   B. Egger, 'Women and Marriage in the Greek Novels', in Tatum, *The Search*, 260-80 at 272f.

have made them more palatable for the male readers (or their authors). Admittedly, Morgan has defended the paleness of the pro- tagonists: 'The colourless heroes are perhaps blank screens onto which the reader can project himself more easily than on to a more individualised character'[87]. But if this extremely weak argument were valid, surely the most popular works of literature, or of the cinema for that matter, would abound with colourless heroes!

None of the recent contributors to the debate on female reader- ship of the novel has taken the *AAA* into account. Yet, the result of our discussion strongly supports the case for the defence, since it immediately raises an important question. Why would Christian male authors think that women would suddenly become interested in a genre in which they had not been previously interested? It seems much more natural to accept that these authors had noticed the con- temporary interest of women in the novel. I stress the word 'contem- porary'. There is no need to think that the novel was 'invented' for women. The examples of the *Iolaus* or the so-called Protagoras novel (above) clearly militate against such a view. But nothing prevents us from accepting that, with the emergence in the first and second cen- tury of the wealthy female upper-class in Asia Minor, a new audience had developed which comprised males and females, for whom some novelists introduced female protagonists instead of male ones. The female protagonists of the contemporary *AAA* and their female read- ership strongly support this view.

[87]   Morgan, 'The Greek Novel', 145.

XII. Bibliography of *Acts of Thomas*

JAN N. BREMMER

Texts[1]

Bernard, P., 'Un passage perdu dans *Acta Thomae* latins conservé dans une anaphore mérovingienne', *Revue Bénédictine* 107 (1997) 24-39.

Elanskaya, A.I., *The Literary Coptic Manuscripts in the A.S. Pushkin State Fine Arts Museum in Moscow* (Leiden, 1994) 60-7.

Klijn, A.F.J., *The Acts of Thomas. Introduction, Text, Commentary* (Leiden, 1962).

Lipsius, R.A. and M. Bonnet, *Acta Apostolorum Apocrypha* II.2 (Leipzig, 1903; repr. Hildesheim, 1959).

Lucchesi, E., 'Additamentum ad Martyrium s. Thomae apostoli coptice', *Analecta Bollandiana* 106 (1988) 319-22.

Poirier, P.-H., *L'hymne de la perle des Actes de Thomas* (Louvain-la-Neuve, 1981).

--, *La version copte de la prédication et du martyre de Thomas*. Avec une *Contribution codicologique au Corpus copte des "Acta Apostolorum Apocrypha"* par Enzo Lucchesi (Brussels, 1984).

Thilo, J.C., *Acta S. Thomae Apostoli* (Leipzig, 1823).

Wright, W., *Apocryphal Acts of the Apostles*, 2 vls (London, 1871; repr. Amsterdam, 1968).

Zelzer, K., *Die alten Lateinischen Thomasakten* (Berlin, 1977).

---

[1] I have limited myself to the more recent literature. For the older bibliography see Moraldi, *Apocrifi*, 1237-42. The *ATh* are of course also frequently discussed in studies of the gnosis, Manichaeism and Syriac theology.

Concordance

Lipinski, M., *Konkordanz zu den Thomasakten* (Frankfurt, 1988)

Translations

Bovon, F. and P. Geoltrain (eds), *Ecrits apocryphes chrétiens* I (Paris, 1997) 1321-1470.
Drijvers, H.J.W., in Schneemelcher, *NTA* II, 322-411.
Elliott, J.K., *The Apocryphal New Testament* (Oxford, 1993) 439-511.
Erbetta, M., *Gli Apocrifi del Nuovo Testamento, II: Atti e Leggende* (Torino, 1966) 313-74.
Esbroeck, M. van, 'Les Actes apocryphes de Thomas en version arabe', *Parole de l'Orient* 14 (1987) 11-77.
Festugière, A.-J., *Les Actes apocryphes de Jean et de Thomas* (Geneva, 1983) 41-117.
James, M.R., *Apocryphal New Testament* (Oxford, 1924) 364-438.
Klijn, A.F.J. (ed), *Apokriefen van het Nieuwe Testament* II (Kampen, 1985) 56-160.
Moraldi, L., *Apocrifi del Nuovo Testamento* II (Torino, 1971) 1125-1350.

Apocryphal Acts in general

Bovon, F., *et al.*, *Les Actes Apocryphes des Apôtres* (Geneva, 1981).
—, 'Miracles, magie et guérison dans les Actes apocryphes des apôtres', *J. Early Chr. Stud.* 3 (1995) 245-59.
—, (ed), *The Apocryphal Acts of the Apostles* (Cambridge MA, 1999).
Del Cerro, G., 'Los Hechos apócrifos de los Apóstoles: su género literario', *Estudios bíblicos* 51 (1993) 207-32.
Elliott, J.K., 'The Apocryphal Acts', *Expository Times* 105 (1993-94) 71-7.
Hock, R. *et al.* (eds), *New Perspectives on Ancient Fiction and the New Testament* (Atlanta, 1998).
Junod, E., 'Créations romanesques et traditions ecclésiastiques dans les Actes apocryphes des Apôtres. L'alternative fiction romanesque – vérité historique: une impasse', *Augustinianum* 23 (1983) 271-85.
Lipsius, R.A., *Die apokryphen Apostelgeschichten und Apostellegenden. Ein Beitrag zur altchristlichen Literaturgeschichte* II.1 (Braunschweig, 1887).
Ljungvik, H., *Studien zur Sprache der apokryphen Apostelgeschichten* (Uppsala, 1926).
Plümacher, E., 'Apokryphe Apostelakten', in *Paulys Realencyclopädie der*

classischen Altertumswissenschaft, Supplementband XV (1978) 11-70.

Rordorf, W., 'Terra Incognita. Recent Research on Christian Apocryphal Literature, especially on some Acts of Apostles', in his *Lex orandi – Lex credendi* (Freiburg, 1993) 432-48.

Rostalski, F., 'Die Gräzität der apokryphen Apostelgeschichten', in *Festschrift zur Jahrhundertfeier der Universität Breslau am 2. August 1911* (Breslau, 1911) 59-69.

Söder, R., *Die apokryphen Apostelgeschichten und die romanhafte Literatur der Antike* (Stuttgart, 1932).

Warren, D.H., 'The Greek Language of the Apocryphal Acts of the Apostles: A Study in Style', in Bovon, *Apocryphal Acts*, 101-24.

Zachariades-Holmberg, E., 'Philological Aspects of the Apocryphal Acts of the Apostles', in Bovon, *Apocryphal Acts*, 125-42.

Acts of Thomas

Abouzayd, S., 'The Acts of Thomas and the unity of the dualistic world in the Syrian Orient', *Aram* 1 (1989) 217-52.

Adam, A., *Die Psalmen des Thomas und das Perlenlied als Zeugnisse vorchristlicher Gnosis* (Berlin, 1959).

Attridge, H.W., 'The Original Language of the Acts of Thomas', in H.W. Attridge *et al.* (eds), *Of Scribes and Scrolls* (Lanham and New York, 1990) 241-50.

—, 'Paul and the Domestication of Thomas', in E.H. Lovering and J.L. Sumney (eds), *Theology and Ethics in Paul and His Interpreters* (Nashville, 1996) 218-31.

—, 'Intertextuality in the *Acts of Thomas*', *Semeia* 80 (1997 [1999]) 87-124.

Blond, G., 'L'encratisme dans les actes apocryphes de Thomas', *Recherches et Travaux* I.2 (1946) 5-25.

Boone, E., 'L'onction pré-baptismale: sens et origine. Un exemple dans les *Actes de Thomas*', *Studia Patristica* 30 (1997) 291-5.

Bornkamm, G., *Mythos und Legende in den apokryphen Thomas-Akten* (Göttingen, 1933).

Bousset, W., 'Manichäisches in den Thomasakten', *ZNW* 18 (1917-18) 1-39.

Bussagli, M., 'The Apostle Thomas and India', *East and West* NS 3 (1952) 88-94.

Cartlidge, D.R., 'Transfigurations of Metamorphosis Traditions in the Acts of John, Thomas, and Peter', *Semeia* 38 (1986) 53-66.

Colless, B., 'The Letter to the Hebrews and the Song of the Pearl', *Abr-Nahrain* 25 (1987) 40-55.

Delaunay, J., 'Rite et symbolique en ACTA THOMAE *vers. syr.I, 2a et ss.*', in Ph. Gignoux (ed), *Mémorial Jean de Menasce* (Teheran, 1974)

11-34.

Devos, P., 'Le miracle posthume de S. Thomas l'Apôtre', *Anal. Boll.* 66 (1948) 231-75.

—, 'Actes de Thomas et Actes de Paul', *Anal. Boll.* 69 (1951) 119-30.

Dihle, A., 'Neues zur Thomas-Tradition', *JAC* 6 (1963) 54-70, repr. in his *Antike und Orient* (Heidelberg, 1984) 61-77.

Drijvers, H.J.W., 'Apocryphal Literature in the Cultural Milieu of Osrhoëne', *Apocrypha* 1 (1990) 231-47.

—, and G.J. Reinink, 'Taufe und Licht. Tatian, Ebionäerevangelium und Thomasakten', in *Text and Testimony. Festschrift A.F.J. Klijn* (Kampen, 1988) 91-110, repr. in Drijvers, *History and Religion in Late Antique Syria* (Aldershot, 1994) Ch. IV.

Fiaccadori, G., 'Tommaso in Etiopia', *Studi Classici e Orientali* 34 (1984) 298-307.

Garitte, G., 'Le martyre géorgien de l'apôtre Thomas', *Le Muséon* 83 (1970) 497-532.

—, 'La passion arménienne de S. Thomas l'apôtre et son modèle grec', *Le Muséon* 84 (1971) 171-95.

Germond, P., 'A Rhetoric of Gender in Early Christianity: Sex and Salvation in the *Acts of Thomas*', in S. Porter and Th. Olbricht (eds), *Rhetoric, Scripture and Theology* (Sheffield, 1996) 350-68.

Hopkins, K., *A World full of Gods* (London, 1999) 156-77.

Huxley, G., 'Geography in the *Acts of Thomas*', *Greek, Roman, and Byzantine Studies* 24 (1983) 71-80.

Johnson, C., 'Ritual Epicleses in the Greek *Acts of Thomas*', in Bovon, *Apocryphal Acts*, 171-204.

Kampen, L. van, *Apostelverhalen. Doel en compositie van de oudste apokriefe Handelingen der apostelen* (Diss. Utrecht, 1990) 165-200.

Köbert, R., 'Das Perlenlied', *Orientalia* 38 (1969) 447-56.

Kruse, H., 'Das Brautlied der syrischen Thomas-Akten', *Or. Christ. Per.* 50 (1984) 291-330.

—, 'Zwei Geist-Epiklesen der syrischen Thomas-Akten', *Oriens Christianus* 69 (1985) 33-53.

—, 'The Return of the Prodigal', *Orientalia* 47 (1978) 177-84.

Lafargue, M., *Language and Gnosis: The Opening Scenes of the Acts of Thomas* (Philadelphia, 1985).

Leloir, L., 'Le baptême du roi Gundaphor', *Le Muséon* 100 (1987) 225-33.

Marcovich, M., 'The Wedding Hymn of Acta Thomae', *Illinois Class. Stud.* 6 (1981) 367-85, repr. in his *Studies in Graeco-Roman Religions and Gnosticism* (Leiden, 1988) 156-73.

Matthews, C.R., 'Apocryphal Intertextual Activities: A Reframing of Harold W. Attridge's "Intertextuality in the *Acts of Thomas*",' *Semeia* 80 (1997 [1999]) 125-35.

Omodeo, A., 'I miti gnostici degli Atti di Tomaso', *La Parola del Passato* 1 (1946) 323-37.

Poirier, P.-H., '*L'Hymne de la Perle* des Actes de Thomas: Étude de la tradition manuscrite', *Or. Chr. An.* 205 (Rome, 1978) 19-29.

— '*Évangile de Thomas, Actes de Thomas, Livre de Thomas.* Une tradition et ses transformations', *Apocrypha* 7 (1996) 9-26.

—, 'Les *Actes de Thomas* et le Manichéisme', *Apocrypha* 9 (1998) 263-89.

Riley, G.J., 'Thomas Tradition and the Acts of Thomas', in E.H. Lovering (ed), *SBL 1991 Seminar Papers* (Atlanta, 1991) 533-42.

Rouwhorst, G., 'La célébration de l'eucharistie selon les Actes de Thomas', in Ch. Caspers and M. Schneiders (eds), *Omnes Circumadstantes. Contributions Towards a History of the Role of the People in the Liturgy* (Kampen, 1990) 51-77.

Salles, J.-F., 'La tradition de saint Thomas apôtre en Inde', *Monde de la Bible* 1119 (1999) 59-61.

Siegert, F., 'Analyses rhétoriques et stylistiques portant sur les *Actes de Jean* et les *Actes de Thomas*', *Apocrypha* 8 (1997) 231-50.

Smelik, K.A.D., 'Aliquanta Ipsius sancti Thomae', *VigChris* 28 (1974) 290-4.

Tissot, Y., 'Les Actes apocryphes de Thomas: exemple de receuil composite', in Bovon, *Les Actes apocryphes*, 223-32.

—, 'L'encratisme des Actes de Thomas', *ANRW* II.25.6 (Berlin and New York, 1988) 4415-30.

Valantasis, R., 'The Nuptial Chamber Revisited: The *Acts of Thomas* and Cultural Intertextuality', *Semeia* 80 (1997 [1999]) 261-76.

Vellian J. (ed), *The Apostle Thomas in India according to the Acts of Thomas* (Kerala, 1972).

Waldmann, H., *Das Christentum in Indien und der Königsweg der Apostel in Edessa, Indien und Rom* (Tübingen, 1996).

Zelzer, K., 'Zu den lateinischen Fassungen der Thomasakten', *Wiener Studien* NF 5 (1971) 161-79 and 6 (1972) 185-212.

—, 'Zu Datierung und Verfasserfrage der lateinischen Thomasakten', *Studia Patristica* 12 (1975) 190-4.

Zur, Y., 'Parallels between Acts of Thomas 6-7 and 4Q184', *Revue de Qumran* 16 (1993) 103-7.

Index of Names, Subjects and Passages

Weeden, T.J. 25
widow 82, 89
women 40-1, 47-8, 51, 78-90; in the *AAA* 88-90; reading 160-8

Xenophon of Ephesus 163-4

PRINTED ON PERMANENT PAPER • IMPRIME SUR PAPIER PERMANENT • GEDRUKT OP DUURZAAM PAPIER - ISO 9706

N.V. PEETERS S.A., KLEIN DALENSTRAAT 42, B-3020 HERENT